POLES APART

POLES APART

BEYOND THE SHOUTING, WHO'S RIGHT ABOUT CLIMATE CHANGE?

Gareth Morgan
&
John McCrystal

RANDOM HOUSE
NEW ZEALAND

A RANDOM HOUSE BOOK
published by Random House New Zealand
18 Poland Road, Glenfield, Auckland, New Zealand

For more information about our titles go to www.randomhouse.co.nz

A catalogue record for this book is available from
the National Library of New Zealand

Random House New Zealand is part of the Random House Group
New York London Sydney Auckland Delhi Johannesburg

First published 2009. Reprinted 2009.

© 2009 Gareth Morgan and John McCrystal; photographs by Gareth Morgan;
graphs as credited

The moral rights of the authors have been asserted

ISBN 978 1 86979 045 5

Random House New Zealand uses non chlorine-bleached papers from sustainably
managed plantation forests.

Cover design: Seven
Design: IslandBridge
Printed in Australia by Griffin Press

Contents

If the facts change, I change my mind.
What do you do, sir?

— John Maynard Keynes

Introduction

Beginning a book with a list of Frequently Asked Questions isn't the usual convention. It's more like something you'd find on a website than between the covers of a traditional book. But we're going to do just that — let's say we're moving with the times, and note that it's appropriate in a book covering a phenomenon that owes much of its character to the internet.

The Intergovernmental Panel on Climate Change (IPCC) releases its monumental Assessment Reports — containing the aggregated results of the work of countless scientific researchers, lead authors, reviewers and editors — onto the internet on average once every four and a half years. Between drinks, hundreds of titles by scientists, commentators, journalists, politicians, industry magnates, right-wing think tanks, left-wing cabals, free-market enthusiasts and environmental activists emerge like ticker tape, taking one stance or another on the state-of-the-climate debate. Newspapers crammed with op eds, editorials and major features and magazines with dramatic covers and shocking new revelations on climate cram the news-stands.

Meanwhile, a veritable blizzard of scientific papers are making their stately way through the peer review process and emerging (or not) in academic journals in the fullness of time, and only after extensive revisions and rewrites. It's become customary for sneak previews of these to be made available on the internet, even if it's only a hearsay report on some blog or another claiming that the results from the work of such-and-such a team shortly to be published in respected 'Climate Journal X' will make the author of some post or another look like a monkey.

And then, of course, there are the blogs. Little research, so far as we are aware, has been done into quantifying the heat generated in the blogosphere by computer servers labouring to keep up, but it's likely to be a fruitful area.

All the while, science happens. Robotic instruments sweep silently across the heavens, fixing the Earth, its oceans and its atmosphere in their glassy stare, transmitting the data they're gathering in real time back to Earth. Others plumb the depths of the ocean and surface like whales to blow a stream of data to remote monitoring stations. Thousands more bob about on the ocean's surface or stand sturdily in forest and desert, on mountaintop and valley floor, on farmland or on urban streets, uptown, downtown and in the 'burbs, thermometers taking the temperature of sea and air, anemometers whirring, barometers testing pressure, hygrometers tasting air for moisture, radiometers recording the sun's radiation as it plays upon the surface, spectrometers breaking light into bits and recording the patterns.

Twice a day every day, all over the world, huge, wobbling balloons swell as they ascend into the upper atmosphere, the little boxes of sophisticated instrumentation slung beneath them transmitting yet more data.

Intrepid teams wait and stamp their feet and slap their arms across their chests to keep warm in temperatures far below freezing as somewhere, hundreds of metres beneath their feet, a drillhead nears the bedrock beneath an ice sheet.

Bored graduate students peer at the displays of scanning electron microscopes and compare what they see in a rock sample with a well-thumbed guide to the various species of oceanic plankton that had their day in the sun hundreds of thousands of years ago, and enter their observations into a spreadsheet — more data.

More bored graduate students painstakingly transcribe values originally handwritten in big, dusty, leatherbound ledgers or on sheafs of brittle, yellowing official forms, noting perhaps how the writing goes from smooth, confident and elegant to shaky and spidery, recording not only the weather as it happened a hundred years ago in some benighted corner of the world, but also the decline into old age of the postmaster who arrived in the bloom of youth and promise and who performed his daily weather observations as mechanically as he performed his ablutions, day after day, year in, year out, recording the data without hope or expectation of thanks, let alone reward.

More data.

And still more bored graduate students, wishing they'd done science instead of classics at varsity and could even now be doing cool stuff with lasers and isotopic mass spectrometers instead of performing painstaking sight translations of Latin and Norse and Old English in the hope they'll find some reference to later-than-usual frost or snow under the wheels of Caesar's chariots in Gaul, or a bumper wheat harvest in Greenland, or unseasonable heat bothering the horses as they dragged drays of Cornish wine to the monastery . . .

All this data, from a dizzying multiplicity of disciplines, is generated, uploaded, downloaded, entered, stored, extracted, sorted, massaged, interrogated into yielding up eigenvectors and running stochastic averages and graphs that show means and modes and two-sigma confidence intervals, and finally turned into the kind of information that a modern-day analyst will deign to consider. If there's one thing the climate change field is not short of, it's information. And there's more of it every day. It takes the internet and its virtual assembly of interested parties to keep abreast of it all.

Anyway. Frequently Asked Questions. Since we first began working on this project and summoned the courage to tell people about it, we've fielded a few. We present the following list to satisfy some measure of our readers' curiosity, allowing them to proceed through the rest of the text without distractions. So without further ado . . .

Poles Apart: Frequently Asked Questions

What's all this about then?

The authors intend this book to be the reasonable, interested layperson's guide to the debate over what we will usually call **anthropogenic**

global warming. The word 'anthropogenic' means 'caused by human activity', and that's really the crux of the hypothesis. Human activity — especially the consumption of fossil fuels such as oil and gas since the industrial revolution got under way in 1750 — has generated an increase in 'greenhouse gases', which trap in the lower atmosphere heat otherwise destined to be re-radiated into space. This causes warming (we'll look at how and why in depth in the next chapter).

I've heard about global warming, and it sounds lovely. I mean, where I live we could use a bit of warming . . .?

Part of the hypothesis is that the quantities of greenhouse gases that we've emitted and will continue to emit (unless some kind of concerted action is taken to limit those emissions) could raise the Earth's temperature to the point where undesirable, even catastrophic, effects will result (see the last section of Chapter 3, 'Is Anything Agreed?' for the kinds of things we're talking about). These, it's suggested, will more than likely outweigh any regional benefits that there might happen to be.

This book's a bit behind the times, isn't it? Isn't the debate over?

Sure, one side — we've chosen to call them 'the Alarmists' — would have you believe the debate's over, that 'the science is settled'. But just because one side in an argument is shouting that it's all over doesn't necessarily mean they're right, or that we should listen to them. There are plenty of people around — scientists and laypeople of one sort or another — who believe the science of global warming is far from settled. In this book, we call these people 'the Sceptics'. Part of the reason we've written it is precisely to test the Alarmist assertion that the argument's over, as well as the strength of the Sceptics' assertion that the science isn't yet settled. And while we won't give away too much at this early stage, suffice to say that if the argument were well and truly over, we wouldn't have seen the need for the book, either.

Ooh — the labels 'Alarmist' and 'Sceptic' sound kind of inflammatory . . .?

You'll find them in the literature. The Sceptics call the IPCC and those who subscribe to the theory of anthropogenic warming 'Alarmists', because it's their contention that the whole issue is a beat-up (a conspiracy, a mistake, an overstatement); they say the calls for immediate, drastic action on a global scale to cut emissions of greenhouse gases and to prepare to mitigate the effects of global warming are creating unnecessary fear and anxiety in the general public.

The term 'Sceptic' is trickier, because people on this side of the argument occupy a wide range of positions. There are some who, in the genuine spirit of scientific enquiry, question aspects of the theory of anthropogenic global warming and have yet to be convinced. They deserve the scientifically respectable title of 'Sceptics'. There are others who seem scarcely interested in addressing the science, and who appear instead to be attempting to raise doubt over the reality of global warming in order to buy time for corporate concerns that have a stake in the energy status quo and are prepared, for this reason, to pay big dollars to create confusion around the topic. These people are more properly termed 'deniers'.

But to keep it clean and simple, we've used these two labels to represent the opposing sides in the debate. Like all exercises in taxonomy, it's not perfect, and it isn't even-handed: the respectable term 'Sceptic' makes deniers appear more sincere than they deserve to appear, whereas the term 'Alarmist' paints all subscribers to the theory of anthropogenic global warming as insincere and irresponsible. We apologise for any offence or inconvenience to the Alarmists.

But let's remind ourselves: this is an argument where one side must be right, the other side wrong. If the Sceptics are right, the IPCC et al. *are* being alarmist, in the dictionary sense of someone who creates false or unnecessary alarm. If the cap fits, and all that — it's the purpose of this book to work out who gets the headgear.

Whose side are **you** on then?

We've tried to approach the topic from a position of perfect agnosticism. After all, neither of us knew the answer at the start, even though we began with our individual suspicions. Along the way, on this, our epic voyage of discovery, it's been surprisingly easy to maintain this agnosticism, because whereas we'd both expected reason to be drawn unerringly to the correct answer like a compass needle to magnetic north, we found throughout the process that our faculties flapped about like weather vanes, pointing to wherever the latest gust of information happened to have originated.

All this talk about two sides who are 'Poles Apart' suggests bitter and diametric opposition. Surely you're making it seem worse than it is? I mean, scientists are grown-ups — they're only interested in the merits of a theory and the quality of evidence, aren't they?

Yeah, right. That's what we thought, too. But this topic, unlike any other in recent memory (or at least, in our recent memory) — perhaps unlike any since the debate over Charles Darwin's theory of evolution by natural selection (and its modern adversary, the theory of intelligent design) — just seems to get danders up. Neither side can quite abide the other, and you'll see some pretty immoderate things written and said on both sides of the divide. It's not just the quality of the arguments that get trashed: neither side is above indulging in out-and-out ad hominem mud-slinging as well. Perhaps wounded professional pride is part of it. After all, it's impossible to make an assertion one way or the other without at least implying your opponents lack sincerity, or competence, or both. (Not that there's any shortage of *explicit* statements that any given writer's opponents are insincere and incompetent.) But the depth of feeling is both surprising and disappointing.

The Sceptics would have you believe the vehemence of the Alarmists is calculated to deflect attention away from the weaknesses in their case, and to suppress dissent. The Alarmists retort that it's hard to keep your cool when you're dealing with malicious peddlers of disinformation who aren't qualified to speak, let alone be taken seriously . . . You get the picture.

Talking about qualifications, what makes you think you can decide who's right and who's wrong in a debate between highly trained scientists?

Good question! In the end, we believe we're about as well qualified to form an opinion as anybody else you care to name. The sheer complexity of climate science, and the breadth of the range of disciplines it crosses, means that practically everyone is all at sea when considering most of it, and that includes scientists.

After all, modern science is highly specialised. The age of the polymath has passed, and the more specialised you are, the less likely you are to be competent in a field other than your own, let alone all of them. Even the leading expert in any given aspect of climate science will be ill-equipped to gauge the merits of other aspects in their fine detail — the most revered authority in atmospheric chemistry will stand about as much chance of picking up erroneous assumptions, experimental blunders, exaggerated claims and falsified figures in the work of an oceanographer as would an economist, or a political philosophy graduate — or a plumber, or a nurse, for that matter, or more relevantly, a policy analyst or a cabinet minister — although they might have a greater familiarity with technical writing and a better knowledge of basic physical science.

No individual has a sufficient grasp of climate science to claim to be able to pronounce the theory of anthropogenic global warming right or wrong in all its particulars. That means everyone's in the same boat, even if some have a slightly better view of the horizon.

That said, we firmly believe the sheer complexity and extreme technical difficulty of climate science shouldn't be allowed to be a barrier to gaining a working knowledge of the theory of anthropogenic global warming, or to assessing the quality of the evidence for or against it. If such a barrier exists, it must be removed. Specialist knowledge that can't be communicated intelligibly to the non-specialist is of no more practical use to humankind (in a democracy, at least) than ignorance.

Why do we need to understand anthropogenic global warming? Why don't we just believe what the IPCC is telling us?

The implications of the theory of anthropogenic global warming make it the most important issue our generation will face — far more important than workaday war, famine, pestilence, or tax hikes. After all, every single one of these things — even tax hikes — will follow in the train of global warming, if it eventuates. Few generations, if any, have faced anything quite like it, if indeed any have. Even those generations that saw major transformations in scientific understanding — those living around the time of Galileo, for example, or Darwin — were confronted with new ways of thinking about the universe rather than with the discovery of a scientific fact that demanded action, with otherwise potentially dire consequences. In other words, previous scientific revolutions have been mainly theoretical, rather than practical, in their implications.

In Western democracies, we're currently being asked to say yea or nay to policy that is being formulated as a response to the theory of anthropogenic global warming, and the ramifications of our choice are far from trivial. It's imperative, for this reason, that we make an informed choice rather than one based on blind faith. The stakes are simply too high for us to ignore the consequences of getting it wrong. It stands to reason that if we're to judge the merits of the action proposed by our leaders and policy-makers, we must understand what it is they're contemplating and why (and hope our leaders and policy-makers have been at least as diligent in framing their understanding, too).

I've heard there's a consensus of scientists on the subject of global warming. Surely that's good enough for me?

Last time we looked, 'consensus thinking' was considered to be the antithesis of good scientific method. You only resort to consensus in a world where the truth isn't clear and you need the comfort of numbers to help you deal with your insecurity — or the weight of numbers to ensure dissenters fall into line. Scientists, by contrast, are supposed to have regard only for the evidence — whether observations of the real world support or contradict the prevailing theory. Consequently, when it's scientists who are appealing to a 'consensus' — real or aspirational — as the validating principle of a hypothesis, alarm bells ought to start ringing. Hence the need for scepticism.

Australian zoologist Tim Flannery, a wonderfully eloquent writer on the subject of climate change and someone who is convinced that human-induced catastrophic climate change is upon us, nevertheless acknowledges in his bestselling book *The Weather Makers* that 'deep scepticism has a particularly important role to play in science', and that 'many people have reacted with rightful caution to news about climate change. After all, we have in the past got things badly wrong.'

History is littered with the wrecks of bandwagons, which ran off the road despite the sheer numbers of eminent scientists, philosophers, politicians and academics who jumped on to await Rapture, or Armageddon, or Utopia, or whatever else was supposed to come next.

Predictions of global catastrophe are especially notable in this hall of shame. There seems to be something about the message of doomsayers that appeals to us, or at least to some deep-seated streak of craven millennarianism within consumers of modern mass media. Think of all the scares you've known in your own time: cancer epidemics from chemicals in widespread use in the production of food we've been eating for half a century now; the imminent (two decades ago) death of the world's forests from acid rain; the mass extinction of birds and other species from pesticides; the Y2K prediction; the clear and present danger of the extinction of all life on Earth due to the impact of an asteroid, and (poignantly, given the present topic) a number of earnest warnings in the 1970s of a looming new ice age.

Perhaps the most pathetic example of imminent death by consensus was the panic following the 1972 publication of 'The Limits to

Growth', where a group cosily named 'the Club of Rome'— 'scientists, economists, businessmen, international civil servants, heads of state and former heads of state from all five continents' — told us that the world was running out of energy resources, portending certain catastrophe within decades. Far greater exploitation of the world's resources than the Club of Rome ever imagined has occurred every year since that infallible group of luminaries met, yet within 15 years of their pronouncement, the known reserves of oil on the planet had doubled, because the actions of the cartel of oil-producing nations spurred the rest of the world into exploring for (and discovering) more and more of it.

In light of this track record, scepticism over claims that a 'consensus' exists on the menace du jour is not only understandable, but to be encouraged.

Indeed, recent examples can be found of scepticism helping rather than hindering scientific understanding. In 2003–4, to take one highly relevant instance, there was serious debate over whether the flood of fresh water from a melting of the Greenland ice sheet had in the past caused the shutdown of the so-called Atlantic 'ocean conveyor' (the system of oceanic currents by which heat is transported from the tropics to the Arctic, beneficially warming the coastlines of North America and Europe as it passes), and whether it might happen again. Why did anyone care? Well, the suggestion was that the shutdown of the conveyor in the past had plunged Europe into a mini ice age. The debate gained an edge in 2005 when a team of researchers (Bryden et al.) published a paper in *Nature* that suggested the conveyor was slowing.[1] The popular press got wind of it, and put it about that Europe was going to get dramatically colder. However, a paper by Cunningham et al. (2007) revealed that the recently observed slowdown was merely part of a pronounced natural variability in the conveyor system.[2] The IPCC subsequently proclaimed, on the strength of the new research, that a North Atlantic Conveyor shutdown was unlikely. That kind of self-correction is what science is all about.

Panel Discussion

The Intergovernmental Panel on Climate Change was established in 1988 by the World Meteorological Organization and the United Nations Environment Programme, and was charged with assessing the state of the science on the question of climate change. Or perhaps this is a little inaccurate: as its very name suggests, the IPCC was pretty convinced of the *fact* of climate change right from the outset, a reflection, no doubt, of the collective belief of the scientists of the World Meteorological Organization (WMO). It's also responsible for compiling inventories of the greenhouse emissions of nations, and for publishing the findings of its assessments.

The IPCC comprises the plenary panel, which meets annually, and three working groups, which are responsible for assessing the physical science bases of climate change (WG1), the particular risks facing human and natural systems from climate change (WG2) and the possible responses to limit greenhouse gas emissions, to mitigate and to adapt to the effects of climate change (WG3). There's also a secretariat and a bureau responsible for the administration of all this work.

The IPCC published the first of the four Assessment Reports that it has so far produced in 1990, and this largely informed a meeting of international governmental representatives at Rio de Janeiro in June 1992 (properly known as the United Nations Conference on the Environment and Development, but slightly more sexily nicknamed 'the Earth Summit'). It gave rise to a treaty called the United Nations Framework Convention on Climate Change, which 154 countries ratified.

The agreed purpose of this convention was 'to achieve stabilization of greenhouse gas concentrations in the atmosphere at a low enough level to prevent dangerous anthropogenic interference with the climate system'. It divided signatories into two groups, industrialised and developing nations, and placed the greater burden upon the former.

Trouble is, the emissions targets stipulated by the UNFCCC were non-binding; in light of the international community's track record of voluntary compliance, a binding set of targets was substituted by a conference of the parties in the former Japanese imperial capital, Kyoto, in December 1997 (the so-called Kyoto Protocol). This came into force in early 2005, although it still has not been ratified by the world's largest emitter, the United States — a minor emission omission!

Meanwhile, the IPCC went about its business, producing its second Assessment Report in 1992, the third in 2001 and the fourth in 2007. Each is a monumental document, hundreds of dense pages long and crammed with scientific detail, technical language and colourful, baffling graphs. The findings are presented in carefully calibrated language, usually signalled with italics. A scientific assessment of the probability that any given statement is correct is labelled as *likely*, *very likely*, and so on, and pieces of information presented to the IPCC (or by one part of the IPCC to another) may be *approved*, *adopted* or *accepted*, in descending order of conviction.

The Assessment Reports themselves are the work of an international community of scientists — the Fourth Assessment Report distilled the work of 800 contributing writers coordinated by 450 lead authors and rigorously checked by 2500 expert reviewers, all drawn from 130 countries.

IPCC meetings likewise bring together scientists and political representatives from all WMO member countries. It's preferred that the political representatives have some 'relevant expertise', even if in many cases this amounts to little more than having had hands-on experience of the climate control feature in the governmental limousine. Even the more dedicated and informed political reps are hardly likely to get to grips with the content of the Assessment Reports, and thus, each report has also appeared in a kind of Reader's Digest edition, the Summary for Policymakers. Whereas the Assessment Reports themselves are assembled by scientists, the politicians have a hand in the compilation of the Summaries for Policymakers.

How much gets lost — or found — in translation at the hands of the politicians is the most controversial aspect of the IPCC and its activities. A Select Committee of Britain's House of Lords made precisely this criticism in a report published in 2005, and there have been a few high-profile defections from the IPCC process itself: Richard Lindzen, MIT professor of atmospheric chemistry, who was lead author of a chapter of the IPCC's Third Assessment Report published in 2001, is probably the best-known (and most respected). Lindzen was critical of the way in which the content of his chapter was précised in the Executive Summary.

On the other hand, it is striking how little respectable scientific dissent there is both from within and from outside the IPCC. Much of the rest tends to get stuck into the IPCC message on the grounds that it *understates* the danger from anthropogenic global warming.

The IPCC's next magnum opus, the Fifth Assessment Report, is due for release in 2014.

So we should just sit back and wait for the scientists to work it all out, right?

Wrong. This is yet another respect in which the climate change debate differs from other, theoretical disputations. If the Alarmists are correct, we can't afford to let the science proceed at its own stately pace until all reasonable doubts are silenced, because the longer we delay action, the closer to futile our actions will become. It's like trying to decide whether there's a god or not when you're on your deathbed. If you wait until you have irrefutable proof — that is, until you've either guttered out into nothingness or you're face to face with the Big Guy who's holding a list of your transgressions and frowning at it — it's all too late. So you've got to cut your losses, forsake certainty and decide on the basis of the evidence available to you whether there's any real need to get down on your knees and repent.

So how can we know if we should be scared?

Unlike most scientific propositions, this one can't be demonstrated in a laboratory. We have only one Earth, and only one shot at understanding what's going on in this, our grand-scale, high-stakes experiment with the air conditioning. We don't have the luxury, as scientists usually do, of demanding repeatability.

Our approach in this book — and we recommend it to anyone who's interested enough to try it — has been to try to gather, from a committed survey of the available sources, whether there's a coherent theory of anthropogenic warming, and whether observations of the natural world corroborate it. We expected that once we'd finished our survey we'd be in one of three positions:

1. On the balance of evidence, observations of the natural world support a coherent theory of why increased concentrations of greenhouse gases due to human activity will produce significant global warming. Accordingly, policy initiatives to address global warming and its consequences are worth evaluating.

2. On the balance of evidence, observations of the natural world do not support the theory of why increased concentrations of greenhouse gases will produce significant global warming. In this case, policy initiatives to address global warming and its consequences are not worth evaluating.

3. On the balance of evidence, observations of the natural world do not support the theory of anthropogenic global warming, but the theory of anthropogenic warming is more coherent than the alternatives. Policy initiatives to address global warming and its consequences are therefore worth evaluating.

How did you go about finding out?

We read a lot, and to put it mildly, there's a lot to read — scientific papers, books, magazine and newspaper articles, blogs, online articles . . . there's an endless supply, before you even begin to consider the slab-like Assessment Reports produced by the IPCC. And because the material is highly technical, we needed guidance. So we approached eminent climate scientists working on both sides of the question (Sceptics and Alarmists) and asked them to help clarify the science for us. Our request was received with far greater enthusiasm and generosity than we could possibly have hoped for, let alone expected, and our muddled, wrongheaded and obtuse questions were treated with patient courtesy throughout. The impromptu panels we assembled went further still, and solicited input from their friends and colleagues on our behalf, so that we finished up in contact, one way or another, with some of the most eminent climate scientists on the planet. We are deeply indebted to all involved; and the principal contributors are named in the acknowledgements. By the time we reached the point we recognised as the end of our research, we felt we'd had the best possible instruction and were in the best possible position to reach a decision.

And the verdict is . . .?

In Chapter 8. But getting there is half the fun!

I've had a flick through the book, and I saw some graphs. I'm a bit scared of graphs. And I'm a little bit afraid there might be big words and maths and stuff.

While it's pretty much impossible to achieve what we've set out to achieve without recourse to numbers, technical terms and the occasional bit of maths, we've tried to keep it all as simple as we could. We've presumed a bit of familiarity with very basic scientific terms, but we've included a glossary at the back of the book that explains all terms, both basic and not-so-basic. And while we are well aware that graphs can be a bit of a judder bar in the reading journey, the graphs we've used aren't gratuitous: they actually help to show at a glance what a whole array of otherwise meaningless numbers are trying to tell us. We've done our best to explain within the text or the caption what you're looking at in every case.

What if I don't agree with your conclusion?

We hope that by the time we reveal our considered opinion on the theory of global warming, you'll have reached a considered opinion, too. We're not out to tell anyone what to think, but rather to show how we reached our own position. But you may feel you want to read more on the subject. We've tried to keep references to a minimum, but those we've included will direct you to the sources of our information. Since a lot of the material that has informed the text has taken the form of email correspondence, we've chosen to make much of this stuff available on a website: www.polesapart.com, and we encourage interested readers to check it out. Doubtless the lively controversy that we've been privileged to be in the middle of these last few months will rage on. It's compelling viewing.

Whatever you decide, we hope you enjoy the journey.

Gareth Morgan & John McCrystal
Wellington, New Zealand
February 2009

Chapter 1

What Is 'Global Warming'?

Even the most complacent citizen of the developed world will have heard of 'global warming' or 'climate change' by now. But ignorance of what the phenomenon actually is — and you'll hear it described as 'climate change', 'global warming', the 'greenhouse effect' — is not confined to the complacent and the uninterested. And the way it has been discussed has changed through time. When it first appeared on the anxiety radar of the developed world, it was almost universally referred to as 'global warming'. But that didn't sound so bad, particularly to people who found their local conditions left a little to be desired, and whose stock response to the prospect of another degree or two on the thermometer was 'Bring it on!'

Quite apart from the marketing difficulties, use of the term 'global warming' stood to cause confusion and promote scepticism, because while the overall global effect is a warming of the planet, individual localities might experience little or no change, or even a change for the cooler, depending upon the complex combination of drivers that determine their regional climate. Similarly, and as we'll see, few scientists use the term 'the greenhouse effect', because this, too, potentially causes confusion with a natural, beneficial property of the atmosphere. Before we proceed, then, it's necessary to establish from the outset what we're talking about.

'Anthropogenic' global warming — what it's not

Pollution

Ever since the 1970s, and the rise of the environmentalist movement, the wider public has been aware of the notion of 'pollution'. We've all seen a deterioration in the quality of our waterways, and if you live in any of the major cities in the world, or even in any small centre of population snuggled up under the lee of a mountain range, you can periodically see air pollution happening. It's that yellow haze that wreathed the tops of skyscrapers and obscured much of our view of the Beijing Olympics; it's that smoky fog — popularly known as 'smog' since the term was coined in 1905 — choking the streets of London of a winter. It consists of a mixture of gases (which you can't see), and 'particulates'— microscopic particles of soot and other chemicals — (which you can see), and it comes from such sources as industrial smokestacks, vehicle exhausts, domestic fireplaces, forest fires and volcanoes, and the reaction of all of these with atmospheric constituents and sunlight.

Technically, this kind of pollution affects 'local air quality' without having any global significance (although the sources named above are also sources of the gases that are of concern to anthropogenic global warming). Indeed, and perversely, particulates have been credited with mitigating the full effects of global warming at times in our recent past, although that's not quite the same thing as saying air pollution is a good thing. In fact, inhalation of particulates is known to affect your health and even to measurably shorten your life.

For the purposes of our discussion, however, the only link between local air quality pollution and anthropogenic warming is that in both cases it is human activity that has degraded the natural environment.

Ozone depletion, or 'the ozone hole'

Most people are dimly aware that there was a panic some years ago about a 'hole' scientists had discovered in a layer of the atmosphere over the Antarctic ice cap that was letting in harmful radiation. The part of the atmosphere that was affected was the 'ozone layer', and the reason for its depletion was the release of certain long-lived manufactured gases — mostly a group called chlorofluorocarbons, or CFCs for short — that reacted with ozone and destroyed it.

Ozone, we learned, was a trace constituent in the atmosphere as a whole, and was primarily concentrated in the lower reaches of the region known as the stratosphere (that is, approximately 20 km from the Earth's surface) — the so-called 'ozone layer'. In fact, ozone is found throughout the atmosphere, from the Earth's surface to the atmosphere's outer reaches, but in this part of the atmosphere it's created by a reaction of oxygen with sunlight. And it's a good thing, we learned, that all that ozone is up there, because it shields the Earth's surface, including all other living things and us, from some of the more dangerous forms of radiation that reach us from the sun.

Ozone is destroyed by a range of natural processes, too. But more significantly, it turned out that all those CFCs that were being used as propellants in aerosol cans and as the refrigerant in refrigerators and air-conditioning systems were escaping into the upper atmosphere where, due to the patterns of atmospheric mixing and circulation, they were becoming concentrated over the South Pole during the winter. Here, they were broken down to release their chlorine, which concentrated on ice crystals high in the atmosphere. Each spring, as the sun returns to the Antarctic, the area of chlorine-rich (and ozone-depleted) air breaks up and spreads northwards.

Stories of looming environmental catastrophe are two a penny. Stories of looming environmental catastrophe with a happy ending, on the other hand, are impossibly rare. Despite protests (and denial) from industries that produced and relied upon CFCs, scientists and policy-makers moved swiftly to address the problem, with a round of meetings and summits culminating in a ban on the production of CFCs and a set of steps to limit their release, signed in Montreal in 1987 (the Montreal Protocol). The growth of the ozone hole, which had been rapid every year since its detection in 1985, slowed, and although it continues to grow (the hole of 2008 was of record extent) we may even begin to hope that the atmosphere will heal. Suppose there's no resumption of CFC manufacture or release, and once those long-lived chlorine (and bromine) molecules have finally dissipated, we might just have dodged a bullet.

While there are broad similarities between the ozone-hole drama and the alleged looming environmental catastrophe that is climate change — both involve potentially disastrous damage on a global scale as a result of human activity, and both have to do with the release of gases that perturb the delicate balance of trace atmospheric constituents — they are not strictly related. The two — global warming and ozone depletion — are frequently confused. It doesn't help that ozone is actually a greenhouse gas in its own right (but only a minor player in climate change). Nor does it help that climate scientists talk about 'aerosols' a lot, although they're referring to particles in the atmosphere rather than spray-on deodorants or flyspray.

The ozone-hole story has some further relevance to the matter at hand. It provided a model for swift, decisive and (above all) effective action on environmental damage caused by human activity. Much of the way in which the IPCC has proceeded was modelled on the Montreal Protocol experience.

The greenhouse effect

One of the most popular names for anthropogenic global warming is not quite accurate. The 'greenhouse effect' actually refers to a beneficial property of the atmosphere, namely its ability to trap thermal energy (heat) that would otherwise be dissipated from the Earth's surface into deep space. Without this property, life as we know it would be all but unsustainable. The mechanism involved in anthropogenic global warming — and we'll examine it in more detail shortly — is the same, but it is misleading to refer to 'the greenhouse effect' as a bad thing.

Anthropogenic global warming — what it is, and how it works

What *is* meant by all the loose talk of 'global warming', 'climate change' and 'the greenhouse effect' is what you might call the 'enhanced greenhouse effect', or human changes to the natural greenhouse effect that are alleged to give rise to deleterious effects. In the simplest possible terms, the theory of anthropogenic global warming states that human activity is enhancing the natural tendency of the atmosphere to trap heat ordinarily radiated from the Earth's surface into space. According to the theory, this must lead to increases in atmospheric and surface temperature, and to changes in the various systems that comprise the Earth's climate. Many, if not most, of these changes are expected to be regrettable at best, and catastrophic at worst.

In order to understand both the theory and the various objections to it, it's necessary to understand how the 'greenhouse effect' — both the benign, natural version and the anthropogenically enhanced version — is supposed to work. Some basic scientific knowledge is presumed in what follows, but if you're inclined to muddle your atoms with your molecules, your infrared with your ultraviolet, we refer you to the glossary at the back of the book.

A short history of the atmosphere

One of the absolute preconditions for the existence of life on Earth — by which we mean *any* life, not just human life — is the presence of the atmosphere. Simply put, and as the name suggests (*atmos* is Greek for 'vapour', and *sphere* needs no explanation), the atmosphere is the thin envelope of gases and particles clinging to the surface of our home planet, held there by the Earth's gravity. It serves several essential purposes: it shields us from the bulk of the harmful radiation emanating from the sun and from deep space; it maintains the surface of the Earth at a relatively constant temperature; and it supplies the gases upon which most life processes depend.

There are plenty of planets with atmospheres floating around. Indeed, 'gas giants' such as Jupiter consist almost entirely of atmosphere, and most stars have an atmosphere of sorts. But not any old atmosphere will do when it comes to supporting life. Even the Earth's atmosphere has been hostile to life as we know it for most of the planet's history. We're currently reckoned to be on our third configuration of the atmosphere. The first, which is thought to have consisted of hydrogen and helium, disappeared into space soon after the birth of the planet. The second, the result of the outpourings of volcanoes in the newly formed solid crust (and possibly bequeathed by the collisions of comets and meteors containing volatile compounds), consisted of ammonia, methane, carbon dioxide and water vapour, and wouldn't have been much use to us, either. You might as well have tried getting a lungful on Venus or Jupiter as breathing the local air of four billion years ago.

The photolysis (literally, the breakdown by sunlight) of ammonia eventually reduced concentrations of that gas in the atmosphere, and produced in its stead the most abundant of the gases in the present set-up — nitrogen. The appearance of organisms that were capable of using water and carbon dioxide to produce the complex compounds upon which they subsisted started an aeons-long transformation of the atmosphere. The by-product of this process (called photosynthesis) is oxygen, and once the Earth's air began to feature significant proportions of this gas, it began to be possible for organisms more complex than the algal slimes that had hitherto ruled the world to develop.

Third time lucky

The dry composition of the third atmosphere (it usually contains around 1% water vapour) — the remarkably hospitable and stable arrangement of gases we enjoy at the moment — is roughly 78% nitrogen, 21% oxygen and just under 1% argon. Other gases, such as carbon dioxide (CO_2) and ozone (O_3), are mere traces.

It's arranged in layers, each defined by certain properties. The lowest of these (that is, the one adjacent to the Earth's surface and extending upwards for as much as 18 km) is the **troposphere,** so named (*tropos* means 'to turn' or 'change' in Greek) because it's a dynamic zone of convection (the rising and falling of hot and cold air masses) and it's where all the weather happens. Heat, as we'll see, is produced by the influence of solar radiation on the Earth's surface, and hence just above ground level is the warmest part of the troposphere. As you rise through the troposphere, moving away from the source of the heat, the air temperature decreases.

At a certain point (around 18 km above the surface of the Earth at the equator, and around 8 km above the North and South Poles) that cooling trend reverses: as you continue to rise, the air now begins to warm up (as molecules that are heated by the shortwave radiation from the sun, particularly ozone, become relatively more abundant). The point at which the cooling trend stops and the warming trend starts is termed the **tropopause,** and this comprises the boundary between the troposphere and the next layer out, the **stratosphere.**

The stratosphere (from *stratos,* meaning 'spread out' in Greek) is a comparatively stable region, and its component gases are quite different from those of the troposphere. Most of the gases in the troposphere consist of fairly reactive molecules (that is, they react with one another, or are susceptible to breaking down in sunlight), and are therefore quite short-lived. Longer-lived molecules tend to find their way into the stratosphere. Perhaps the most significant stratospheric gas, found in its highest relative concentrations in the upper stratosphere, is — as we've seen — ozone, a type of oxygen comprising three rather than the usual two atoms. When high-energy radiation from the sun encounters stratospheric ozone, much of the radiation is absorbed by the destruction of ozone molecules. If it weren't, the surface of the planet would be inhospitable for much of life as we know it.

Above the stratosphere (beginning at an altitude of roughly 90 km above the Earth's surface) lie the **mesosphere** (*meso* meaning 'middle' in Greek), the **ionosphere** (sometimes called the thermosphere) and the **exosphere.** Each serves its purpose — the ionosphere, for example, reflects radio waves, and it's because we can bounce radio waves off it that we can send signals from one side of the Earth to the other — but these regions are less well understood. (Indeed, so poorly understood is the mesosphere, which is too high for aircraft to operate in and too low for orbital craft to enter, that it's sometimes called the 'ignorosphere' by scientists.) They are, at any rate, largely irrelevant to the topic at hand, which involves the troposphere and (to a very small degree) the stratosphere.

Besides gases, the atmosphere also contains aerosols (as we've already noted, not to be confused with flyspray or deodorant cans), which are small particles or droplets such as soot, dust, sulphates and what are known as volatile organic compounds (usually referred to as VOCs). These are most abundant in the troposphere, which most of the sources — industry, the combustion of forests, fossil fuels and so on — adjoin, although all those scientists and politicians tooling their way around the world to and from global-warming conferences and summits tend to cruise about in airliners which fly in or just above the tropopause to avoid the worst of the world's weather, and dump soot, sulphates and VOCs into the stratosphere. Events such as volcanic eruptions can inject huge quantities of dust and particles directly into the stratosphere, too.

The stratosphere also contains water vapour, both from the troposphere (although the elevation of water beyond the tropopause is comparatively infrequent) and from a chain of reactions involving methane gas, but water is a relatively minor constituent.

Let there be light

Visible light — the stuff we can see — is a form of electromagnetic radiation. There are other kinds, ranging from the type of radiation that makes our televisions and radios work through to nasties such as gamma rays, produced by the burst of atomic weapons, for example, and by many heavenly bodies. What all forms of electromagnetic radiation have in common is that they comprise **photons**. These are best thought of as packets of mobile energy, and they are peculiar, in that they behave both like a stream of particles and like a series of waves all at the same time. It's the wave-like properties of electromagnetic radiation that we use to differentiate between the various species, because each is defined by its 'wavelength' or 'frequency', which can actually be measured. The shorter the wavelength, the higher the frequency; and the higher the frequency, the greater the energy of the radiation in question. Radio waves have a long wavelength (as much as a kilometre, even more), a low frequency and therefore low energy. At the other end of the spectrum, gamma rays have a very short wavelength (0.01 of a nanometre, one-hundredth of one-billionth of a metre, or even less), a very high frequency and therefore pack a lot of energy. Radio waves are completely harmless, as they have little effect on the atoms and molecules they impact upon, whereas gamma rays cause catastrophic damage to living tissue because of the amount of energy they impart and the havoc they can cause to the molecular bonds of complex molecules such as DNA.

It so happens that the human eye is adapted to react to the impact of electromagnetic radiation within a certain range, namely from 400 to 700 nanometres (blue to red respectively). The likely reason the eye has evolved to be sensitive to these wavelengths, incidentally, is that most of the radiation reaching the surface of the Earth from the sun occurs within this band. The range of wavelengths that can be detected by the human eye is usually referred to as 'light' or the visible spectrum (although just to confuse matters, both infrared and ultraviolet radiation, while invisible to the naked eye, are commonly called 'light' as well). The visible spectrum itself lies just a little to one side of the middle of the broader electromagnetic spectrum. Immediately above it is ultraviolet radiation, and immediately below it is infrared radiation.

Electromagnetic radiation is the means by which energy from the chemical reactions occurring on the sun is transferred across space to the Earth. Millions of complex chemical and physical processes are caused in the atmosphere, in the Earth's crust and in the oceans by the various incident forms of radiation. Many of them are essential to life:

the energy in blue-violet and orange-red visible light, for example, is used by green plants to break the bonds of carbon dioxide and water to create the complex molecules called carbohydrates (with which every diet-conscious citizen of the world is familiar) which, in turn, are used by animals that eat the plants to power their own life systems. There are millions of complex reactions and effects produced by the solar irradiation of the Earth and its atmosphere, but we're chiefly concerned here with just one: heat.

The heat is on

Among the many and variously convoluted technical definitions of heat, the most useful one is probably that heat is 'energy in transit'. One of the properties of the universe is that it is seeking a state of equilibrium where the same amount of energy exists at every point, and one of the ways in which energy is transferred from one point in the universe to another is by heat. There's a kind of gradient, that is, between hot and cold bodies, and heat moves from one to the other as surely as air will move from an area of high pressure to an area of low pressure, or a ball will roll down a slope.

The scientific definition of a hot body (and here you can readily see the difference between scientists and the buyers of shrink-wrapped magazines) is one in which the molecules are in a state of excitement, moving vigorously; a cold body is one in which there is less movement of its constituent molecules. The difference between a hot glass of water and a cold one, that is, consists in the level of excitement of the water molecules in each. This is why you'll occasionally hear 'heat' defined as 'molecular energy' — it's the energy that causes molecules to move randomly in space.

Heat moves in three ways: by convection, by conduction and by radiation. Convection is the process at work when hot air (or water, or other fluid) rises and its place is taken by cold air (or water, or other fluid). You can see it at work when you look at the movement of tea leaves in a cup of tea: some leaves move upward as hot water rises, carrying them along with it. Some fall, as the cooler water they're borne in is displaced by the warmer. Conduction is the movement of heat from a hot part of a body to cooler parts, as where the handle of a frypan placed on a hot stove will heat up although it's the pan that is being directly warmed. Radiation is the emission of photons, and in this case, the radiation of heat is the emission of photons in the infrared spectrum. (See Figure i in the first colour section for an illustration of the electromagnetic spectrum.)

As mentioned above, infrared radiation is the band of the electromagnetic spectrum immediately below (in terms of frequency) the longest wavelength component of the visible, which is red light (*infra* means 'beneath' in Latin). Within the broad definition of infrared, there are higher- and lower-wavelength radiations — in other words, there is an entire infrared spectrum. As a body is warmed, it begins to emit photons. At first, these are comparatively low in energy and of longer wavelength, occupying the 'far infrared' end of the infrared spectrum. Heat the body further, and the photons emitted are of proportionately higher energy and their wavelength shortens. Heat it further still, and some photons will be of sufficient energy to fall in the visible spectrum. In this state, the object is both hot (and emitting infrared radiation) and glowing red (emitting red light). Carry on heating it, and it will emit light of progressively shorter wavelengths in addition to infrared and red: the body will change colour from red to orange to yellow and finally to white ('white hot', emitting the entire visible spectrum).

Much of the radiation emitted by the sun is very high in energy. Most of this doesn't reach the Earth at all, being intercepted in the upper atmosphere — gamma and X-rays by the ionosphere, ultraviolet radiation by the ozone layer in the stratosphere — although a proportion does reach the surface. Some of it is reflected, but the energy of a further fraction is absorbed by the surface, whether it be the solid crust or the liquid ocean, and the effect is to heat up what it strikes. The substances so warmed, like all hot bodies, emit infrared radiation (or 'heat') in their turn.

The greenhouse effect (again)

If there were no atmosphere, the heat produced by the irradiation of the Earth's surface would be largely lost to deep space in the form of the re-radiation of infrared. This is, indeed, the fate of much of it; but the atmosphere traps a proportion, through the agency of the so-called 'greenhouse gases'.

The major constituents of the atmosphere, nitrogen and oxygen, are simple biatomic gases — that is, their molecules comprise pairs of strongly bonded atoms. These are completely transparent to infrared radiation, allowing it to pass without reflecting or absorbing it. But many of the minor constituent gases consist of more complex molecules. Carbon dioxide, for example, comprises a carbon atom bonded to two oxygen atoms, arranged in a straight line; water vapour is a 'Mickey Mouse' molecule, with two hydrogen 'ears' bonded to an oxygen atom; the methane molecule comprises a carbon atom bonded to four hydrogen atoms in a tetrahedral arrangement. And then there are other, even more complex molecules, such as the so-called halocarbons, which comprise combinations of carbon atoms and atoms of halogens, such as chlorine, fluorine and bromine.

When infrared radiation strikes the right kind of complex molecule, it is absorbed. That is, the energy of the photons is transferred to the molecule, by creating a 'flexing' of its molecular bonds — radiant energy is converted to molecular energy.

The configuration of the atoms and the nature of the bonds within the molecule determines what form this 'flexing' takes, which in turn determines precisely which wavelengths of the infrared spectrum are absorbed; carbon dioxide, for example, which can be imagined as three atoms in a straight line, can either wobble up and down (like a skipping rope) or stretch and retract (like a spring). Each kind of flexing requires the absorption of infrared radiation of a different wavelength. Needless to say, there are more ways in which more complex molecules may flex, and thus more complex molecules can absorb a broader range of infrared radiation.

Having absorbed some proportion of the infrared radiation emanating from the Earth and heading for the deeps of space, these wobbling, stretching molecules re-emit it in random directions. Some ends up in deep space after all. Some is absorbed by adjacent molecules of greenhouse gases. Some is directed back toward the Earth's surface.

So in simple terms, what we have is the sun irradiating the Earth's surface, the Earth's surface radiating infrared, and greenhouse gas molecules absorbing it and re-radiating it furiously, some toward the Earth, some into space. Where the amount of sunlight coming in and the number of greenhouse gas molecules remain constant, an equilibrium exists between the amount of radiation coming in, the amount of radiation going out (that is, being lost into deep space) and the temperature of the Earth's surface. But alter either side of the equation (it gets called the Earth's radiation 'budget') by altering the amount of sunlight coming in or by decreasing the amount of longwave radiation going out, and that equilibrium is disturbed. The Earth's temperature must rise or fall until a new equilibrium is established.

Think of it like this. You've got a heater going in your room, and you've also got a window open. The room temperature is constant, because the amount of heat produced by the heater is offset by the amount lost through the window. This is a state of equilibrium. If you turn on another heater, the temperature in the room will rise until it, too, is offset by the heat loss through the window. Or, alternatively, if you close the window a bit, the heat will also rise until a new equilibrium is established. The heater is the sun's rays. The amount the window is open or closed is equivalent to the number of molecules of greenhouse gases available to absorb infrared radiation.

As already noted, while the term 'greenhouse effect' has solely negative connotations in the popular mind in this day and age, it is actually a positive thing. Without the heat-trapping effect of greenhouse gases in the atmosphere, it has been estimated that the average surface temperature of the globe would be −17°C, as opposed to the +15°C it currently is. The 'trapping' of heat close to the surface that would otherwise be lost to space is one of the functions of the atmosphere that makes life on Earth (at least as we know it) possible. No scientist that we're aware of disputes the existence of the greenhouse effect or how it works. It bears repeating that contrary to what is widely believed, the greenhouse effect is not the problem at work in global warming; rather, what is feared is an *enhanced* greenhouse effect, where an *excess* of greenhouse gases traps an excess of heat.

Living dead carbon

So what constitutes 'an excess of greenhouse gases'? The theory of anthropogenic global warming states that human activity has been adding greenhouse gases to the atmosphere, where they do what they do — namely trap infrared radiation — over and above the levels that would be trapped by the fraction of greenhouse gases already present naturally. The chief, but not the only, villain is carbon dioxide. It's not the fact that we produce carbon dioxide that's the problem — after all, carbon dioxide is a by-product of the very act of breathing, and it is one phase of what gets called the 'living carbon cycle'. The problem apparently arises when we contribute to the atmosphere carbon dioxide generated from sources outside the living carbon cycle, most notably from the burning of fossil fuels and the production of cement. And as these have been favourite human activities since the industrial revolution, the problem has been gathering momentum at the same rate as industrial activity. Most of the standard of living enjoyed by the developed world has therefore been produced through the burning of fossil fuels; and if the theory of anthropogenic global warming is correct, all that prosperity has come at a price — the climatic stability that is essential to most of the Earth system. And it's that very stability on which humankind depends, not only for a cosy standard of living, but ultimately for its very existence.

Let's look at this in a little more detail, because the difference between living and fossil carbon is crucial to understanding the theory of anthropogenic global warming.

The basis of all life on Earth — with the arguable exception of weird, chemical-eating bacteria hanging out around volcanic vents in the abyssal depths of the oceans — is the sun. The blue-violet and orange-red fractions of the visible spectrum are used in the process of photosynthesis, whereby plants 'fix' carbon dioxide from the air and water from the soil into carbohydrates (complex sugars which, as their name suggests, are combinations of carbon and hydrogen atoms). Carbohydrates are stored energy, which is why plants make them. The energy stored in them is released when they are 'burned' in living cells, whether that's in the cells of the plant that made them, or in the cells of animals that eat the plants, or animals that eat the animals that ate the plants (and so on, up the food chain). This 'burning' requires oxygen, which both plants and animals draw in from the atmosphere, and its by-product is carbon dioxide. So some of the carbon originally fixed in photosynthesis is released back into the atmosphere; the rest is used to build the other complex molecules (proteins, fats and oils) that comprise living tissue. When a plant (or animal) dies, it undergoes another complex set of chemical processes known as decomposition, and some of the carbon involved in its body tissues finds its way back into the atmosphere. The rest remains in the ground. This round of capture, use and release of carbon is the basis of the so-called 'living carbon cycle'. There are other elements to it, as well. Free carbon dioxide is also dissolved in the oceans, in proportions that depend upon the temperature of the water (ever noticed that warm fizzy drinks are much fizzier than cold?), and carbonates are used by some living organisms (such as corals, plankton and shellfish) to produce the solid structures in which they live.

This cycle — photosynthesis, metabolism, tissue-building, decomposition — and the cycles involved in shell- and coral reef-building have been going on for aeons, and as each generation of plants and animals has lived and died, some proportion of the carbon that was fixed in tissue or in reefs and shells has been deposited (the fashionable term is 'sequestered') in this way. Over time, deposits of carbon-bearing compounds have grown enormously concentrated, and when subjected to the right combinations of geological pressures and temperatures, ancient reefs and shellfish beds have formed chalks

and limestones, and deposits of dead plants have produced reservoirs
of sludgy, carbon-rich liquids (better known as crude oil), seams of
solid, almost pure carbon (coal) and pockets of natural gas.

Under natural conditions (that is, without human intervention),
the living carbon cycle has tended to maintain an equilibrium between
free carbon, carbon locked up in living tissue, carbon dissolved
in the oceans and carbon fixed in minerals, and the whole balance
has depended upon temperature. The equilibrium has always been
vulnerable, and each shock, most notably a rise or fall in temperature,
has required a new equilibrium to be established.

Human activity has assaulted the equilibrium of the latter-day
living carbon cycle in two main ways. As the industrial revolution got
under way, it changed the way land was used. Deforestation and the
intensification of agriculture had the potential to perturb the balance.
The burning of forests returned to the atmosphere the proportion of
carbon fixed in trees that was otherwise destined to be sequestered in
the ground, and it replaced the carbon-fixing capacity of the forest
with the lesser capacity of crop and pasture.

And the story of the industrial revolution really boils down to the
story of the exploitation of fossil energy. The development of the first
practical steam engine by the English inventor James Watt, which he
patented in 1775, ran on coal, and this marked the beginning of what
has been called 'the carbon economy'. The perfection of techniques
for recovering crude oil and refining it into liquid fuels represented
a massive escalation in the process of dumping fossil carbon into the
contemporary living carbon cycle. And meanwhile, the production of
cement, a process that uses another fossil form of carbon and releases
carbon dioxide, went into overdrive. Look around you and note how
much of the built environment comprises concrete.

Water, water, everywhere

All of this — the reanimation of fossil carbon, combined with the
biosphere's reduced capacity for its sequestration — looks ominous

enough to those inclined to believe that adding CO_2 to the atmosphere is a problem. But it gets a whole lot worse, because of the interconnectedness of various elements of the climate system.

As we've already had occasion to note, much of the free carbon abroad at any given point in time is dissolved in the world's oceans, and the cooler the water, the more carbon dioxide it can hold in solution. Warm the water, and the ocean's capacity to absorb is reduced, meaning more CO_2 remains in the air. Warm the water further and it releases some of its dissolved carbon dioxide into the atmosphere, where it too can contribute to the enhanced greenhouse effect. Not only that, but water vapour is a greenhouse gas in its own right, and the warmer the world, the more evaporation and the more water vapour in the atmosphere. So carbon dioxide may serve as a mere trigger to the much greater warming effect of water vapour.

Rotten luck

But wait, there's more. Vast reserves of methane, another potent greenhouse gas mostly formed by the decomposition of dead tissue, lie beneath the oceans in peculiar structures known as clathrates, and in semi-decayed matter deep-frozen in the permafrost of the northern tundras. It's been argued that it won't take much warming of the seabed and the frozen tundra to liberate all that methane.

Low albedo

And we haven't finished yet. Much of the Earth is covered by 'permanent' ice in its various forms, notably ice sheets and caps, and glaciers. These have the effect of reflecting solar radiation (a property known as 'albedo'), and deflecting much of the energy that might otherwise be converted to heat and retained by greenhouse gases. But there will be less ice in a warmer world, and therefore reduced albedo. The ground (or ocean) exposed where ice has melted will convert into heat all that radiation that the ice formerly reflected into space, warming the world. And the warmer the world, the faster ice will melt, and so on.

The cumulative effect of these various 'feedback' mechanisms is accelerating global warming, with the enhanced greenhouse effect leading to warming, and the warming enhancing the greenhouse effect.

All very scary, isn't it? But remember, this is the theory. Now that we know what *can* go wrong, how do we establish what *is* going on with the Earth's climate?

Chapter 2

Taking the Earth's Temperature

Whatever the weather

Human beings have always been interested in the weather. For much of the history of our species, we had to be. After all, if you are a hunter-gatherer, farmer, gardener or fisherman, knowing what the heavens are going to throw at you is essential to the success of your enterprise, and often to your very survival.

Once people became civilised enough to fight wars on a national scale and to crave empires with which to dominate trade, the weather loomed as a critical variable in military endeavour. Much of what we know about the weather in far-flung regions of the Earth was collected by people trying to work out whether favourable winds would bless their fleets of merchantmen or warships, and whether the sun would shine on manoeuvres.

Even in the modern world, where technology has all but insulated us from rain, hail and shine, the fascination endures, and the nightly weather bulletin is one of the most watched items on prime-time television. And few topics rival the weather as the stuff of casual conversation.

Programmes for the systematic observation of weather were set up in several locations and among several different dynasties in the pre-industrial era, notably among the Arabs around the tenth century AD and in Renaissance Florence, where the science-minded Medici family organised the first regular weather report from a network of observers. Other such networks were established subsequently, but it wasn't until the 1800s, with the invention of the telegraph, that it became possible to establish an observation network on a national scale. The first such organisation was the United States national weather service, which commenced relaying the observations of volunteers by telegraph in 1849. The British Meteorological Office was set up as a unit within the Board of Trade in 1854, and when newspaper weather forecasts were inaugurated with the publication of the very first report in *The Times* in 1861, they relied upon information provided by the Met Office.

Other countries soon followed in establishing national meteorological services. In 1871 an international meteorological congress was held in Vienna, and when two years later the International Meteorological Organization (IMO) was set up, countries began to share information. The study of global weather — as distinct from a kind of comparing of notes — began in earnest in 1950 with the transformation of the IMO into the World Meteorological Organization (WMO), under the auspices of the United Nations, and it was from these global datasets that the very much younger science of climatology later sprang.

'Climate is what you expect; weather is what you get' — Mark Twain

The study of climate was thus slow to get under way. Climate is different from weather, even if the two are related. 'Climate' is the aggregate of weather observations made at a particular site and averaged over a period, usually 30 years. Whereas weather is local and highly variable, climate is less localised, steadier and slower to change. It's like the movement of a sharemarket index compared to the day-to-day volatility in individual stocks. For climatologists, weather is a distraction — the noise that fudges a clear climate signal.

The notion that there was such a thing as climate — a tendency of the entire Earth to warm and cool quite separately from the day-to-day vicissitudes of local and regional weather — arose in the first instance from a dawning awareness of the age of the Earth among nineteenth-century geologists, who realised that certain rock- and landforms had been generated not by the action of water but by the slow, inexorable grinding of ice.

This was news to a world which had accepted more or less without question that the whole show had been created in 4004 BC — as you could discover for yourself by carefully adding up the generations that begat other generations in the Old Testament — and which had supposed such anomalous geological features as the Grand Canyon to be evidence of the Deluge that Noah had ridden out in his ark. And once it was accepted that the Earth was not thousands but billions of years old, and that it had been covered with ice not once but many times in its history, the unsettling question emerged: what is there to stop the Earth experiencing another ice age?

Much of the effort of early climatologists was devoted to determining what caused glaciation — and ironically enough, it is to the data compiled in this undertaking that contemporary climatologists studying anthropogenic global warming are indebted. This might seem strange — as it still seems strange when you reflect that as recently as the 1970s, there was a body of respectable opinion abroad that was warning us of the global cooling crisis and the impending new ice age, even as other scientists were concluding that the theoretical link between increasing atmospheric concentrations of carbon dioxide and global warming was becoming a reality. The history of science, however, is littered with such little ironies.

So what kind of evidence bears out the theory of anthropogenic global warming, and how is it being gathered?

The direct approach

The most basic and reliable method of measuring temperature is, of course, with a thermometer. In their simplest (and most familiar) form, thermometers consist of a sealed reservoir connected to a sealed glass tube and part-filled with a liquid such as alcohol or mercury. They function on the well-known principle that heat causes liquids to expand: as the liquid in a thermometer expands or contracts in response to warming or cooling, the column creeps up or down the tube. By reading the column's position in relation to a scale on the tube, the ambient temperature can be determined.

The mercury or alcohol thermometer has been with us since 1742, when the first attempt to put a scale on the instrument known as the thermoscope — in all respects the same as a thermometer, but capable only of registering change in temperature rather than quantifying the magnitude of that change — was made by Swedish astronomer Anders Celsius.

Naturally enough, many more sophisticated versions of the thermometer have been devised, most of them electronic. Some use the known variation of the electrical resistance of a material (a metal or a ceramic) to generate an electrical signal that is interpreted by a voltmeter. Some use what is known as the Seebeck Effect, or the thermoelectric effect — the tendency of conductive materials to generate a voltage when heated — to produce an electrical signal. Yet others rely on the peculiar capability of electrical charge to 'tunnel' through a layer of insulating material between two conductors, which varies according to the temperature of the materials in question, in order to produce that electrical signal.

The fine details of the more sophisticated thermometers are difficult to explain, let alone understand, but thankfully, they're not important here. The feature all thermometers have in common is that they directly measure the temperature of the material under scrutiny. It doesn't matter which kind of thermometer you dunk in water, or expose to the air: the point is that it is reacting directly to the thermal energy in the material itself and it is conveying that reaction through a simple interface to you, the observer. A dataset generated by the consistent, attentive use of a thermometer will therefore be about as reliable a set of numbers as you can get.

There are many different datasets used in climate science that have been generated by direct instrumental measurement, and some of them are only slightly younger than the technology of the thermometer itself. Let's have a look at some of these.

The air that I breathe

As noted earlier, the direct instrumental measurement of surface air temperature (that is, of the air closest to the ground) was coordinated into a national programme in the United States in 1849 and in Great Britain in 1854. Other nations followed suit. Attempts to dust off the old record books and extract data comparable with more contemporary records began as climatology's stocks rose in the latter half of the twentieth century, notably by the British Meteorological Office's Hadley Climate Research Unit (HadCRU) and the American National Oceanic and Atmospheric Administration (NOAA) and National Aeronautics and Space Agency's (NASA) Goddard Institute for Space Studies (GISS).

The traditional, standard equipment with which national meteorological programmes monitored temperature was a simple maximum/minimum thermometer mounted in a Stevenson Screen, a white-painted, louvred box designed to protect the thermometer (and other meteorological instruments) from the elements and from direct sunlight while still allowing the free circulation of air. The Stevenson Screen was the brainchild of Thomas Stevenson, a British civil engineer (and, incidentally, the father of Robert Louis Stevenson, of *Treasure Island* fame) who devised it at the Met Office's behest in the mid-1800s. These were sited, again according to tradition, outside post offices across Great Britain (and America), and it was part of the job description of postmasters to take regular readings and record them in a 24-hour cycle from 9 am to 9 am. In the early twentieth century, Stevenson Screens were mostly moved to new sites at airfields.

The virtue of the global dataset derived from meteorological observations based on the traditional network of Stevenson Screen-housed thermometers is obvious: it has been derived from simple instrumentation consistently situated and handled, and it extends back almost to the beginning of the period of interest in the study of climate change, namely the industrial revolution.

The human factor

This global dataset is not without its obvious limitations, however. Records kept prior to (roughly speaking) the 1960s were only ever intended for local uses, such as to inform farmers or fishermen about what weather pattern was prevailing and therefore what crops were likely to succeed or what sea conditions to expect. These have proved difficult to reconcile with datasets focused on compiling a picture of global climate. For much of the history of organised meteorology, less than meticulous care was taken with the positioning of Stevenson Screens. It was common — and indeed, as climate Sceptics delight in pointing out, it's still common — to find a Stevenson Screen sited next to a building bristling with air-conditioning exhausts, or adjacent to a runway consisting of a large tract of tarmac. Screens were frequently shifted from one site to another as other demands (such as construction) required, or the nature of a site changed (trees grew, buildings and fences were constructed or demolished, grass airstrips were tarsealed), and the changes weren't necessarily recorded and duly compensated for.

And as with all observation, its accuracy and integrity was a function of the diligence of the observers themselves — including tired, harassed or overworked postmasters, and lazy, sloppy or insouciant airport workers — who were responsible for maintaining the equipment and taking and recording the readings. And, of course, for much of its history the dataset was not truly global. Good coverage existed in developed, politically stable nations. Coverage outside such countries was rather poorer, and in the isolated regions of the world, especially the climatologically significant poles, it ranged from sporadic to non-existent.

Hot in the city

There are less obvious limitations, too. It was argued that even in those areas where surface air temperature readings were consistently and meticulously taken over the entire period of the history of instrumental records (the 'instrumental period', as it gets called), they were subtly biased by the effect of what were called 'urban heat islands'. The tendency of built-up areas to warm up more than their rural hinterland had first been described in 1820 by British chemist and amateur meteorologist Luke Howard (who also developed the system of cloud classification in general use today). The results of a study published in 1982 confirmed the effect.[1] Tall buildings obstruct the night sky, and thus reduce the amount of re-radiated energy escaping to space (which is why the urban heat island effect is supposed to be strongest at night, when the loss of thermal energy into space is at its greatest). Buildings also reduce the movement of wind, and paved surfaces are not subject to the cooling effect of evapotranspiration. What's more, much of what goes on in cities — lighting, air conditioning, the burning of fuels in internal combustion engines — produces heat as a waste product.

Noting that most weather stations are sited in or near urban centres, and that most of the world's towns and cities grew over the twentieth century, it was argued that the general rise in global temperatures could be attributed to the burgeoning urban heat island effect. Naturally enough, this idea enjoyed considerable currency in Sceptic circles for the better part of two decades, and attracted an equivalent amount of attention from those who sought to debunk the notion that observed temperature rises were merely an artifact of urbanisation. Two influential methods of correcting for the urban heat island effect were devised as a response. Karl et al. (1988) used an average of the data gathered from the United States Historical Climate Network (essentially the surviving network of 1062 Stevenson Screens across the 48 contiguous states) to offset the presumed heat island effect.[2] And in 2001 arch-climatologist Jim Hansen used satellite night photography to quantify the urbanisation surrounding each of the USHCN sites (on the presumption that more intense lighting indicated the presence of urban agglomeration and hence more warming; absence of lighting indicated the absence of buildings and less warming) and to serve as a basis for a system of case-by-case corrections.[3] In this monumental effort, Hansen found that 42% of the weather stations he studied could indeed misrepresent true temperature trends — by *under*-measuring local temperature. Regardless of the urban heat island effect, that is, many weather stations were actually sited in cool zones, such as parks, and their data needed to be warmed to make it more representative of reality.

Cooking the books

And that brings us to the other subtle source of error in instrumental surface temperature data, namely the need to 'adjust' most historical datasets to render them compatible with one another and with contemporary records. Moreover, even the most complete temperature series contain gaps, and these are customarily filled with estimates developed from averages of other, closely correlated series. It's commonly objected that the processes involved in such adjustment are fatally dependent upon the adjuster's assumptions and, some go so far as to add, motives.

Thanks to the diligent efforts of Sceptics to discredit the way in which climate data is gathered and handled, many examples of errors and dubious number-crunching practices have been shown up. A leading light in this field is John Goetz, a regular contributor to Steven McIntyre's influential sceptical blog, http://www.climateaudit.com. In 'Adjusting Pristine Data', a post to a different site in September 2008, Goetz traced the fortunes of data collected at Mohonk Lake as it was passed up and handled in turn by the NOAA and the GISS.[4] In the same month the Mohonk Lake site in upstate New York had featured in a *New York Times* story as a paragon of the USHCN's method: temperatures had been taken from the maximum/minimum thermometer housed in its Stevenson Screen every day since the first reading on January 1, 1896. In all that time, only five people had ever taken the readings, ensuring as much consistency of method as could be hoped. The screen's site had never been changed, and the sleepy little settlement of Mohonk Lake hadn't changed much in all that time, either. The temperature series from Mohonk Lake, that is, was likely to be as pristine as any temperature record anywhere in the world. Goetz 'wondered', as he rather disingenuously put it, 'what happens to [the] data' after it's collected at the Mohonk Lake site, and he set out to find out. The process, it turned out, was surprisingly convoluted.

The temperatures read (in tenths of a degree Fahrenheit and rounded up or down) from the thermometer each day are recorded by hand on a form that is returned to the NOAA monthly. The data is transcribed into an electronic database, after having been converted to degrees Celsius. It's then converted back into degrees Fahrenheit and checked for quality (that is, for any obviously anomalous and potentially incorrect readings). Once this check has been done, monthly maximum and minimum averages are calculated, and a correction is applied to allow for the time of observation (yielding a set of data known as 'v.2.mean temperature'). A further quality check is run, in which the corrected data is compared to 40 other highly correlated series, in order to identify any non-climatic factors that may have given rise to error. A computer algorithm named FILNET is then run to supply estimates for any missing entries. The resulting temperature series in degrees Fahrenheit is stored (and made publicly available) as the NOAA's official record of the temperature at Mohonk Lake.

The GISS takes the NOAA's data and converts it back to degrees Celsius, and scales it into tenths of a degree. It then performs a series of adjustments designed, Goetz guesses, to reverse the corrections performed by the NOAA:

> For each of the twelve months in a calendar year, GISS looks at the ten most recent years in common between the two data sets. For each month in those ten most recent years it takes the difference between the FILNET temperature and the v2.mean temperature, and averages them. Then, GISS goes through the entire FILNET record and subtracts the monthly offset from each monthly temperature.

The result of this process is a temperature series in tenths of a degree Celsius, and this is the official GISS record of temperatures at Mohonk

Lake. Goetz notes that in Mohonk Lake's case, the effect of all this manipulation is to slightly cool the temperatures actually recorded (that is, the raw data as written down by hand on the NOAA's monthly returns), but his point is made. The data that is presented by both the NOAA and the GISS, and which together with the data series from other weather stations forms the basis of claims made about North American and, ultimately, global temperature trends, is hardly pristine.

The indefatigable Goetz has also highlighted another way in which the apparently fixed and immutable direct instrumental records of temperature are rather less than fixed and immutable. In a post to www.climateaudit.org in April 2008 entitled 'Rewriting History, Time and Time Again', he showed that each update of temperature data actually changes the historical temperature record, because the new data is used to recalculate the estimated values supplied for missing data in the past.[5] New data, that is, has what Goetz calls a 'ripple effect' on the supposedly static historical record. Looking at the GISS temperature record since September 24, 2005, he found '20% of the historical record was modified 16 times' in the two-and-a-half-year period to March 29, 2008. Nor were the changes always trifling:

> The largest single jump was 0.27°C. This occurred between the Oct 13, 2006 and Jan 15, 2007 records when Aug 2006 changed from an anomaly of +0.43°C to +0.70°C, a change of nearly 68%. [See Glossary for a definition of 'temperature anomaly'.]

Goetz also found that the overall effect of this tendency of new data to cause ripples in historical temperature values was to make the years closest to the beginning of historical records cooler and more recent years warmer.

Testing the waters

The heat stored in the first 3.2 metres of the ocean is equivalent to the amount of heat stored in the entire atmosphere. Understanding what's going on energy-wise in the oceans is consequently vital to understanding what's happening — and what's going to happen — to the world's climate.

The trouble with the temperature profile of seawater is that the reading you get in any one part of the ocean depends entirely on the depth at which you're measuring it. The surface warms considerably during the day and cools again overnight, but the influence the warm surface layer has on the deeper layers is complex, and determined by the interaction of convection, currents, salinity, the wind and land masses. Naturally enough, in most parts of the world, the deeper your sample, the cooler will be the temperature. A sample taken as little as a metre deeper than another sample will be considerably cooler.

The first measurements of seawater temperatures were taken by Captain Henry Ellis, the master of an English vessel plying the slave trade, in 1751. While sailing at 25°N in the subtropical North Atlantic, Ellis deployed a 'bucket sea-gauge' that had been designed and supplied to him by Stephen Hales, a clergyman moonlighting as a scientist (and presumably not asking too many questions about his agent's core business). The 'bucket' took samples of water at varying depths through an ingenious series of valves, and these were retrieved and their temperature measured on deck through the use of a built-in thermometer. Ellis was surprised to find that the water got progressively colder the deeper he took his samples, until he reached a certain depth. 'The cold increased regularly in proportion to the depths,' he wrote,

> till it descended to 3900 feet [1189 metres]: from whence the mercury in the thermometer came up at 53 degrees [Fahrenheit: the equivalent of 11.6°C]; and tho' I afterwards sunk it to the depth of 5346 feet, that is a mile and 66 feet [1629 metres], it came up no lower.[6]

The temperature of seawater has been more systematically measured since the mid-nineteenth century. The traditional method was to drag a bucketful of seawater up to the deck of a ship and dunk a thermometer in it. With its large and widely ranging navy, England kept the most comprehensive set of records of sea temperatures in the nineteenth century. Other nations, notably America, were keeping them by the beginning of the twentieth century, when near-global coverage was achieved (although the dangerous and seldom traversed polar waters were only sporadically sampled). In the late 1920s, the Americans began to use insulated buckets to take their samples, out of deference to the change in temperature that water might undergo in transit from sea to deck through warmer or cooler air.

At the outbreak of World War II, an automated system of measuring sea surface temperature was devised whereby a thermometer measured the temperature of water flowing through the cooling water intakes of ships' engine rooms.

Each system had its drawbacks. Even the old bucket and rope system was unreliable, as there was no consistency in the depth to which the bucket was allowed to drop from one reading to the next aboard a single vessel, let alone from vessel to vessel. And while you'd expect measurements of engine intake water to be more consistent, the results of the sampling method depended on the type of vessel (some hulls draw more water than others, and the engine intake will accordingly be lower in the water than on vessels of shallower draught), and even on the lading of a vessel (as a fully laden hull sits lower in the water than it does when under ballast). Since these readings were most commonly taken in proximity to hot engines, they were more than likely biased warm.

Needless to say, changes in the way in which measurements were taken have a profound effect on the resulting dataset, and unless the precise timing and nature of each change is recorded, the quality of the data is irremediably damaged. No such records were kept of the transition — itself less than systematic — from the use of uninsulated to insulated buckets aboard American vessels. Between 1939 and 1941, American ships were progressively converted to the engine-room intake sampling method, and the uncorrected historical record reflects the expected warming bias. More puzzling to those studying the records for the middle years of the twentieth century was a sudden apparent drop in sea surface temperatures in late 1945. In the absence of any other plausible explanation — such as a recent volcanic eruption — this seemed to be a genuine, if mysterious, fluctuation in sea surface temperature, unaccompanied by any similar fluctuation in land surface temperatures. However, a smart piece of detective work by David Thompson et al., published in May 2008, attributed the phenomenon to a change in the make-up of the fleet doing the sampling.[7] Between January 1942 and August 1945, around 80% of measurements were carried out by American ships and only 5% by British. Between late 1945 and 1949, the Americans had substantially handed over to the British: only 30% of measurements were conducted by US vessels, compared with 50% by British. Thompson and his gang noted that in late 1945, US vessels used engine-room intake sampling, whereas the Brits used uninsulated buckets.

Buoy oh buoy

In the 1960s, the US Coastguard began deploying a range of moored buoys around the American coastline, and this network was later extended across the equatorial Pacific to monitor the Southern Oscillation (the more or less regular weather pattern based on warmer and cooler ocean temperatures known as El Niño and La Niña). Other moored and drifting buoy networks were established subsequently by the US NOAA National Data Buoy Center (which took over the administration from the Coastguard in 1970) and by other countries. The buoys carry a number of meteorological and oceanographic instruments, including thermometers to measure sea surface temperature and the air temperature just above the sea's surface. These days, the data so collected are transmitted by satellite to monitoring stations that compile them. The major advantage of this method, of course, is that there is consistency between the measurements taken at different sites. The disadvantage is that the change of measurement method requires still more correction to the historical record in order to align the buoy-generated datasets with those generated by older methods.

Deeper and deeper

So much for direct measurement of sea surface temperatures. Tossing a bucket over the side, or measuring the temperature of the engine intake, can't tell you anything much about the temperature of the deeper layers of the oceans. Instruments to do that were developed from 1910, when the great Norwegian explorer Fridtjof Nansen developed what became known as the 'Nansen bottle'. This was a canister that was lowered on a cable to a predetermined depth, whereupon a brass weight (named a 'messenger') was dropped down the cable. Upon impact, the messenger caused the bottle to invert, trapping a water sample and also 'fixing' the reading on a thermometer enclosed in the bottle. A series of Nansen bottles on the same cable could take a succession of readings at different depths. A new, improved version of the Nansen bottle was developed in 1966 by an American, Shale Niskin, and a new, improved version of the Niskin bottle is still in use today.

As one of the many scientific silver linings that accompanied the clouds of war, instruments were developed to measure subsurface temperatures in the interests of assisting submarine warfare (the temperature of water being a key determinant of how effective submarine-detecting sonar is). A South African-born physicist named Athelstan Spilhaus developed a device that he called a bathy-thermograph for the US Navy in 1936. It consisted of a torpedo-shaped brass housing containing instruments that fed data to the surface via a tether that included fine copper wires. The bathythermograph operated by measuring the pressure of the surrounding water; since it sank at a known rate, and since water pressure varies according to temperature, the ambient temperature of the water through which it passed could be calculated. As it could be operated from a moving ship, it was able to be conveniently deployed on any old surface ship passing through the area of interest (termed 'vessels of opportunity' by scientists) without affecting their operation.

In the 1960s, an expendable version of the bathythermograph (nicknamed the XBT) was developed. This uses a thermistor to measure temperature, feeding data to the surface via wires. When it reaches the end of its tether, this simply breaks and the instrument is allowed to vanish into the abyss. And more recently again, a sophisticated robotic float named the ARGO has been developed, which can be programmed to traverse at a stipulated depth (as deep as 2000 metres) and to surface at 10-day intervals to transmit oceanographic data gathered in the interim to monitoring stations via satellite. The ARGO project is an international initiative, involving over fifty countries (although the US provides the lion's share of its funding). Since its inception in 2000, a total of 3274 probes have been deployed. Again, like the buoys measuring sea surface temperatures, XBTs and the ARGO probes provide consistent records across a globally comprehensive network of measuring sites.

But that's not to say that the data they provide are foolproof. The raw data from both XBTs and ARGO probes require correction for various potential sources of error, such as depth and pressure effects. In 1998, when an upgraded version of the XBT was distributed, not everyone noticed that its accompanying software already performed this correction. This saw the same correction applied twice to the data values for 1997 and 1998. This over-correction has since been corrected! And in a study of the integrity of the vast dataset generated by ARGO probes, it was found that 15% of probes had a deficiency of one sort or another, requiring another set of corrections and data sorting.[8]

Up in the air

Flying a kite

The first meteorological observation taken from above Earth's surface is considered to have been American polymath Benjamin Franklin's celebrated 1752 demonstration — by flying a kite in a storm — that lightning was electricity. In fact, Franklin may never have actually performed this experiment, as his writings indicate he was well aware of the real danger of being barbecued should his theory prove to be right. A Frenchman performed it safely, using an iron rod instead of a kite; a Russian who tried to do it Franklin-style with a kite *was* barbecued.

Up, up and away . . .

Following Franklin's suggestion, however, kites became the method of choice for carrying instruments aloft to measure atmospheric parameters, until the first manned hot-air balloon flight took place on November 21, 1783, using a balloon designed by French brothers Joseph and Etienne Montgolfier. Ten days later, a manned flight in a hydrogen balloon by a pilot hired by the brothers Montgolfier carried a passenger, a barometer and a thermometer aloft, the first use of a balloon to take atmospheric temperature readings. In 1785, an English doctor named John Jeffries took a thermometer, a barometer and a hygrometer (a device that measures humidity, or atmospheric water vapour content) to 9000 metres and made the first instrumental study of the upper reaches of what came to be called the troposphere.

It was customary for balloonists to release small paper balloons (nicknamed 'pilot balloons'; 'pibals' for short) to gauge wind speed and direction before they threw caution to the wind, as it were, and went up themselves. Pilot balloons tracked with theodolites began to be used by meteorologists for gathering high-altitude wind current data, and unmanned balloon flights carrying measuring and recording devices such as meteorographs (which use the movement of a temperature-sensitive bimetal strip to record temperature changes on a rotating paper drum) began in the 1890s; scientists offered rewards to anyone who found and returned a meteorograph that had fallen to Earth (its descent slowed by parachute) after its carrier balloon had burst. (It was by using this technique, and the painstaking series of 600-odd soundings he carried out between 1898 and 1904, that Frenchman Léon Philippe Teisserenc de Bort established that at a certain point above the Earth's surface the air ceased to cool and began to warm, and so the troposphere, tropopause and stratosphere were identified.) Pilot balloons are still used today, although the methods of tracking them have improved since the advent first of radar and then of the Global Positioning by Satellite (GPS) system.

What's that sonde?

The first experiments with a device that could measure temperature and transmit that data by radio from high above the Earth's surface were conducted by Colonel William Blaire of the US Signal Corps in 1924. A Frenchman and a Russian independently developed much more sophisticated versions of the device five years later. The world's very first weather bureau, Robert Bureau, named his invention 'radiosonde', from the French word for a probe, 'sonde'; the name stuck, but it was Pavel Molchanov's version, which converted the data from weather instruments into Morse code, that was adopted as the standard meteorological tool of the next few decades. Radiosondes were (and are) carried aloft by balloons, and they transmit their data by radio to surface monitoring stations. The United States government inaugurated a national radiosonde programme in 1937, with temperature and pressure (and, later, humidity) sensors added to the instrument package. Today, a synchronised release of radiosonde balloons takes place at 0000 and 1200 hours UTC (Universal Time Coordinated) from over a thousand sites worldwide, with the data compiled into a twice-daily 'snapshot' of the atmosphere. Each balloon rises to a maximum height of around 35 km before it bursts, and the instrument package and shredded balloon descend on a small parachute (to minimise the chances of causing death or destruction on the ground).

A variety of other balloons are used in meteorology, too, the type depending on the purpose of their individual mission. New materials and the miniaturisation of electronics permit balloons and radiosondes to reach the outer limits of the atmosphere and conduct a variety of chemistry and physics experiments beyond the reach of aircraft and beneath the reach of satellites.

Progress, however, is a mixed blessing, because the introduction of new instrumentation technologies has once again introduced a potential source of error into the historical record of radiosonde observations. Efforts are under way to identify and correct biases present in the record, but the NOAA concedes that,

the temporal homogeneity of many radiosonde time series is suspect due to historical changes in instruments and measurement
practices. Such changes may introduce artificial inhomogeneities
to the time series, making them unsuitable for the study of long-
term climate variations, such as through trend analysis.[9]

What's more, a glance at the global distribution of radiosonde balloon
sites shows that it is biased toward the northern hemisphere (where
very many more of the sites are located) and toward continental rather
than maritime sites.

Beyond the reach of balloons, scientists must rely upon sounding
rockets — essentially ballistic missiles carrying a payload of scientific
instruments rather than things that go bang in the night — which
have been in use in atmospheric research since the 1950s.

Implying we're frying: indirect measurements of temperature

The view from space

The idea of placing artificial satellites into orbit around the Earth
has a long history, but it was the Russians who were first to put the
theory into practice, successfully placing their little round Sputnik
(the word means 'satellite' in Russian) into a low-altitude elliptical
orbit in October 1957.

It was a momentous event, and it took the USSR's rival in the
stakes for superpower boss of the world, the United States, completely
by surprise. Not only was it a bit of a blow to national pride, it also
demonstrated the Soviet superiority in rocket technology. Since space
rockets and intercontinental ballistic missiles are essentially the same
thing, this was tantamount to declaring the Soviet Union to have
a greater capability of delivering nuclear weapons to America than
America could resort to in reply. The result was the so-called 'space
race', with each side in the Cold War scrambling to build bigger and
better spacecraft.

Some good came of this rather childish attack of rocket envy: rockets and satellites became the new 'vessels of opportunity' in scientific exploration. The first satellite intended to make observations of the Earth's weather from space was the United States' Vanguard 2, which carried a pair of optical scanners aloft in late 1959. The scanners were intended to measure cloud cover, and were linked to a tape recorder and transmitter, which could be operated from mission control back on Earth. The satellite was successfully placed in orbit, but the value of the observations it was able to perform was limited by a problem with the orientation of its spin axis.

Still, it had been shown that it was technically possible to put weather instruments in space, and the TIROS-1 (the name is an acronym for Television Infrared Observation Satellite) that the Americans put in orbit the following year is regarded as the first successful weather satellite. The TIROS sent back high-quality, dynamic images of weather systems, and was the forerunner of the Nimbus programme, with which the era of satellite 'telemetry' (literally, 'measuring from afar') began in earnest. Nimbus-1, carrying an array of instruments for studying clouds, was placed in orbit in April 1964, and generated 27,000 high-quality cloud images in its three-week lifespan. Successive Nimbus craft — there were seven in all — carried more and more sophisticated scanning equipment for measuring different parameters of the Earth's surface and of the atmosphere.

By the time Nimbus-3 was launched in 1969, by using an instrument called MUSE (monitor of ultraviolet solar energy) and another called IRIS (infrared interferometer spectrometer) scientists could at last measure both the quantity and the spectral quality of incoming and outgoing radiation. With high- and medium-resolution infrared radiometers, they could analyse both the distribution and the intensity of the infrared radiation emitted by the Earth and its atmosphere. With a satellite infrared spectrometer, they could take cross-sections through the atmosphere and determine its temperature at different altitudes. With Nimbus-4, launched the following year, they could use a temperature-humidity infrared radiometer to measure the temperature at the Earth's surface and at the tops of clouds, and measure the water vapour content of the atmosphere, and with a back-scatter ultraviolet detector they could map ozone distributions.

Soon enough, there were filter wedge spectrometers, selective chopper radiometers, microwave spectrometers and limb radiance inversion radiometers whizzing around up there as well, subjecting the Earth to their cool, optically coated scrutiny. The seventh and final vehicle in the programme was launched in late 1978, and was still sending back data 11 years later.

Since then, Earth observation satellites have proliferated, and other players besides the United States have begun launching and operating them, too. The European Space Agency (ESA), Roscomos (the successor to the Soviet space programme) and JAXA (the Japanese space agency) have all been involved, and the range and quality of data available to science has improved dramatically. As fast as scientists could dream up some aspect of the Earth system they'd like to study, instruments were developed, built, bunged into rockets and hoisted into the heavens to perform the necessary measurements. Specialised oceanographic satellites first appeared with the short-lived SEASAT in 1978, then with TOPEX/Poseidon in 1992 and JASON-1 and JASON-2 in 2001 and 2008 respectively. These permit precise measurements of ocean surface temperatures, tides, current circulation and wave heights, among other parameters. There are even satellites capable of mapping the movement of wind.

Orbital drawbacks

There can be no doubt about the importance of satellite telemetry to the task of understanding the Earth and its climate. Satellite instrumentation yields precise, consistent and — above all — globally comprehensive measurements, including (for the first time in history) data from the polar regions. But like every other tool available to humankind, these instruments are not without their limitations.

First, many readings taken from satellites are not a *direct* measure-ment of the parameters they test. Instead, instruments such as radio-meters measure radiation, principally in the infrared and visible spectra, emanating from the Earth. The data thus generated need to be converted according to algorithms that are critically dependent on our understanding of the physical processes that generated the radiation. This presents the opportunity for error, not just in the complicated calculations that must be performed, but also in the underlying assumptions themselves. It has by no means been uncommon for flaws to be identified in the processes by which raw data from satellite telemetry is converted to climatological data. It's therefore quite likely that others remain to be discovered and corrected, with obvious implications for the data series.

Second, due to their reliance upon electromagnetic radiation such as infrared and visible light, satellites are (perverse as it seems) at the mercy of weather conditions, and many measurements can only be performed when cloud cover is thin or absent. This produces what is known as a 'fair weather bias' in much of the data available from satellites, which requires correction.

Third, correction and adjustment is needed in order to render data series from satellite telemetry compatible with data generated by more traditional measurement techniques. How does one reconcile the record of ocean 'skin temperaure'— that is, the temperature of the first 10 microns of seawater, as measured by a satellite infrared radiometer — or even the 'subskin' temperature — the first 1 mm, as measured by a microwave radiometer — with temperature data gathered by slinging a bucket over the side of a ship, or by drawing water from 10 metres beneath the surface where the engine intake is located, or (in the best case) from records gathered using Nansen or Niskin bottles? Any such reconciliation will depend on a detailed understanding of how the 'skin' and 'subskin' temperatures relate to the 'surface' and 'foundation' temperatures (anything from the first metre to the first 10 metres) traditionally studied by direct measurement techniques.

Proxy music

While instrumental records of world temperatures began in the mid-nineteenth century, records of global average temperatures go back hundreds of thousands of years — back not only to the days way before the invention of the thermometer, but also long before there was anyone around with the intellectual capacity to use one. How, you might wonder, can this be?

Many aspects of the Earth and its systems vary according to temperature. Some of the relationships between temperature and its effects are comparatively simple, and thus if a reasonably intelligible record of those effects through time can be discovered, then past temperatures can be deduced.

It's in this field — the study of what's known as the 'paleoclimate' (from the Greek word *palaios*, meaning 'old') — that the sheer, breathtaking ingenuity of scientists becomes apparent. The range of the weird and wonderful objects of study that yield meaningful information about past climates just about defies belief. Let's have a look at a few of them.

Boring ice

Oxygen occurs in three stable isotopes, namely ^{16}O, ^{17}O and ^{18}O. In ^{16}O, the atomic nucleus consists of eight protons and eight neutrons. In the other isotopes, the number of protons is still eight, but there are more neutrons. As you'd expect with those extra particles thrown into the mix, the ^{17}O and ^{18}O isotopes are heavier.

The Earth's oceans and the vapour in the atmosphere contain water that comprises a mixture of the three isotopes. Although ^{16}O is very much more abundant than either of the others, with ^{18}O the scarcest, the precise ratio depends upon temperature, as the heavier water molecules incorporating the heavy isotopes of oxygen behave differently to ^{16}O. Light water evaporates more readily than heavy water; heavy water condenses more readily than light.

As a general rule, when the Earth is cooler, the oceans will contain more heavy water and the water falling as rain and snow in the higher latitudes (that is, those farthest from the equator) will be proportionately richer in light oxygen. (It has been shown that the isotopic ratio in the tropics does not vary with temperature, for reasons that needn't trouble us here.)

There are several places in the world where the precipitation that has fallen every day for the last hundred thousand years is still there, notably in the ice sheets covering Greenland and Antarctica, and in some of the alpine glaciers that have survived since the last ice age. Using a long (often hundreds of metres) cylindrical drill, a sample core of ancient ice can be taken, the rod of ice gently teased out and analysed. Annual layers of precipitation can be identified under a microscope. The ice in each layer can be analysed using a device called an isotope ratio mass spectrometer, and the ratio of oxygen isotopes measured and plotted against a standard (arbitrarily designated as the ratio found in the contemporary ocean at a depth of between 250 and 500 metres). From there, it is a matter of extrapolating from the isotopic ratio to the global climate that must have prevailed when the ice was formed.

What's more, because last season's snow (technically known by an Old German word, 'firn') lying on the ground contains air gaps that are progressively sealed off as more snow falls and pressure increases, ice cores also contain microscopic bubbles of the air through which the snow fell. Carefully handled, then, ice cores can also yield samples of the ancient atmosphere itself for analysis, so that a continuous record of the concentrations of greenhouse gases can be compiled from direct measurement. Any dust settling on the snow is preserved in the cores, too, and measurements of certain ions in dust samples enable scientists to identify markers that link the ice stratigraphy to geological records from elsewhere in the world. These markers in turn make it possible to date the ice layers. Little wonder, then, that ice sheets are sometimes referred to as the world's 'climate museum'.[10]

The first ice cores were drilled in the 1970s at sites high on the Greenland ice sheet and at the Soviet Vostok station in one of the more remote and inhospitable reaches of Antarctica. The core retrieved from Vostok was deep enough to yield climate information extending back over 400,000 years. Another Antarctic core, drilled at Dome C by the European Project for Ice Coring in Antarctica (EPICA), is even longer (3270 metres), and extends records back to 720,000 years, incorporating several glacial/interglacial cycles.

Soon after the Greenland Ice Sheet Project (GISP) began yielding results, an American scientist named Lonnie Thompson began his heroic 30-year career drilling ice cores from glaciers high in the mountains in tropical regions, beginning in the Peruvian Andes. These, it was hoped, would shed light on the dynamics through time of the tropical climate, which comprises (among other phenomena) the globally significant North Atlantic and Southern Oscillations and the monsoons.

There are difficulties associated with using ice cores as a proxy measurement of global climate. They are critically dependent on the observer's ability to date the strata accurately. Counting annual layers can be complicated where snowfall has failed or more than one substantial fall has occurred in any given season. The distinction between annual layers in the deeper reaches of the cores is harder to identify, as the ice is compressed, and close to bedrock, the strange hydraulic effects of pressure render the record useless. Dating can, in any case, only reliably be done by aligning traces of volcanic events with the more firmly dated geological record; where these traces are absent, dating becomes problematic. In other words, while ice cores can provide a high-resolution snapshot of the past climate, the picture begins to pixelate as you survey the remote past.

More fundamentally, there are a number of variables that must be taken into account when developing an algorithm to convert the quantity measured (namely the ratio of light oxygen to heavy oxygen) into temperature, since the isotopic ratio is itself a function of a complex set of weather processes. This concern is best answered by showing how temperature as measured by isotopic ratios during the instrumental period looks against the instrumental record. Figure 1 shows a graph of the results from a Greenland core superimposed on the directly measured temperature record from its nearest surface station. You'll note that the dots (representing proxy measurements) almost always fall on the line (representing directly measured temperatures), indicating very good agreement.

Another objection is that each ice core is at best only a regional proxy, a reliable indicator of such parameters as local temperature and precipitation rates, without necessarily being indicative of the wider global climate. However, against these quibbles, it can be shown that

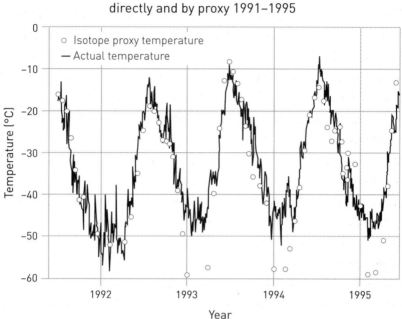

Figure 1. Who needs a thermometer to measure temperature? Proxy measurements of temperature deduced from a Greenland ice core (circles), superimposed over the instrumental measurement record from a nearby surface station.

Source: Christopher Shuman, Associate Research Scientist, NASA Goddard Earth Science and Technology Center, Greenbelt, Maryland, USA.

where the same methodologies are applied to snowfall that overlaps with the instrumental record, good agreement between global average temperatures and ice-core data is observed, suggesting that they provide a realistic guide to the paleoclimate.

And while each core is a product of regional variables, taken in combination the ice-core records from the northern and southern hemispheres and from polar, tropical and subtropical regions show an impressive level of agreement, suggesting that they are individually capable of reflecting global climatic variations.

Boring silt

Ice is not the only repository of ancient climate information. Many living organisms build shells from compounds of carbon and silicon, the most common being calcite (calcium carbonate) and silicate. Perhaps the most useful organism in paleoclimatology is the group known as foraminifera (literally, 'hole bearers', as their shells feature pores through which their squishy inmates used to stick pseudopods into the outside world). These have been around in various incarnations throughout much of the history of life on Earth. They are primarily marine organisms (although some live in fresh water and still others in humus in rainforests). The marine species tend to live the planktonic good life, drifting about in the upper regions of the ocean subsisting on other plankton and diatoms. They're short-lived, and when they die, their shell (or 'test') drifts to the seafloor where, with millions of others of their kind, they are laid down in layers that are destined, in the fullness of geological time, to become limestone.

Oil prospectors quickly learned to look out for certain species, or combinations of species, of foraminifera in rock samples drilled from the seabed, as these were indicators of the conditions under which oil and gas deposits form and are trapped. It wasn't long before foraminifera became the subject of scrutiny in their own right. Scientists studying the layer-cake of fossilised foraminifera tests in seabed samples were able to produce a chronology of their evolution, and this has proved useful in dating rocks (and also, by calibrating which species seem to favour which conditions, in reconstructing the conditions prevailing in ancient oceans). And since the foraminifera build their shells from calcium carbonate, they are proving pretty handy as a proxy measure of the atmospheric and oceanic conditions that prevailed in the remote past.

Calcium carbonate ($CaCO_3$) is formed from calcium and carbon dioxide in the presence of water, which provides the extra oxygen atom. Since the carbon used by foraminifera comes from the atmosphere and the oxygen from the water in the surrounding sea, studying the isotopic constituents of the calcium carbonate in fossil foraminifera tests can give a snapshot of both the temperature of the ocean (as judged by the ratio of ^{16}O to ^{18}O, and by the isotopic ratio of other elements, such as magnesium and calcium) and of the carbon dioxide profile of the atmosphere (as judged by the ratio of carbon isotopes). More or less the same information can be gleaned from drilling cores from coral reefs or from the limestone formations that ancient coral reefs become, and from measuring the isotopic ratios in the minerals deposited in the growth of speleotherms (stalagmites and stalactites).

Sediment can yield other information, too. Lakebed sediments contain the pollen of the plants that were growing in the vicinity of the lake in the remote past, and by identifying the succession of species occupying the landscape, a profile of the local climatic conditions can be developed.

Like ice cores, sediment samples from any given site are proxies for regional climate only. A core drilled in the Sargasso Sea, for example, may indicate an unusually warm period at the same moment in history that a core drilled from the Ross Sea indicates the opposite. Yet as initiatives such as the Integrated Ocean Drilling Program generate more data from sites scattered across the world's ocean basins, it is to be hoped that a broad pattern of agreement between sediment cores can be detected, thus building up a picture of the global climate.

Other physical proxies
Just plain boring

It took some bright spark of a geologist to work out that the way the Earth's surface warms is pretty consistent throughout the world, and has remained pretty consistent through time. Not only is the crust warmed by the heat from the molten mantle beneath it, but it's also warmed by the heat in the atmosphere, the effect of which creeps slowly downward through the crust over time. Once you've corrected for the background effect of the heat of the mantle emanating outwards, and providing you know the thermodynamic profile of the material you're examining, measuring the temperature at different levels in the crust is like winding the clock backwards and measuring the heat that was absorbed from the atmosphere years ago.

As a technique, it has certain advantages over other proxy measurements, in that it's directly measuring a second-order effect of surface air temperature itself. But there are a few variables involved, and some insanely complicated equations are required to extrapolate from readings taken deep underground to reach an accurately dated surface temperature series. And once again, boreholes are a regional, if not local, proxy only; still, as there's a network of thousands of bores being examined worldwide, the expectation is that a global signal will emerge from the noise of local and regional datasets.

Tracking ice

Geologists can also track the advance and retreat of glaciers with a reasonable degree of precision, and glacier extent is regarded as a useful indicator of climate. Happily, too, there are glaciers right around the world, even in the tropics, which means they give good global coverage.

However, the extent of glaciers depends on the delicate balance of factors that determine the rate at which they grow as against the rate at which ice is lost through melting. A glacier is a river of ice, flowing down from its névé (the basin at the head of an alpine valley where snow collects, feeding the ice tongue) to its terminal face, where ice melts as fast as the glacier behind it is moving. An advance may be caused either by a slowdown in the rate of melting, or by an increase in the supply of ice. Conversely, a retreat can be due to a succession of lean snow years in the névé, or increased temperatures that accelerate ice loss through melting. And just to complicate things, precipitation (of which snowfall is a form) is influenced by temperature, so that a warmer global climate may drive increased regional precipitation and actually cause glaciers on the receiving end to advance faster than the warmer lowland temperatures can melt them. All things to bear in mind when making bold claims about what the advance or retreat of a glacier implies for past and present climate.

Reading trees

We've already noted that fossilised pollen in sediment samples can give clues to changes in local vegetation. The responses of living organisms to climatic change can be useful in other ways, too. Noting that the growth rate of some species of tree varies according to climatic conditions, scientists studied the annual rings of living and petrified examples of those species. A good growing season shows up as a broad annual ring; on the other hand, trees record a forgettable year as a narrow band. A popular target for this type of study has been the Californian bristlecone pine, a long-lived upland species of which some living examples are known to be over 3000 years old (one, nicknamed 'Methuselah', is over 5000 years old: they're not called *Pinus longaeva* for nothing!). Even dead examples are useful, as their remains can be dated using radiocarbon technology. What's more, since plant tissue is constructed from atmospheric carbon, samples taken from each growth ring can yield carbon isotopes to serve as a proxy measurement of the constituents of the past atmosphere. And it's not just annual rings that are useful: one set of studies has exploited the tendency of western hemlock needles to produce more or fewer stomata (the pores on the underside of leaves) according to the concentration of atmospheric carbon dioxide, using this knowledge to reconstruct past carbon dioxide levels from needles preserved in swamp sediment samples.

As proxies go, however, tree rings and stomata are more problematic than most. Plants — and bristlecone pines and western hemlock are no exception — have good or bad growing seasons according to a number of different variables, of which temperature is just one. Rainfall is another, at least as significant; intensity of sunlight is another; as is the level of nutrients in the soil; and increased atmospheric concentrations of carbon dioxide can have a fertilising effect, too. Indeed, a comparison of bristlecone ring width over the instrumental period revealed a twentieth-century growth spurt that was poorly correlated with temperature and rather better correlated with rising CO_2.[11]

The dwindling level of confidence in tree rings as an indicator of temperature suffered a further blow with the 2008 publication of research that showed green plants maintain a constant internal temperature regardless of the ambient temperature (suggesting the relationship between ambient temperature and growth is not as simple as supposed).[12] Nonetheless, as an indicator of local and regional climate, tree data still have a place in tracking the aggregate effect of climate variables — how favourable or not a growing season was.

Countless other biological responses to past climatic changes can chime in, too. The range of bowhead whales, for example, tends to be limited to the edges of the Arctic ice pack, where the species they target for food exclusively live. The presence of bowhead whale remains on the seabed and on raised coastal deposits is thus presumed to be an indicator of the extent of the pack.[13]

Lies, damned lies and statistics

Climate is a fickle beast. It is the function of an enormous number of variables, and consequently, the job of teasing a signal out of the cacophony of noise in climate data is extremely difficult. This is true of the recent past, where the data has been gathered using direct instrumental measurement. How much harder, then, when we are considering the remote past, where climate data is compressed and confused with other signals, and still other sets of noise.

That a signal can emerge from the vast, noisy datasets provided from the examination of climate proxies at all is thanks to the sophisticated statistical tools at the disposal of the modern scientist. Techniques such as regression analysis and multivariate analysis can assign different weights to the different variables that bear upon a measured parameter, and correct the data in such a way that the desired variable is brought to the foreground and other, irrelevant variables recede into the background.

Such filtering of data is not only desirable, but essential. However, there is a point at which the manipulation of data for the purposes of clarification strays into the domain of data falsification. Both sides of the climate change debate have been guilty of over-enthusiasm in their use of data-handling techniques to produce results that suit their case, and these have led to occasions where the argument has shifted from the obscure field of climate research and into the arcane world of maths. Perhaps the most celebrated is the controversy over the so-called 'hockey stick' graph that featured in the first IPCC report and (more famously) in Al Gore's influential piece of Alarmist cinematography, *An Inconvenient Truth*. (See 'Data Hockey' panel, in the first colour section.)

If that regrettable episode proved nothing else, it served to throw a spotlight on the layer of high-flown applied mathematics that interposes between the data as gathered and the consumer (that is, the layperson reading the findings of this or that scientific study). It's not just the scientific methodology involved in gathering data that needs to be considered when trying to assess the quality of research findings: the way in which that data has been handled subsequently is at least as important. The history of the debate on global warming is strewn with papers that have been discredited on the strength of the statistical shenanigans — data-sifting and -mining, smoothing and filtering, curve-fitting, cherry-picking among data series and values, the deployment of unjustifiable averages, et cetera — involved in assembling them.

The world's next top model

It would be remiss to leave a discussion of the tools used to explain climate past and present without having a look at those with which climate scientists these days peer into the future — namely models. The rise of climate science has coincided exactly with the rapid rise in computer technology, and at each step of the way computers have provided a platform for extracting sense and order from the apparent chaos that is climate in the making. These abstractions from reality reflect the sum total of our knowledge about climate and hence, while certainly not perfect, they are useful frameworks with which to study the likely consequences of oddball shocks to the climatic system, such as pumping oodles of CO_2 into the atmosphere, changes in the Earth's orbit, fluctuations in solar irradiance and so on. As 'virtual Earths', models are the nearest thing we can get to planetary lab rats, upon which to perform experiments.

Weather forecasters have long used computer models to represent the processes that create local weather. When the present state of the weather is fed into these intricate programs, they can run forward and produce representations, based on probabilities, of the future. These can be quite accurate in the short term (out to, say, three days). But because of the impossibility of initialising the model with a perfect representation of present weather, longer-term forecasting is notoriously less reliable.

The recent development of supercomputer technology has permitted the construction of the granddaddies of computer models, what are commonly termed Atmosphere–Ocean General Circulation Models (AOGCMs) — unspeakably complicated programs that attempt to represent the mechanisms involved in the real climate system, and to simulate the way the climate works in real time. Typically, they divide the Earth's surface into grids, and the atmosphere above and the ocean beneath the grids into different levels. Each iteration of the model begins with incoming solar radiation and works through the various processes that transfer heat through the Earth's atmosphere and oceans — re-radiation and reflection from the surface, absorption and re-radiation by atmospheric gases, reflection and absorption by clouds, movement from one grid to the next through circulation, absorption by the ocean and movement around the Earth and into the depths due to currents and convection, and so on. Needless to say, an astronomical amount of computing power is needed to run full-scale AOGCMs — you know someone's using one when the lights in the district surrounding the institution go dim — and there are simpler versions available, some simple enough to be run on a PC. (There's even one very cool project which enlisted PC owners willing to permit the processing power of their machines to be accessed via the internet when they're not using them, creating a kind of geographically dispersed supercomputer to run climate-modelling iterations.) Simpler models use larger grids, or replace the ocean with an undifferentiated slab, or ignore the ocean altogether.

Full-scale AOGCMs such as the UK Hadley Centre's HadCM3 (Hadley Centre Coupled Model version 3) or the US NOAA's GFDL.CM2 (Geophysical Fluid Dynamics Laboratory Coupled Model version 2) have reached a degree of sophistication where they can reproduce not only seasonal variations, but also longer-phase cycles such as the Pacific Decadal Oscillation and the North Atlantic Oscillation, which are patterns that emerge in weather trends in their respective ocean basins. They can reproduce the past and present climate quite accurately, and this gives a measure of confidence that their predictions for the future are likely to be accurate — there are no guarantees in this game; welcome to the wonderfully uncertain world of modelling. (They successfully predicted, without having to be told, the cooling effect of the injection of aerosols from the massive volcanic eruption of Mt Pinatubo in the Philippines in 1991.) At the very least, the best and biggest climate models represent the state of our knowledge of what the climate is and how it works. Leaving the human-induced increase in atmospheric levels out of modelling runs sees them fail to reproduce the behaviour of the climate over the last 250 years. Including that effect, by contrast, improves their tracking. We'll have a look at just how closely in Chapter 6.

There have been instances, what's more, where models have pre-dicted certain climate effects that have not manifested themselves in data generated from real-world observations. Satisfied that the models were functioning correctly, scientists have occasionally sought to locate errors in the methodology used to generate the observational data itself. It's generally considered to be poor scientific form to try to make the evidence fit the theory rather than the other way around — yet close scrutiny of the instrumentation has in some instances led to the discovery of errors. This hasn't done the credibility of models any harm at all.

'All models are wrong. Some are useful.'

But permit us a word — or let's be accurate, several words — of caution.

By definition models are not reality, as the above quotation from one of the world's greatest statisticians and modelling theoreticians, George Box, suggests. They are an abstraction and a representation of the state of knowledge of the salient characteristics of the system under study. The Earth, after all, isn't divided into 300 km² squares; nor is the atmosphere composed of 24 discrete layers, or the ocean 50. The very best a model can achieve is to test our knowledge against reality, and project that knowledge forward to make a guess (albeit a highly educated guess) about the future. Modellers and most scientists are aware of their limitations.

To listen to some of the claims made on behalf of AOGCMs by the ill-informed or the over-enthusiastic, however, you'd believe that the results produced when the data is run through climate models somehow have the status of 'evidence' in the global warming debate. In almost all fields of scientific enquiry there's a massive divide between those who build models and understand their limitations, and those who use models as if they were reality. And modellers themselves are far from infallible. There are tempting traps for young players: to illustrate them, we'll consider two extreme, hypothetical examples of misguided model-building.

At one extreme, we have Crazy Climate Scientist I who discovers in his laboratory a bilateral relationship between CO_2 concentration and temperature. He finds that CO_2 absorbs infrared radiation at a certain rate. The researcher then concludes that this relationship is sufficient to represent the impact of rising CO_2 concentrations on the world's temperature. In other words, all other 'real world' influences on temperature are deemed immaterial; any reinforcing feedbacks or offsetting effects from weather systems or any solar or natural variations are subjugated to the supremacy of this one relationship.

Such a model would clearly be over-simplistic, too much of an abstraction from reality to be that useful in predicting the future. Further, if we tried to 'simulate' the past climate from a data series of, say, 100 years' worth of observations of CO_2 concentrations simply by using this model to 'predict' what the temperature would have been, we'd find the 'fit' of the predictions to the actual temperatures pretty poor — too poor to have any confidence that this model could predict the future. And that, in fact, is the case. The year-by-year correlation of CO_2 concentration with world temperature is not strong (see Figure 2).

Now let's go to the other extreme. Let's say Crazy Climate Scientist

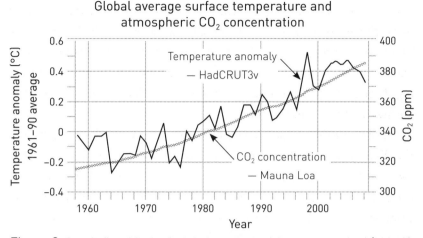

Figure 2. Rough fit: while both global average surface temperature (black line) and atmospheric carbon dioxide concentrations (pale line) have risen since 1958 (when measurements of the latter began), the progression of CO_2 has been smooth and steady whereas temperature has been all over the place. There is clearly no simple, linear relationship between the two.

Source: Data from HadCRUT2 and R.F. Keeling et al, Carbon Dioxide Research Group, Scripps Institution of Oceanography (SIO), University of California.

II is equally determined to 'explain' these 100 observations of real-world climate, but finds that there is a 'special' event that accounts for whatever the temperature turned out to be in each year — whether it be a volcanic eruption, an oil-crisis-induced rationing of petrol, a world-war-induced shutdown of factories, a 9/11-crisis suspension of air transport, the impact of a meteorite, or whatever. His approach is to construct a model of 100 separate 'explanatory' (or dummy) variables, each one to account for one year of temperature but to have no part in explaining the temperature in other years.

Ironically, although this model would simulate the past record of world climate to perfection, it would be as useless as the previous model in predicting the climate of the future. Crazy Climate Scientist II would demonstrate far superior ability to explain the past climate, but wouldn't know where to begin to look at the future.

Now somewhere between these useless extremes lies every climate model ever built, each with its strengths, each with its weaknesses, and all with absolute limitations. Not one of them is reality, and the author of any model who knows his or her business should be the first to point that out. Unfortunately, though, in all fields of science there are fellow travellers — those who know very little about the construction, testing and limitations of models — who claim far, far more for models even than good old common sense would permit. Climate science is not unusual in this regard: it's a sad reality of most fields of scientific enquiry where modelling is involved.

What if we averaged the predictions from the models of Crazy Climate Scientists I and II? Would that help?

No, it would not. If you add rubbish to rubbish, you get only rubbish. Now a consensus of model outcomes, such as that produced by the IPCC in its 2007 report, for example, doesn't necessarily add weight to the credibility of predictions. The whole point of a model is that it's based on a rationale; so if you average the predictions of two models with two quite different rationales, what are you really saying? It's far safer just to consider the range across models of their predictions in response to some shock or another. Averaging the predictions is to dumb things down to a potentially meaningless level.

So much for the pros and cons of models from a theoretical stand-point. Let's look at how climate models are constructed in practice. Underpinning all climate models are certain physical laws, such as the principles of the conservation of energy and momentum, the laws of thermodynamics and so on. These account for the basic similarity of the major General Circulation Models. After that, however, there's an element of subjectivity, depending on the author's choice of what the fundamental relationship or relationships are that determine climate. If the author is a fan of the greenhouse gas effect, this relationship will take centre stage. If they're a disciple of solar variations, then expect solar variations to be to the fore. If they get off on cosmic rays, then we have a different form. If atmospheric/oceanic coupling is viewed as a critical part of the equation, it gets the nod too, and so on. No one phenomenon will provide an entirely adequate explanation for the past data, so next the modeller adds other relationships that they think are relevant, along with second-order effects, or feedbacks — some that reinforce an initial shock and others that offset it.

A full system-wide model will try ambitiously to combine all of these relationships and laws so that a full representation of everything material to a description of the world's climate system is included. Of course, the manner in which the various simple and multivariate relationships are brought together differs between models and is a function of the author's understanding of the interrelationship, based on belief mixed with such empirical validation or estimation techniques as are available to tell us what the multitude of sensitivities or elasticities are.

Let's next consider how model builders most often bring their structures together. Once they've been assembled from a few simple principles and relationships — in the case of climate models, these will largely be basic laws of physics and chemistry — and some scope to accommodate the extent of the sensitivities of these has been built in using data from the real world, they are tested against reality. Ironically, one of the standard tests to validate a model is to see whether it can simulate the same datasets that have been used to calibrate many of its operating parameters. This approach is valid, but limited — the 'predictions' that come from such an exercise are *ex post* (after the event, or within the sample of observed data) rather than *ex ante* (before the event, or beyond the sample of data observations). It doesn't do much to prove the efficacy of the model beyond providing some confidence in the 'tractability' or 'tracking error' (the way model results fit real-world data) of the complex structure the modeller has concocted.

In most cases, the tracking error of models over the same dataset upon which their parameters were estimated is pretty high. What this is telling the researcher is that either the relationships they've postulated are insufficiently robust to explain the variation across the dataset, or there are other factors, not included in the model, that must be included in order to provide adequate tractability.

This is often where the trouble starts. In order to make their model fit the data better, the researcher proceeds to augment the basic theoretical framework with second-, third- and fourth-order effects, each one of which reduces the tracking error of the model over the whole known dataset. Now remember Crazy Climate Scientist II

— he added in 100 of these effects in order fully to explain the 100 observations in his dataset. Of course, most modellers stop short of that extreme because they'd be laughed out of court; nonetheless, elements of this 'kitchen sink' approach — biffing more and more into the mix — can get incorporated. And the trouble with this approach is that it prioritises the reduction of tracking error even at the expense of the theoretical underpinnings, or 'story', of the model.

So once the model has been sufficiently expanded to deliver a reasonably small tracking error, the temptation is to believe you've got the climate system sussed. But care is needed. The fact that a model can approximate the past is not that impressive — a necessary but not sufficient condition for credibility. More important is its performance when subjected to shock treatment, as we'll see.

Another potential source of error is the datasets that are used in the parameterisation of models. We've already seen how common it is for even supposedly simple and pristine sets of data such as historical thermometer readings to be filtered, adjusted and normalised for all manner of variations that analysts don't want ruining their results. To coin a phrase, the evidence should speak for itself, because it's the raw data, in all its random, stochastic, naked, chaotic glory, that most closely represents the quantity we're seeking to understand. Smoothing, averaging and other filter methods are valid in their place, but not when they are pushed too far and violate the first principles of data integrity, introducing a subjective quality to the data from the outset. Data series that have been subjected to this level of interrogation should not be used as the source for model parameters, but it's not unusual to find modellers who are blasé — or, to put it delicately, enthusiastic — enough to do it anyway.

The above is intended to serve as a warning to the consumer of modelling. Models are not infallible (if a model were found that *was* infallible, it would be reality rather than a model!). They are occasionally treated with a kind of reverence they don't deserve. The experience in other fields — yes, even in such a deeply respectable and empirical science as economics — shows that models can be and are pushed beyond their limits.

But that doesn't mean models are useless. Far from it. They play an important role in defining the state of our knowledge about the phenomenon we seek to explain, and in extrapolating from that knowledge into the future. So how do we tell whether a model-based piece of analysis is worth the paper it's written on?

The best technique that we are aware of is to perform an 'attributions analysis', by watching carefully to see what happens at each step along the way when the model is subjected to a shock. In short, what you're looking for is the cause or causes of the projected outcome: what is the role of every element seen as material to the net outcome? If, for example, the model is suggesting that the world temperature will rise by 3°C should CO_2 in the atmosphere be doubled, then let's see *why* the model is saying that. What are the contributions to the overall impact — how much of the effect is immediate impact, how much is 'committed' (delayed), what are the mechanisms that can delay the committed effect, what are the offsetting impacts and how large or small are they, what are the reinforcing effects and how large or small, and over what time period? Why does doubling CO_2 concentration not cause a runaway impact on temperature, and why doesn't the impact of doubling CO_2 get totally offset by natural stabilising effects, either?

Any modeller worth their salt should be able to present a full attributions analysis of any of their model predictions. Without this they are giving their readers nothing but a story out of a black box and asking them just to believe it. This is modelling alchemy of the worst type and deserves no place in a serious discussion. Attributions analyses are straight out of Modelling 101, and their value can be seen in Chapter 6, where we go looking for the precise numerical value (or rather, the precise degree of imprecision in the numerical value) of the various feedbacks presumed in climate models. Understanding the nature and extent of the attributions in a climate change prediction that a model makes is the only way we can have any level of confidence in that prediction. This is the richest contribution that models can make to the climate debate — they throw the nature and extent of our knowledge of key drivers and their uncertainties into sharp relief.

Summary

So what can we say, in summary, about the methods used to produce evidence of climate change?

A couple of aspects are immediately obvious.

First, the data become less reliable and precise as you move backward through time. Even the records for the 'instrumental period' leave much to be desired, due in the first instance to the fact that most of the data gathered were intended for a different purpose than that which they are now being asked to serve. Silent changes in instrumentation and methodology have distorted data series to greater and lesser degrees. And beyond the instrumental period, where we are forced to fall back on proxies for our information, the resolution of the picture falls away further (and in the case of a global result, must be constructed from a group of regional datapoints). The Sceptics maintain a steady, skirmishing pressure on these points, arguing that so much of what the Alarmists claim is based on unreliable data that their conclusions are worthless.

But while precision is desirable, the next best thing is knowing where the uncertainty lies, and how critical it is to the enterprise that relies on the information. While there's plenty of reason to doubt the absolute veracity of any bold line representing global average temperatures for the last 200,000 years, it's harder to quibble with the instrumental record, some fuzziness notwithstanding, and with the broad, shadowy bands that show general trends in graphs of the remote past without making claims to Swiss watch precision. What's more, there's a large element of educated guesswork in reconciling the historical record prior to satellite telemetry with records since, but that doesn't mean the hybrid record is worthless. Any judgement on how well or badly this reconciliation work has been done rests on your opinion of the sincerity of those doing it.

The second thing that's noteworthy in this survey of measurement techniques is that climatology is a science that, while not quite in its infancy, can't really claim to have outgrown its pimply, awkward stage. Curiosity about climate dates back to the realisation of the ice ages. Anything resembling systematic study dates only to the 1950s, and it wasn't really until the 1970s that the tools adequate to study so large and shifty a beast as climate became available. New tools are becoming available all the time. The self-assurance with which climatology presently speaks may have more to do with the brash presumption of youth than with wisdom.

Speaking of the tools available, it has to be said that some of the tools that modern climatology has at its disposal must be used with care, and we, the consumer, must be wary when taking anything that has been produced with them at strict face value. Numbers can be made to mean practically anything with the application of a little sophisticated statistical analysis. Both sides gild the lily here and there, and sometimes downright dishonesty can be detected in the way data are handled, sifted and presented. It often pays to look behind the headlines, and it would greatly assist the lay public in making decisions about the credibility of scientific 'findings' if there were complete transparency regarding the data-handling that has gone on at every step along the way.

Transparency is vital, too, where models are wheeled out. Given we don't have the luxury of a few spare planet Earths lying about the lab, models are the only means we have to test our understanding of the climate system. But to say that the climate behaves a certain way because it behaved that way in modelling is no more convincing than to say a drug works on human disease because it worked that way on some hapless rat. To know how credible the results of any given model are, we need to know how it ticks — which cogs turn and which levers trip when you press a certain button. In short, the findings of models should be accompanied by attributions analyses — transparency.

Again, the evidence of the way the climate behaves speaks for itself, but hardly ever clearly and distinctly. It pays to know this when you're deciding how much to trust anyone who claims to be speaking on its behalf.

Chapter 3

Is Anything Agreed?

Now that we've looked at the main methods by which scientists can take the Earth's temperature, and their limitations, and before we ship out for the front lines of this little spat between Alarmists and Sceptics, let's spend some quality time on that small tract of climate science real estate where peace reigns — at least in the main, because even here there's still the odd diehard prepared to take a potshot or two.

We're pleased to report that there are five areas of common ground between those who look at the data and warn of 'impending climatic catastrophe' and those who look at the same data and shrug, 'No worries, mate.'

1. The Earth's climate is, and has always been, changing

a. Ancient history

You'll still find people around who will assure you that the Earth was created over six days in 4004 BC, but let's disregard them. Scientists on both sides of the climate debate prefer to think of the Earth as some 4.6 billion years old, as judged by the geological record. And over that time, there's indisputable evidence that the climate has varied enormously, even if you're considering only the period in which the Earth has been blanketed by what we called its 'third atmosphere' in Chapter 1. As we've already noted, this realisation came as a bit of a shock to the nineteenth-century geologists who were trying to work out why it looked so very much as though most of the Earth's surface had been scoured by ice at some point in our past, yet there was no mention of such a monumental cold snap in the Bible. When, in the early twentieth century, fossils were discovered deep in the Antarctic interior that suggested plants and animals had lived there, the scale of the changes the Earth's climate must have undergone became even more apparent.

So let's begin with a trip down geological memory lane. Scientists like to talk of three general phases of the paleoclimate:

▷ A Snowball Earth, where ice covers the whole planet, and it is practically uninhabitable. The last of these was some 635 million years ago, and nobody is expecting another soon.

▷ A Greenhouse Earth, where it is tropical, even at the poles, with no ice present on our planet at all and things are sufficiently snug for exothermic (that is, needing warmth from outside their bodies to power their metabolism) dinosaurs to saunter about. The global average temperature on Greenhouse Earth was 4 to 7°C warmer — some new techniques are suggesting up to 10°C warmer — than we're used to. And apparently atmospheric CO_2 concentrations of six times pre-industrial levels were not uncommon. The last Greenhouse Earth was around 70 million years ago.

▷ An Icehouse Earth, a state the Earth entered around 34 million years ago, where it is cool enough for ice sheets to persist in the polar regions and for glaciers to lie on high mountains at low (that is, tropical) latitudes. Icehouse Earth is the only version humanity has ever known, so let's look at it in a little more detail.

The shift to Icehouse Earth began with a sharp drop in temperature around 34 million years ago, permitting the growth of the glaciers and the first of many Antarctic ice sheets. Glaciers and ice sheets in Icehouse Earth expand and contract, or 'pulse', and these pulses are referred to as 'glacial' and 'interglacial' periods (respectively, ice ages and the warmer intervals in between). For most of Icehouse Earth's history, this cycle had a period (frequency) of 40,000 years.

The first Antarctic ice sheet and Icehouse Earth's brand-new glaciers came and went with the glacial–interglacial pulses every 40,000 years, until a further drop in temperature around 14 million years ago established a permanent core to the Antarctic ice sheet. A mere seven million years ago — it seems like only yesterday — the first ice sheets formed on Greenland, and 2.6 million years ago, huge ice sheets formed over the European and North American land masses, also pulsing every 40,000 years.

About 800,000 years ago, however, and for reasons that await a convincing explanation, the period of the glacial–interglacial pulses changed to 100,000 years. We presently inhabit an interglacial phase — a warm spell between big freezes — one that has so far lasted around 11,000 years. Scientists refer to this interglacial as the 'Holocene', which means 'entirely recent'.

The Holocene interglacial began at the end of the Pleistocene, a period from 1.8 million years ago until 11,550 years ago. The Pleistocene was characterised by repeated glaciation, with 30% of the Earth covered by ice at its maximum, including all of New Zealand. During this period the continents were more or less in the same position as they are today.

Since 65 million years ago (when the dinosaurs and 70% of all species on Earth became extinct), atmospheric CO_2 concentrations have trended down (from a whopping 2000 parts per million at the beginning of the Icehouse Earth, around 34 million years ago, to around 300 ppm throughout most of the rest of history).

So what's with all that pulsing that ice sheets and glaciers go in for? Surely the regular 40,000- and 100,000-year cycles are a clue that there's a powerful natural driver of climate at work?

Indeed there is, and here we need to recognise and pay tribute to one of the most substantial contributions to our knowledge of climate, namely the work of Serbian civil engineer, mathematician and card-carrying oddball Milutin Milankovic. Taking a break from his workaday contemplations of the properties of reinforced concrete, Milankovic decided he was going to solve the mystery of the ice ages using nothing but a pencil, paper, presumably an eraser, and definitely some pretty heavy-duty maths. Perhaps the vast series of calculations he performed later formed part of the series of 'letters' he wrote to a young Austrian woman, who had apparently asked him to 'explain the mysteries of the universe' to her. Milankovic took her rather more literally than she probably had in mind. Contrary to his wife's lifelong insistence that the young lady was 'a literary device', Milankovic's charming interrogator was a real person.

We can only imagine how her heart must have gone pitter-patter every time she wandered down to the letterbox and recognised his handwriting on an envelope during the heady phase when he was explaining the mysteries of climate to her. In breathless prose, the incurably romantic Milankovic would have described to her how eccentricities in the Earth's orbit caused fluctuations in the amount of solar radiation reaching the planet, and that these fluctuations were what triggered ice ages and thaws. He identified three aspects of the Earth's orbit, each of which had an impact on global climate: a 100,000-year cycle due to the fact that the Earth's orbit is not a perfect ellipse, and takes us further away from the sun in some iterations than in others; a 41,000-year cycle caused by shifts in the tilt of the Earth's spin axis; and a 26,000-year cycle arising from the way the Earth wobbles on its spin axis. If she was really lucky, he might even have showed her his maths.

Perhaps all that talk of throbbing ice masses was supposed to serve as a come-on along the lines of Andrew Marvell's seduction poem 'To His Coy Mistress', intended to urge his beloved that time was short: we've only got another 89,000 years of the interglacial left, so why not make, ahem, hay while the sun still shines, at least at the present level of intensity — he was an engineer, after all. If so, alas, the success or otherwise of this tactic remains one of the unknowns of climate science.

We do know, however, that Milankovic's work was published in 1920 to hoots of derision. He had his defenders over subsequent years, but it wasn't until the 1970s that ocean sediment data produced a historical record of climatic variation that showed practically incontrovertible evidence of the cycles he had predicted; and a little over a decade after his death in 1958 the work of the Serbian engineer finally won the universal acclaim it deserved. The glacial–interglacial cycles corresponding to the vagaries of Earth's orbit and spin are known as Milankovic cycles in his honour.

Today his seminal work is one of the few areas of common ground between Alarmists and Sceptics who otherwise shout at each other across the divide. The deep sea sediment cores show, as Milankovic's work postulated, that we've had eight 100,000-year glacial–interglacial cycles in the last 800,000 years, and about thirty 41,000-year glacial pulses in the previous 1,200,000 years. They vary a bit in the area covered by ice and in the volume of ice lying on land, and the reasons for this variation in the extent of the changes are not understood. The role of changes in composition of atmospheric gases, sunspot activity, and the unique role of water vapour and its precipitation are all candidate explanations for what played variations on Milankovic's orbital theme, and for what might cause lower-order climate variability in the meantime; we'll evaluate these later on. Yet the basic engine of climate remains — solar radiation as modulated by variations in the Earth's orbit.

b. Merely the last million years

Figure 3 shows another graph, which presents a reconstruction of the paleoclimate for the most recent fifth of the Icehouse World. These data for the last 800,000 years are derived from the ice core drilled at Dome C by EPICA, the longest ice core currently available to us.

Once again, Milankovic's cycles are plain to see in the sawtooth cycle of glacial and interglacial. The eight major temperature minima

Global surface temperature reconstruction for the last eight millenia

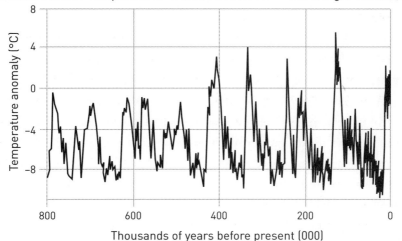

Figure 3. Rapid to rise, slow to sink: global surface temperature anomaly (as deduced from the EPICA Dome C ice core) from 800,000 years before the present (BP) to the present day. Note the distinctive 'sawtooth' pattern of the glacial–interglacial cycles, where abrupt warming to a sharp peak is followed by a rather gentler decline into an ice age. Note also that since 450,000 years ago, the warm periods have been getting warmer.

Source: Data from Lüthi et al (2008). 'High-resolution carbon dioxide concentration record 650,000–800,000 years before present'. *Nature*, 453, 2008, 379–382.

(at some 8°C below current temperatures) start at about 50,000 years ago and repeat about every 100,000 years back from there. Similarly, the temperature grand maxima (of some 3°C higher than present) can be seen going back from about 20,000 years ago and recurring every 100,000 years. It's interesting to note that the 100,000-year variability undergoes a change about 450,000 years ago, with the amplitude of variation greater since that point than it was before. In other words, warm phases (interglacials, such as our current Holocene) have been warmer in the last 450,000 years, whereas cold phases (glacials) don't seem to have changed.

The really interesting aspect of temperatures from ice-core records is the way they move, with the exit from a glacial proceeding very rapidly until temperatures hit a maximum — somewhere between 2 and 3°C above the current global average temperature — before a long, slow decline from that sharp peak into the next glacial. What accounts for this weird sawtooth pattern — sudden, steep climbs and gentle declines? It turns out that the explanation for this asymmetry, where the warming phase of the pulse is so much faster than the cooling, tells us much about the way the natural, solar-driven cycles in the Earth's climate operate.

A glacial is reckoned to come about when a succession of northern hemisphere summers delivers less 'insolation' than normal — the term 'insolation' is constructed from the words 'incident solar radiation', the amount of the sun's rays reaching the Earth's surface. This means that snow and ice from the previous winter is lying about in June, and this escapes the thaw. Successive weak thaws allow a build-up of ice, and this in turn reflects a greater proportion of solar rays to space (whereas usually they would be absorbed by the darker ground exposed by the thaw), precipitating a regional cooling. The regional cooling becomes global, and the ice starts piling up. And pile up it does: once our Earth is into a full glacial, these ice caps typically build up to a depth of 3 km — fully the height of all but the tallest peaks in the Rocky Mountains, a runaway climate effect if ever there was one.

On the other hand, when a Milankovic cycle creates conditions favourable for warming, the thaw begins, from the bottom up. This is because the lower atmosphere gets progressively cooler the higher you rise above the surface (because after all it's the surface, acted upon by the sun's radiation, that is the source of the warming). At 3 km above the surface, the height of the summit of these colossal ice caps, the temperature is 20°C cooler than at their foot. But as the foot warms and the ice melts, the entire ice mass descends through the atmosphere, entering warmer air as it goes and melting proportionately faster. The smaller it gets, the higher its surface-area-to-volume ratio becomes, and the faster again becomes the melting. And the smaller it gets, the more dark ground (or ocean) it reveals, which warms more effectively than the snow and ice. Needless to say, with all that ice out of the picture, both the Earth's surface and the air warm faster. So whereas the build-up of ice is a long, slow process, its disappearance — and global warming — is pretty quick by comparison.

c. Our cosy little interglacial — the Holocene

Twenty thousand years ago, at the peak of the last glacial, when the ice sheets pulsed out to a maximum before retreating, the global average temperature was a little more than 5°C lower than that of the present day and the ice sheets in North America and Europe reached down to the latitudes occupied by present-day New York, London and Berlin. These began melting around 18,000 years ago and were mostly gone by around 11,000 years ago, when our present interglacial, the Holocene, commenced. Since then, if the various paleoclimate proxy measures (graphed in Figure 4) are to be believed, the prevailing climate has been like something out of Goldilocks — not too cold, not too hot, just right. During the Holocene the global average temperature has varied only by around 1°C. It was a little warmer around 8000 years ago, in the so-called Holocene Climatic Optimum, and has been declining gently ever since.

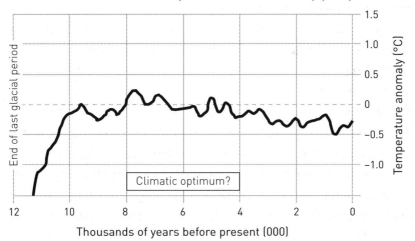

Mean Holocene temperature variations (by proxy)

Figure 4. Boring and stable: global surface temperature anomaly (as deduced from the average of multiple climate proxies) from the end of the last ice age circa 12,000 years BP to the present. Note how stable the Earth's climate has been in that period, the Holocene, coinciding with the rise of human civilisation.

Source: Adapted from Robert A Rohe, http://www.globalwarmingart.com/wiki/Image: Holocene_Temperature_Variations_Rev_png#Data_Sources

It's the sheer, unexcitable predictability of climate throughout the history of civilisation that gave rise to the old, complacent attitude (and reinforces the contemporary, complacent attitude among some Sceptics) that climate, along with death, taxes and unrest in the Middle East, is one of those few things in life that can be relied upon. But let's put recent climate trends into the context of ancient climatic variation. Figure 5 shows the 'best guesses' of temperature range throughout the ages — and gives an indication of just how small the temperature range has been in the recent era compared with the swings the Earth has previously gone in for.

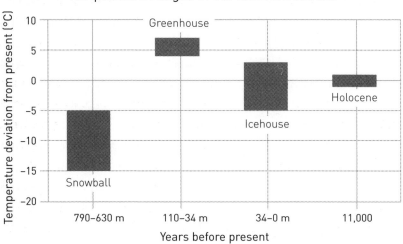

Figure 5. Converging to constant: the wild swings of the Earth's climate in the remote past have settled down through time. The Holocene looks decidedly unexciting by comparison with what's gone before.

Source: Peter Barrett.

2. The world is warming

We can take two points from the foregoing discussion. First, we can say with absolute certainty that the climate has varied drastically in the past. And second, we can say that nature has driven it. Human beings hadn't been invented for much of the Earth's history, let alone seven-litre sport-utility vehicles, or the plasma televisions driven by coal-fired electricity grids on which we comfortably watch reruns of *An Inconvenient Truth*. On these two points, both sides can agree.

Not that you can take much comfort from either fact, however. The climate as we know it has very little in common with earlier incarnations, and very few of the climates that have prevailed on Earth in the remote past would support the ecosystems that we know, love and depend upon. Any return to those climates would quite literally mean the end of life as we know it. On this, all sides agree.

It's time to forsake the sandbagged safety of remote antiquity and take a peep over the parapet. What we're surveying now is the battle-scarred, contested ground of the temperature record of the recent past, extending back over the last 1000 years. For much of that period, we must rely on proxy data, as discussed in the previous chapter. We'll deal with that part of the record shortly. Right now, what we'll look at is one area over which you'd think folks should just be able to get along, namely that period as far back as instrumental records can take us. Of course, individual temperature records that extend further back than 150 years do exist, but they're of little value in determining what global temperatures have been doing, as they're local records only.

There are quibbles — of greater or lesser moment — with each of the components of the series comprising the instrumental period. We've seen difficulties with the old-school thermometer surface air temperature record that extends back to 1850, even for those regions of the globe where coverage existed. We've seen how well-founded reservations about sea surface temperature data are. We've seen that there are problems with the radiosonde data gathered by the weather balloon programme since the 1950s. And there are plenty of people willing to contest the validity of the algorithms used to convert satellite radiation measurements into temperature readings. You'd be forgiven for thinking that assembling all of these disparate datasets into a single, robust series is a task about as formidable as that confronting all the king's horses and all the king's men in the wake of Humpty Dumpty's little contretemps with the concrete.

Temperature is a notoriously variable parameter, as we have discussed. The temperature varies every day in most parts of the world by far greater amounts than the entire baseline hike feared by proponents of anthropogenic global warming. It varies from winter to summer, and from year to year. Temperature also varies according to latitude: the tropics, which receive more (and more direct) sunlight than the higher latitudes, are much hotter. Any value for 'global average temperature' must take all of this into account.

Yet it's vital, if we are to know what's happening with the contemporary climate, to try to develop a global average temperature series. And give or take a bit of desultory sniping from harder-line Sceptics along the way, the evidence of the several versions of global average temperature series that have been constructed is accepted. Figure 6 shows one version of records of global average surface (land and sea) temperature anomaly dating from 1850, developed by the United Kingdom's Hadley Centre. Note the shaded areas that indicate uncertainty arising from the various sources we've identified.

What does it tell us? It shows (and it's almost universally accepted) that there has been a general warming trend (albeit with interruptions) over the last 150 years — a rise of about 0.8°C. One

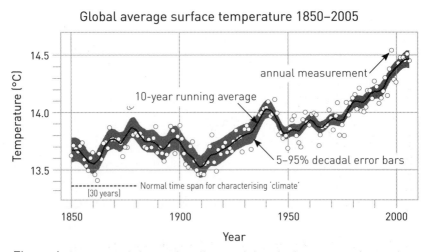

Figure 6. A measured rise: we're all agreed that the instrumental records show global average temperatures have risen during the industrial period, right? Yeah, right.

Source: Data from HadCRUT2.

notable interruption to the trend took place between 1940 and 1970. Another has occurred far more recently, with an apparent slight cooling under way since 1998. Needless to say, the significance of these interruptions has been hotly (no pun intended) debated. The most influential theory for the 1940–1970 cooling is that it was the result of the belching of sulphate particles from coal-fired power plants and industry into the lower atmosphere, which caused 'global dimming' — the reflection of a proportion of solar radiation and hence a cooling of the lower atmosphere. As environmental consciousness gathered momentum, and concern grew over local air quality in the world's major cities, clean-air policies began to be enforced, and pollution-reducing scrubbers were widely introduced. With global dimming reduced, warming resumed. A second, rival theory is that this 30-year cycle of cooling correlates closely with variations in solar radiation, and that this accounts for the more recent cooling, too — more on this in Chapter 5.

Records of ocean temperature, taken in isolation, show the same steady upward trend from 1950 to the near-present — assuming you

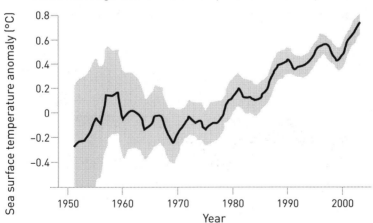

Global average sea surface temperature anomaly 1950–2004

Figure 7. Hot water: the temperature anomaly deduced from measurements of the top 100 metres of seawater since reliable records began in 1950 show the same steady rise.

Source: Adapted from Domingues et al (2008). 'Improved estimates of upper-ocean warming and multi-decadal sea-level rise.' *Nature*, 453, 2008, 1090–1093.

can live with all the correction and adjustment that has been required to make this record hang together. Note the grey shaded area in Figure 7, broadening as you go back to 1950, that represents the potential error.

Let's look now solely at the satellite record, which (with the usual provisos) is regarded as a consistent, reliable, globally comprehensive dataset. Figure 8 shows the temperature anomaly in sea surface temperatures during the satellite era.

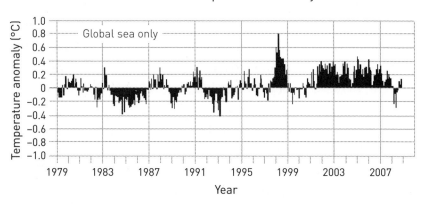

Mean sea surface temperature anomaly 1979–2008

Figure 8. Sea? The ocean is warmer: sea surface temperature anomaly as measured by satellite. The comparative rarity of cooler anomalies since the bumper El Niño year of 1998 indicates generally warmer temperatures.

Source: Data from McLean/University of Alabama at Huntsville, http://vortex.nsstc.uah.edu/public/msu/t2lt/uahncdc.lt

You'll note that sea surface temperatures are distinctly cyclical, as you'd expect given the influence of the Southern and North Atlantic Oscillations, the clearest example of which is the spike representing the 'super El Niño' of 1998. But you'll also note that in the period covered, cooler anomalies have been getting briefer and comparatively rarer, and the period of sustained sea surface warming between 2000 and the present is without precedent in the (admittedly short) era of satellite telemetry.

The graph in Figure 9 shows lower troposphere temperatures, measured using satellite-based microwave sounding units, since the beginning of comprehensive satellite measurements in 1979 and finishing in May 2008, as compiled by the University of Alabama,

Data Hockey

In a 1998 paper, American researchers Michael Mann, Raymond Bradley and Malcolm Hughes used 95 proxy data series (many of them based on tree-ring studies) to reconstruct historical northern hemisphere mean temperatures from AD 1000 to the present.[1] The results were visually dramatic when graphed, with temperatures barely moving above or below a flat line until the twentieth century, when they abruptly flicked upward.

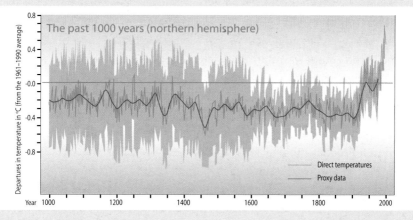

The shape of the graph was likened to an ice hockey stick by the head of NOAA's Geophysical Fluid Dynamic Labs, Jerry Mahlman, and the name stuck.

Mann et al. reported that, based on their analysis, the 1990s were the warmest decade in the last 1000 years, and that 1998 was the warmest single year. The findings and the striking graphic were star features of the IPCC's 2001 Third Assessment Report, and were widely reported in the popular media, especially in Al Gore's influential film *An Inconvenient Truth*. The hockey stick became the equivalent of a logo for anthropogenic global warming — its very own Nike 'swoosh'.

The statistical techniques used in the 1998 paper came under fire from two Canadians, mining industry executive Stephen McIntyre (moderator of the sceptical blog www.climateaudit.org) and economist Ross McKitrick, who accused the authors of fudging the data to produce the dramatic hockey stick shape, which was spurious.[2] A full-scale argument ensued, and after McIntyre accused Mann of peevishly refusing to supply him with the raw data and the algorithms used in his study, it attracted the attention of no less than the US Congress and the National Academy of Sciences, which commissioned independent reports into the validity of Mann et al.'s statistical methods, the value of tree-ring data as a temperature proxy, and other allegations about the scientific peer review process levelled by McIntyre and McKitrick. In 2006 the National Academy of Sciences released a report on Mann's work that concluded:

> The substantial uncertainties currently present in the quantitative assessment of large-scale surface temperature changes prior to about A.D. 1600 lower our confidence in this conclusion [that recent northern hemisphere temperatures have been warmer than at any other time during the last millennium] compared to the high level of confidence we place in the Little Ice Age cooling and 20th century warming. Even less confidence can be placed in the original conclusions by Mann et al. (1999) that "the 1990s are likely the warmest decade, and 1998 the warmest year, in at least a millennium" because the uncertainties inherent in temperature reconstructions for individual years and decades are larger than those for longer time periods, and because not all of the available proxies record temperature information on such short timescales.[3]

In other words, the National Academy of Sciences' view was that Mann pushed his smoothed and error-corrected data of proxy measures of temperature way too far in concluding that 1998 was the warmest year and the 1990s the warmest decade in 1000 years.

Both reports found flaws in the statistical methods used by Mann et al. and expressed reservations about their claims, even though they broadly supported the reconstruction. There was wiggle room here, and, typically in the context of the fraught debate surrounding climate change, both sides proclaimed victory. Yet it is clear that Mann grievously overstated the case. Of course, the hockey stick shape is pretty well identical to that of atmospheric concentration of CO_2, so from the perspective of Alarmists eager to prove their preconceptions, the hockey stick graph was pure gold — nothing more would be necessary to convince the public that anthropogenic global warming was indeed running amok.

And sadly, they were right. Despite the live academic debate on its veracity, Al Gore got hold of it for his 2006 *An Inconvenient Truth* book and movie combo, and at that point the hockey stick became etched in the public mind as truth. Who could forget the enthusiasm of the former vice-president as he rode a hoist up toward the ceiling of the auditorium so he could reach the top of the temperature projection implied by the hockey stick graph?

The debate has continued to simmer, although Mann et al. now have a considerable body of support and a wealth of data to support a much milder version of the story. New versions of the infamous hockey stick are abroad these days, and catchily styled as the findings of 'the hockey team'. The hockey stick graph of the IPCC 2001 report has been replaced by the 'hockey team' version in IPCC 2007. Here it is:

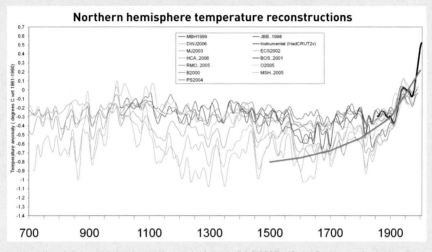

Northern hemisphere temperature reconstructions

Source: Graph is a reproduction of Figure 6.10 from IPCC 2007 WG-1 AR4, drawn from the original datasets the IPCC used.

It's incredible, really, after the humiliation it suffered over the hockey stick, that the IPCC and its much vaunted peer review process still conspire to send a resoundingly false message to the public. The 'hockey team' graph is a chastened version of that bit of statistical over-enthusiasm, but the IPCC is nevertheless determined to vindicate it. The graph is scarcely less misleading in the way it compares present and past.

Note the many wiggly lines, representing individual time series constructed from various proxies. Indeed, to the naked eye, the 13 lines that comprise the graph are individually pretty much impossible to follow from go to whoa — with the notable exception of two of them: the thicker black and grey lines stand out above the tangle of light wigglies. This can hardly be by accident — they both point heavenward, leaving the reader with the impression that temperatures are now at historical record levels and reaching ever further to the sky. 'The hockey stick thesis is alive, and we were right all along,' is what it's saying.

Trouble is, neither of these two heavily promoted series extend very far into the past — which makes them a totally inappropriate basis for comparison with the present; as we've seen in Chapter 2, you can't just graft data collected by new methods to aeons of proxy data that reaches right back into our Earth's past, but is collected on a totally different basis. Statistics 101 teaches students that.

So what are the lines? The black line is the record of direct measurement of world temperature that reaches back only to 1856 and is not comparable to any of the far-reaching proxy measures. The grey Nike swoosh that runs skyward is the more fascinating, not least because it's the only smooth, wiggle-free graph in the picture. Here's why: this temperature proxy is an amalgamation of bore-hole temperatures, each of which provides only two observations of temperature — the years AD 1500 and AD 2000. In other words, each hole can provide only a linear trend (the single line joining the dots) of what temperature has done. So the Nike swoosh is a combo of these linear trends. It is not a year-by-year track of temperature or a proxy for temperature at all, hence the lack of wiggles.

Why on earth would the IPCC even want to superimpose this curve on the same graph as 12 other curves that represent year-by-year changes, let alone highlight it? It's incongruous — unless we suspect the worst.

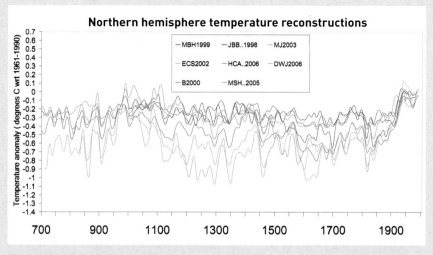

Northern hemisphere reconstructions as reconstructed from the original data but omitting HadCRUT2v and PS2004.

Indeed, only eight of the 13 series of the 'hockey team' graph extend over both recent years and any part of the Medieval Warm Period, roughly between AD 800 and AD 1300 (there's more on this in Chapter 3). So let's have a look at what this data has to say about present compared to past.

Oh dear. The trend seems to be flat. Two of the eight (ECS2002, MSH.2005) indicate the Medieval Warm Period was warmer than the present; four of them (MBH1999, JBB.1998, DWJ2006 and HCA.2006) suggest the 1940s was the warmest period in the series, leaving just two (MJ2003, B2000) suggesting the late twentieth century was the warmest. Further, if we look at the average difference between the temperature maximum of the late twentieth century and the maximum of the Medieval Warm Period, it's a mere 0.09^0C — hardly proof that we live in the world's hottest times in 1500 years! Put away the black and grey biros and there's nothing obvious to suggest the current global warming is outside the range of natural variability, and current northern hemisphere temperatures seem to be at or only a little above those reached during the Medieval Warm Period, according to the majority of the eight proxies. They don't even appear to be rising at an 'alarming' rate by comparison with what they've done before. The temperature rises from AD 850 to AD 1100 don't seem to be much slower than those between 1800 and the 1990s.

Of course, none of this tells us anything about whether anthropogenic factors are causing the current warming, but it does send worrying messages about the IPCC and its peer review process. That Figure 6.10 of the IPCC Fourth Assessment Report of 2007 was ever allowed to run in its over-egged form suggests a lack of objectivity (let alone remorse over the original hockey stick episode!) on the part of both the figure's constructors and its peer reviewers. Worse, Mann et al. published an updated version of the 'hockey team' graph in 2008, which remains as misleading as ever.[4]

It's important to emphasise that the case for anthropogenic warming doesn't stand or fall on demonstrating whether the current extent or rate of the rise in world temperature is unprecedented according to proxy evidence, and catching the Alarmists out on one or two exaggerated pictures doesn't discredit the entire, monumental case. But both the hockey stick and the hockey team serve to remind us that we should look behind the headlines of any claim, no matter how authoritative its promoters.

The electromagnetic spectrum

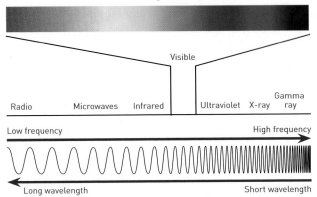

Figure i.The location of the band of visible light is indicated above the spectrum. Infrared lies just to the left of visible red light, showing (in this diagram) that it has a longer wavelength.

Source: www.lcse.umn.edu

A visual representation of warming trends in the troposphere as measured by radiosonde

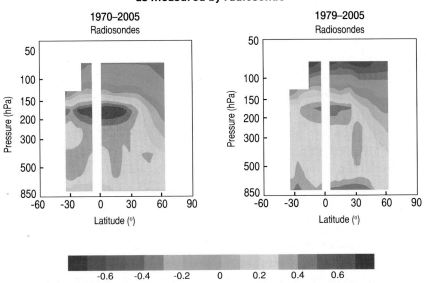

Figure ii. Hot Spot: The pattern of upper tropospheric warming over two time periods, 1970–2006 and 1979–2006, as inferred by the work of Allen and Sherwood. Models have long predicted just such a 'hot spot' to develop in the upper troposphere over the tropics, but evidence has proved elusive. Direct temperature measurements from radiosondes have been equivocal. Allen and Sherwood, studying a second-order effect of warming — thermal winds — believe they've detected it.

Source: Allen, R.J. and S.C. Sherwood, 'Warming Maximum in the Tropical Upper Troposphere Deduced from Thermal Winds', *Nature Geoscience*, 1, 2008, 399–403.

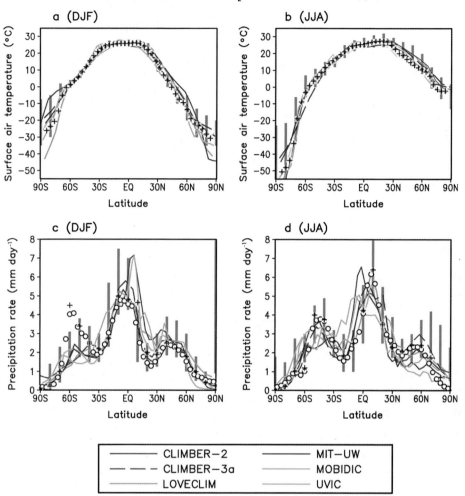

Climate model replications of world temperature and world precipitation (at CO₂ concentration of 280 ppm)

Figure iii. Seasoned campaigners: this is how climate models do when you ask them to replicate world summer and winter temperatures and precipitation rates (top and bottom respectively), and compare them with real-world observations. The model runs are represented by the coloured lines, whereas observed data are plotted using noughts and crosses. They're a pretty good fit, giving confidence that the models have got a good grasp of the processes that make a year's worth of global weather tick.

Source: Fig 8.17 IPCC 2007 WG-1 AR4

Modelled and measured annual mean precipitation

Figure iv. Rain supreme: the models do a pretty good job of simulating a year's worth of precipitation, too, if these two plots are anything to go by. The top figure is the annual mean observed precipitation of the world, with different rain- (and snow-) fall intensities plotted in different colours for the period 1980 to 1999. The bottom figure is the average of the best guesses of various climate models as to the pattern of precipitation over the same period. There are differences, but there are broad similarities, too, suggesting the models replicate the engines of precipitation pretty well.

Source: Fig 8.5 IPCC 2007 WG-1 AR4

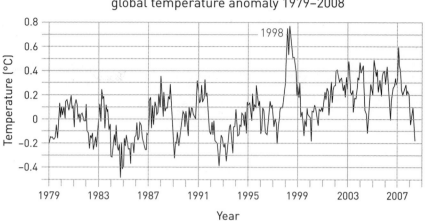

UAH monthly means of lower troposphere LT5.2
global temperature anomaly 1979–2008

Figure 9. It's all over. No trend here: monthly mean lower tropospheric temperature anomaly as measured by satellite since 1979. Although the period from 1999 to 2008 has been slightly warmer than the period from 1979 to 1998, not much trend is obvious in either period. Note the sharp spike in lower tropospheric temperature in 1998, attributed to an intense El Niño cycle that year. That an even more intense El Niño event in 1982/1983 did not cause a temperature change of anything approaching the same magnitude is thought to be due to the effects of the massive eruption of the El Chichon volcano in May 1983, which produced a global 'dimming' that masked the effects of the Southern Oscillation.

Source: Data from University of Alabama at Huntsville,
http://www.nsstc.uah.edu/data/msu/t2lt/tltglhmam_5.2

Huntsville, one of the two major analysts of remote sensing data.

The data suggest that while the years since 1997 have been mostly warmer in most places than the years 1979 to 1996, there has been no warming trend since that bumper El Niño year of 1998. We can see this more clearly in Figure 10, which shows a representation of roughly the same period, this time from 1978 to September 2007.

The average global temperature anomaly (that is, how the temperature has stood in relation to that of 1979) since 1998 was 0.24°C warmer than the average anomaly for the 20-odd years prior to 1998.

How vital 'global average temperature' is to assembling a case for or against anthropogenic global warming is debatable. We've

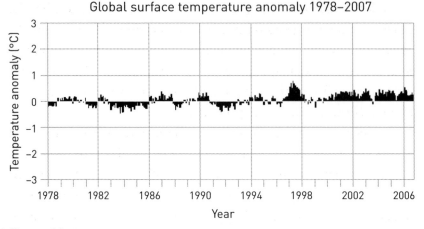

Figure 10. Once was cooler: monthly mean surface temperature anomaly records during the satellite era, showing little continuous trend, even if temperatures have been generally warmer in the period after 1998 than they were in the period before 1998.

Source: Data from McLean/University of Alabama at Huntsville, http://vortex.nsstc.uah.edu/public/msu/t2lt/uahncdc.lt

already noted how hard it is to define, and how hard it is to develop, a universally satisfactory series; more worryingly, it can blur data signals that are better indicators of significant warming. It's the nature of the beast, for example, that the oceans absorb much of the excess energy in the Earth-atmosphere system before that energy makes itself felt in the lower atmosphere. You'll occasionally hear talk of 'committed warming', and mostly this refers to excess energy stored in the oceans that will be transferred to the atmosphere over (roughly) a 50-year period — 'committed', because regardless of what happens with energy in the Earth system from now on, this energy is already latent and must lead to increasing atmospheric and land temperatures over the next few decades. A flat average temperature, that is, need not be an all-clear in terms of warming. Similarly, a flat global average temperature value constructed of temperature values that show a warming over the poles and no change over the inhabited regions of the northern hemisphere will seem superficially reassuring, while at the same time concealing an alarming trend: warming at the poles is bad news, as we rely on all that ice and snow to reflect solar energy back to space.

So let's break down the global picture and have a look at what the satellites reckon is going on in the various regions. The three graphs in Figure 11 show the measurements over the tropics (defined in this instance as the band of the globe between latitudes 20° North and 20° South) and for the southern and northern 'exotropics' (from 20° latitude North and South respectively).

Consider the tropics first. Here, temperatures have displayed no obvious trend over the period for which satellite data have been available. Neither is there much evidence of a trend in the southern exotropics. Temperatures in the northern exotropics, where most population and industry is concentrated, have, by contrast, been consistently higher over the last decade. Even so, 1998 was the warmest year in the northern exotropics, too, and there has been no apparent trend in temperatures since then.

But let's have a look at the poles, which are climatologically far more significant. The loss of Arctic sea ice from year to year or the collapse of Antarctic ice shelves due to warming could have a disastrous effect, as they comprise vast areas of reflective snow and ice; any reduction will mean an equivalent amount of radiation usually reflected to space being absorbed, aggravating warming. Note that the graphs in Figure 12 show satellite temperature data for much smaller geographical areas than the previous graphs, and at least partly for this reason, the variations in temperature anomalies are greater.

As we can see, Arctic Circle anomalies were, despite considerable month-to-month variation, obviously warmer during the most recent decade of satellite temperature readings, whereas Antarctic temperatures were on average slightly colder during the same period. Even if it appears that warming is a regional thing, at its most obvious in the Arctic and also apparent in the northern mid-latitudes, this is consistent with globally warmer temperatures. The Antarctic ice cap is massive — up to two kilometres thick on average — and has a huge thermal inertia. Arctic ice, by contract, is sea ice, a couple of metres thick. Globally warmer temperatures will measurably affect the Arctic long before their effects are detectable in the Antarctic, and once the Arctic pack begins to melt, it will expose tracts of dark ocean to solar

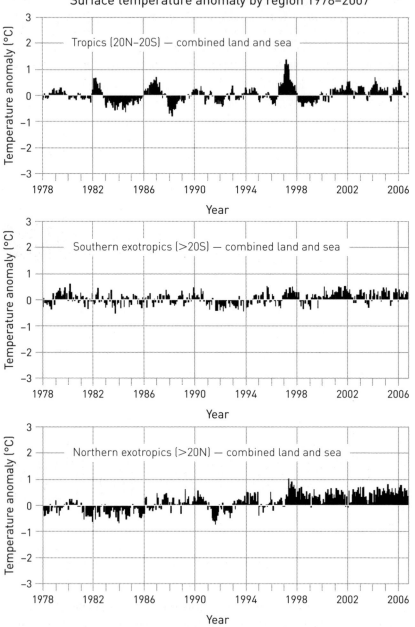

Figure 11. Northern exposure: three panels showing monthly mean temperature anomaly for (from top to bottom) the tropics, the southern hemisphere (south of 20°S) and the northern hemisphere (north of 20°S) as measured by satellite. It's notable that whereas there's a noticeable trend in the tropics (few cooler anomalies after 1999), and a weaker trend

for the same period in the southern hemisphere, there is a distinct trend visible in the northern hemisphere, mostly due to the inclusion of the North Pole region, which is warming faster than any other region on Earth. Note that these three panels and the two comprising Figure 12 are drawn on the same vertical scale, so that it's possible to see at a glance the comparative strength of the trend in each region.

Source: Data from McLean/University of Alabama at Huntsville, http://vortex.nsstc.uah.edu/public/msu/t2lt/uahncdc.lt

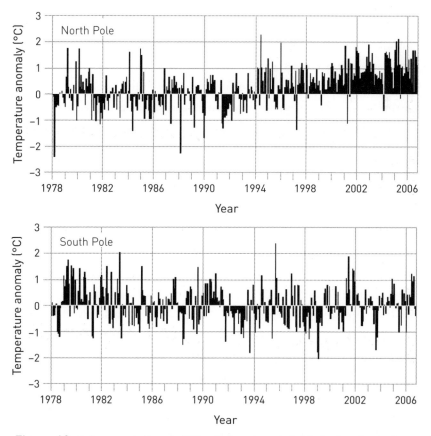

Polar surface temperature anomaly 1978–2007

Figure 12. Poles apart: there's little obvious trend visible in the chart of the monthly mean temperature anomaly at the South Pole (lower panel) as measured from space. By contrast, the relentless and significant warming under way at the North Pole is plain to see in the stack of black lines above zero in the upper panel.

Source: Data from McLean/University of Alabama at Huntsville, http://vortex.nsstc.uah.edu/public/msu/t2lt/uahncdc.lt

radiation that the ice had previously reflected, aggravating warming. So on the one hand, you can say that the global average temperature hasn't shifted significantly over the last 10 years. But in doing so, you ignore the unsettling warming that seems to be under way in the climatologically significant Arctic.

We can say there is agreement that there has been a warming trend over the last 150 years of direct measurement. Both sides agree it's not a steady trend, and it's not uniform across the world — the North Pole shows a stronger trend than average, the South Pole not much trend at all. It's also clear that the trend is clearer for the northern than for the southern hemisphere. Finally, even proponents of anthropogenic global warming concede that the last few years have not continued the trend. The question is whether this is an interruption or the end of the trend. The Sceptics, of course, hail the decade-long decline in global average temperature since the peak of the 'super' El Niño event of 1998 as the predictable cooling phase of a natural warm–cool cycle, and argue that climate variability over the satellite period can be wholly explained in terms of natural drivers without recourse to crazy talk about human agency. The graph in Figure 13 illustrates this contention.

What it appears to show, of course, is that there's an explanation within nature for each and every significant temperature anomaly in the last three decades — El Niño events causing anomalous warming; massive injections of atmospheric aerosols from volcanic eruptions causing anomalous cooling.

Alarmists, as we'll see, argue that the recent cooling is an interruption, and insist that the timeframe over which it has occurred is too short to be meaningful, given how much short-term 'noise' there is in the data. This is why you'll often hear the movement of the 30-year average of world temperature being invoked by the Alarmist camp — 30 years is the standard scientific definition of 'climate' at a measurement site. An average of the 30-year period covered by the graph in Figure 13, for example, will yield a slight rise, and it's this inexorable trend, rather than the short-term volatility, that we must heed.

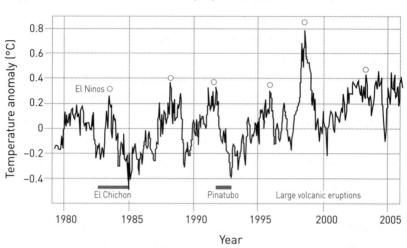

Figure 13. Peak performances: this is an earlier version of Figure 9, except it has El Niño events (circles) and major volcanic eruptions (horizontal bars) superimposed. This suggests that the variability in global temperatures is due to natural causes, and in particular the Southern Oscillation between El Niño and La Niña events (where El Niño events, producing unusually warm sea temperatures in the Pacific Ocean, correspond with elevated global average temperatures) and the eruption of volcanoes (which deposit aerosols in the stratosphere and produce 'global dimming' and thus cooling).

Source: Carter, R.M. (2007). 'The Myth of Dangerous Human-Caused Climate Change', *Proceedings of the AusIMM 2007 New Leaders' Conference*, 61–74.

And never mind the last decade or three decades, what of the last 150 years in the larger picture? Is the warming that both sides agree has occurred significant and unusual (that is, inexplicable in terms of natural drivers), or not? This is where battle is really joined, and since the temperature record back beyond the instrumental period relies upon proxies, the matter becomes much harder to adjudicate and depends upon which proxy or group of proxies you consider to be reliable. Some seem to show, as the IPCC maintains, that the rate and extent of twentieth-century warming is unprecedented in the last 1000 years. Others seem to indicate that there have been periods within that timeframe (and long before human beings were driving

Hummers and watching plasma televisions) where temperatures have been just as high. It's in this context that you'll hear the 'Medieval Warm Period' mentioned (see panel).

So there's broad agreement that the various instruments that have been pointed at the climate for the last 150 years show that the Earth has been warming. There's no agreement that this trend is beyond the pale of natural variability, or even that it's here to stay. Hardly peace in our time, then. Let's return to safer ground, namely what's been going on with carbon dioxide.

Middling Warm

If ever proof were needed that we see past climate as through a glass, darkly, it can be found in the conflicting claims made over the episode variously known as the 'Medieval Warm Period', or the 'Medieval Climate Optimum', or the 'Medieval Climate Anomaly'. There's far more heat generated over just how hot it was back then than there can ever have been radiating at the time.

The period in question is roughly between AD 800 and 1300, so it's well before the times of direct instrumental measurement. It is, however, within the purview of written records, and thus there is some anecdotal evidence of what was going on at the time. And there are, of course, proxy records in the form of sea and lake sediment cores, glacier tracks, ice cores, tree-ring data and so forth.

You'd think, then, that it would be reasonably easy to get a handle on temperatures. Wrong! But the fact there's still some fuzziness around it is not for lack of effort on both sides to arrive at a definitive reconstruction.

We know it was warm back then, because the anecdotal evidence is unequivocal. People were growing wine grapes in the south of England. Apparently tired of the rape-and-pillage lifestyle, the Vikings had turned their hands to farming various localities around the North Atlantic rim, including Greenland, which despite its bucolic-sounding name is hardly prime pastoral real estate these days — and indeed, wasn't looking so good by the 1500s, as the region (and possibly the globe) entered a two-century-long cool spell known as the Little Ice Age.

But exactly where it was warm, how warm it was and for how long is hotly disputed.

Needless to say, the Sceptics are keen on a really warm, global Medieval Warm Period, because that would show (a) that nature was capable of causing instances of warming just as rapid and great as the present warming, and (b) it was a good thing, all told, while it lasted.

The IPCC is just as keen on a tepid, regional Medieval Warm Period, because it is consistent with the assertion that Earth as a whole has not experienced warming of this rate and magnitude any time in the last few millennia.

Interestingly, there is nowhere near the same amount of debate around the depth and duration of the other, closely related climate event of the last 2000 years, the Little Ice Age. But you can bet if we were presently staring down the barrel of global cooling, there would be two camps scrapping over precisely those questions and neglecting the Medieval Warm Period all the while.

Some records indicate a distinct Medieval Warm Period, and these tend to recur throughout Sceptical literature. Look at the graph in Figure 14, for example, which shows it as a pronounced blip between AD 1000 and 1100 in a reconstruction of sea surface temperature from a sediment core drilled from the Sargasso Sea (at the heart of the Bermuda Triangle, coincidentally or not, in the North Atlantic).

But the climate science establishment insists the Medieval Warm Period was not a global but rather a regional

Reconstructed sea surface temperature for the last three millennia

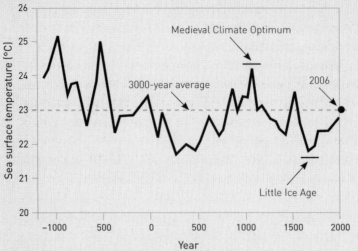

Figure 14. Hot knights: it would have been warm in your suit of armour back in the Middle Ages, if this representation of sea surface temperatures as derived from a sediment core drilled in the Sargasso Sea can be taken as representative of global averages. The Medieval Climate Optimum is plain to see in the peak at around AD 1100, where the Sargasso Sea surface temperature seems to have been over one degree Celsius warmer than it was in 2006.

Source: Robinson A.B., N.E. Robinson, and W. Soon. 'Environmental Effects of Increased Atmospheric Carbon Dioxide'. *Journal of American Physician and Surgeons*, 12, 2007, 79–90.

phenomenon, strongest in the North Atlantic, and in particular in Western Europe. Versions of it — shorter, earlier, later, drier, wetter — have been identified in Africa, Asia, North America and Tasmania, but with too little consistency or synchronicity to be considered a period of global warming. The IPCC tends to use the so-called 'hockey team' graph (see 'Data Hockey' panel, in the first colour section), with a variety of proxies, to refute the notion of a really warm, global Medieval Warm Period.

One or two of the proxies indicate that temperatures rose nearly as high as latter-day twentieth-century temperatures. None show higher temperatures than those recorded during the instrumental period from roughly 1990. And the majority show most of the twentieth century surpassing the hottest the Middle Ages had to offer.

Perhaps the most interesting thing about the whole debate over the Medieval Warm Period is the lack of certainty. The anecdotal evidence is concentrated on a few sites, mostly in Europe, and can't, of course, give numbers. What's more, reviews of the historical sources consulted for this information have raised questions over the reliability of many of them. The proxies are varied, but biased toward the northern hemisphere, and each has it own set of limitations when it's relied upon to yield a definitive answer to the questions 'Was there a Medieval Warm Period, and how warm was it?' Sea sediment cores, boreholes and ice cores struggle to resolve data down to the fineness of the two or three centuries required. Tree rings are intrinsically unreliable, as they are measures of the aggregate of variables that produce a good or bad growing season rather than of a single parameter such as temperature.

Like all the best mysteries, we'll never know the answer. But isn't it fun to see that the significance of the current global climate can be seriously contested with reference to a previous warm period over which we have — and can have — no certainty whatsoever.

3. The atmospheric concentration of CO_2 is rising

There's no disputing the greenhouse effect. It was first proposed in 1824 by Joseph Fourier (who pioneered much of the modern understanding of the concept of 'heat'). Fourier postulated that the atmosphere trapped the kind of radiation that came from the Earth's surface while remaining relatively transparent to the kind of radiation that came from the sun, and that this was why the temperature at the

Earth's surface remained relatively constant. In 1859, John Tyndall demonstrated that complex molecules (in particular, water vapour and carbon dioxide) absorbed heat, and argued that this effect could probably account not only for Fourier's insulating effect, but also for most of the world's climate variations through time. In 1895, as if to prove some kind of principle that behind every great man in climate science there's a woman giving him grief, Swedish scientist Svante Arrhenius sought solace from the fact that his pretty young wife had divorced him, had won custody of their little boy and was torturing our hero with recriminatory postcards from European holiday spots, by seeking the cause of the ice ages through maths (as you do). In particular, he was hoping to work out what would have to happen to atmospheric carbon dioxide to cause the onset or decline of glacials.

'I should not have undertaken these tedious calculations,' the lovelorn Arrhenius wrote, striking a personal note rare in your average scientific paper, 'if an extraordinary interest had not been connected with them. In the Physical Society at Stockholm there have been occasionally very lively discussions on the probable causes of the Ice Age ...'[2]

Arrhenius's estimate that a doubling of CO_2 from 1896 levels (300 ppm) would lead to a 4–5°C rise in global temperature, and that this would take 3000 years, surely caused further lively discussion in the Physical Society. Of course, he didn't reckon on the rate at which humanity would begin to emit the gas — we stand to achieve by 2050 the kind of atmospheric concentrations of CO_2 that Arrhenius imagined if nothing much is done to curb business-as-usual consumption of fossil fuels. And nor (outside certain hardline coal-mongering and -mining circles) is humanity quite so sanguine about the effect of CO_2-driven warming as Arrhenius, who wrote dreamily in 1908 that with increasing CO_2 levels

> ... we may hope to enjoy ages with more equable and better climates, especially as regards the colder regions of the Earth, ages when the Earth will bring forth much more abundant crops than at present, for the benefit of rapidly propagating mankind.[3]

Atmospheric CO_2 received sporadic attention throughout the early twentieth century, but it wasn't until the early 1950s that an ingenious method of measuring 'background' levels of the gas was devised at the California Institute of Technology by the closest thing the IPCC has to a patron saint, Dave Keeling. The effects of elevated CO_2 concentrations on climate began to be discussed again. In 1958, once he'd perfected his methods and instruments, Keeling shifted to Mauna Loa, a volcano on Hawai'i. Here, away from the big industrial emitters on the American mainland, he reasoned that, since CO_2 mixes freely and quickly achieves an average (or background) atmospheric concentration, his samples would be representative of the entire northern hemisphere. Sure enough, Keeling began to produce some astonishing results. Figure 15 shows a graph of his measurements of northern hemisphere atmospheric CO_2.

You'll notice that the dotted trace, representing the actual measurements of northern hemisphere CO_2 concentrations, varies within each year (this is magnified in the inset figure). What Keeling proposed (and it's long since been accepted) is that what he was measuring was the annual decline in CO_2 levels representing the rustle of spring, with the vegetation of the northern hemisphere awakening from hibernation and consuming carbon dioxide during the growing season. It is, as it's been memorably described, a picture of 'the planet breathing'. Compare this pattern with measurements taken in the southern hemisphere (Figure 16), at Baring Head (Wellington, New Zealand, 41° South), a station founded by Keeling's student, Dave Lowe.

Nothing like the same annual seasonality is observed at Baring Head (the solid line) because New Zealand sits in the 'ocean hemisphere', so called because there's a whole lot of ocean and nothing like the same amount of land (and vegetation) as in the northern hemisphere. Note also that the baseline CO_2 level in the southern hemisphere lags behind the north. This is thought to be because most of the emissions are generated by the far denser population of the northern hemisphere, and the air of the two hemispheres takes time to mix, and because the Southern Ocean functions as the world's greatest sink of carbon dioxide.

Northern hemisphere atmosheric CO$_2$ (direct measurement) 1959–2005

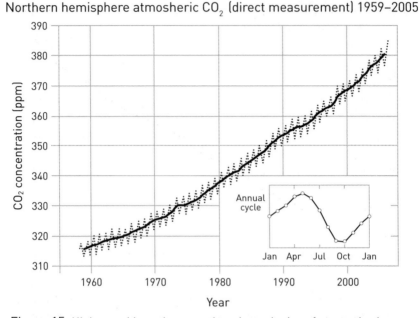

Figure 15. Higher and Loa: the smooth and steady rise of atmospheric carbon dioxide concentrations, as measured by Dave Keeling's observatory at Mauna Loa, Hawai'i. The wavy dotted line records the actual observations, whereas the black line represents the average. The up-and-down pattern visible in the observed data (and amplified in the inset panel) is thought to show the seasonal variation in northern hemisphere CO$_2$ levels, where spring growth of plants removes a proportion of the gas from the atmosphere, and autumn and the hibernation of plants brings a general release of CO$_2$.

Source: http://www.globalwarmingart.com/images/8/88/Mauna_Loa_Carbon_Dioxide.png

So how does this late-twentieth-century rise in CO$_2$ concentrations compare with the more distant past? As we mentioned in the previous chapter, the relative concentrations of the gases in the atmospheres of long ago (sometimes called the 'mixing volumes') can be measured from bubbles trapped in ice cores. Unlike ice-core-based temperature readings, which are reconstructions based on isotopic ratios, these gas measurements are direct, the next best thing to being there. Consequently, there is little dispute over their accuracy (although, as we'll show later, there's some dispute over whether ice cores are of fine enough resolution to accurately represent variability in CO$_2$

Both hemispheres atmospheric CO_2 (direct measurement) 1970–2005

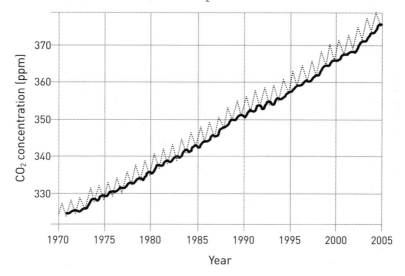

Figure 16. Baring all: a comparison of the variability of the rise of CO_2 in the northern hemisphere as measured at Mauna Loa (light, wavy line) and in the southern hemisphere as measured at Baring Head (solid black line). Levels of CO_2 in the southern hemisphere do not vary by as much as they do in the northern, because there is comparatively less vegetation in the southern hemisphere, which comprises very much more ocean than land. But most relevant to the present discussion is the tight match between the trends for both northern and southern hemispheres: upwards.

Source: Data from R.F. Keeling et al, Carbon Dioxide Research Group, Scripps Institution of Oceanography (SIO), University of California.

concentrations). One glance at the graph in Figure 17 and you get some idea of why the Alarmists are worried about the contemporary increase in greenhouse gas concentrations.

And to silence any criticism of these measurements as methodologically questionable, Figure 18 shows how the ice-core readings (in this case, from a core taken from Law Dome in Antarctica extending back to 1700) look when overlapped with the Mauna Loa data.

Predictably, the main challenge has not been to the CO_2 data, but to its significance. A proxy measurement using the number of stomata on the needles of western hemlock trees (known to vary in accordance with atmospheric CO_2 concentrations) has been produced to suggest

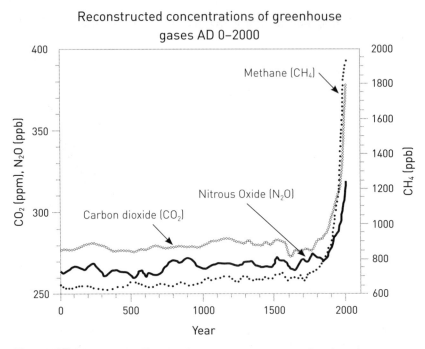

Figure 17. It's a gas; well, greenhouse gases, anyway: the alarming twentieth-century rise in atmospheric concentrations of the three principal greenhouse gases (besides water vapour) — carbon dioxide (grey), nitrous oxide (black) and methane (dots) — is plain to see in this plot.

Source: Forster et al (2007). IPCC 2007 WG-1 AR4.

that current CO_2 levels may have been achieved before in the relatively recent past, and certainly during the Holocene. We'll have more to say about this in Chapter 5, but suffice to say here that it has formed part of an effort to discredit the causal link between atmospheric concentrations of CO_2 and temperatures. But while the causal link is questionable, that there is some sort of link is not, and here we have our fourth item of agreement between Alarmists and Sceptics.

4. Climate and CO_2 are linked

As we've noted, the greenhouse effect — the way in which trace gases in the atmosphere trap heat close to the surface and prevent us freezing — is not disputed. But it's also agreed that Arrhenius's theory that CO_2

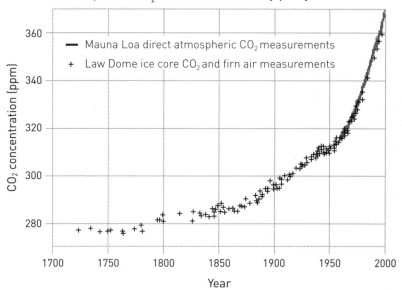

Figure 18. Fits like a glove: discrete measurements of CO_2 concentrations from ice and firn from Law Dome, Antarctica (crosses) laid over the data from direct instrumental measurements at Mauna Loa (grey line). The tightness of the fit is impressive, and gives considerable confidence in the accuracy of the techniques used to measure icebound gas levels, at least for the recent past.

Sources: Data from R.F. Keeling et al, Carbon Dioxide Research Group, Scripps Institution of Oceanography (SIO), University of California, and D. Etheridge, CSIRO Marine and Atmospheric Research.

is solely responsible for the cycle of glacial–interglacial cycles is wrong. Instead, the greenhouse gases (not just CO_2) are thought to serve as amplifiers of the variable signal transmitted by the Milankovic cycles of solar radiation. Reconstructions of temperatures from proxies and measurements of greenhouse gas concentrations from ice cores serve to reinforce this notion. Figure 19 shows how global temperatures as reconstructed from the Vostok ice core look alongside the CO_2 measurements from the same source.

The same elegant correlation can be seen in the data from EPICA's Dome C (Figure 20). This is the same as Figure 3 (page 89), but with curves for the measurements of methane and carbon dioxide added to the temperature trace.

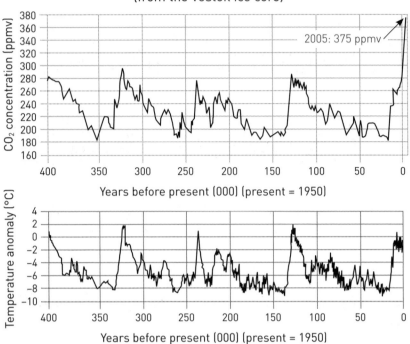

Figure 19. Amped up: the correlation is plain to see between movements in CO_2 concentrations and temperature (as reconstructed from oxygen isotopic analysis — see pages 64–5) from the Vostok ice core, Antarctica.

Source: Data from Petit, J.R./National Climate Data Centre, NOAA.

The Vostok record suggests atmospheric CO_2 concentrations have ranged between 180 ppm and 280 ppm over the 450,000-year period it covers. EPICA's Dome C, covering a much longer period, is in broad agreement.

Another aspect from the ice-core data — and for which there is universal acceptance within the scientific community — is that historically and without exception, temperature rises *precede* rises in CO_2 concentrations, usually by hundreds of years. This is consistent with the theory that greenhouse gases amplify the Milankovic signal. It's supposed that as the Earth's temperature rises as a result of increased insolation due to a wobble or blip in its orbit, greenhouse

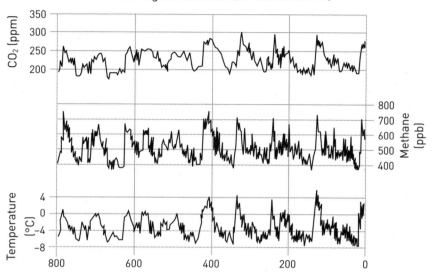

Figure 20. Let's seesaw together: the relationship between temperature, carbon dioxide and methane is just as clear in the ice core from EPICA's Dome C.

Source: Data from Jouzel, J./National Climate Data Centre, NOAA.

gases are released from the oceans and from other natural sinks (such as permafrost and forest floors), enhancing the greenhouse effect and amplifying warming. There's little argument over this theory. Logically, however, it doesn't preclude the possibility that the cart can go before the horse, and a rise in greenhouse gas concentrations can cause warming in its own right.

We'll be looking at this in more detail in later chapters, but it seems opportune to ask whether instrumental records of CO_2 and temperature indicate an answer to this question. Figure 21 shows how the curves of global average temperature and CO_2 since 1850 look juxtaposed.

But wait! There's more! If our world warms too much we're toast, but there's wide disagreement on just how far humankind can adapt to a world of markedly higher temperatures — temperatures unprecedented since civilisation arose. This — the possibilities for

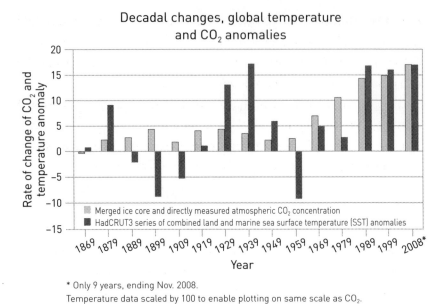

Decadal changes, global temperature and CO_2 anomalies

* Only 9 years, ending Nov. 2008.
Temperature data scaled by 100 to enable plotting on same scale as CO_2.

Figure 21. Ups and downs: the poor correlation between steadily rising CO_2 (light grey bars) and temperature anomaly (dark grey bars), which is all over the show. There is a relationship between atmospheric CO_2 and temperature, but it's clearly not a simple and linear one.

Sources: Data from R.F. Keeling et al, Carbon Dioxide Research Group, Scripps Institution of Oceanography (SIO), University of California, HadCRUT3, and D. Etheridge, CSIRO Marine and Atmospheric Research.

adaptation — is a different story, a different book. Until we've reached a view on whether global warming is real, it would be premature to worry about stopping it, slowing it down or adapting to it. But it's worth looking at why we need to care about global warming at all, and this brings us to the last point of agreement between the Alarmists and the Sceptics: global warming would be a Bad Thing.

5. The consequences

Interestingly, while the Alarmists and the Sceptics agree that there is a warming trend and disagree on what's causing it, there is general agreement on what the consequences of it will be. This implies that unless one thinks the trend either can be halted or will come to an end due to natural causes, then irrespective of which side of the science debate one might empathise with, it's important to know what the consequences of continued warming will be.

And on this issue there is — perhaps understandably — no marked disparity between the scientists' views, whether sceptical of or alarmed by the prospect of global warming. The following are the main elements of a continued warming world that have been identified.

Defrosting

Nothing too hard to explain here. In a warmer world, we won't have so much snow and ice lying around in the winter, and some scenarios predict that within a couple of generations we may have no permanent ice to speak of left anywhere north of the Antarctic land mass. So who needs ice and snow? Skiers, boarders . . . Oh, the tragedy! And a few hundred thousand other folk, too, such as the Inuit and various Siberian tribes of nomads, whose way of life is adapted to the presence of the ice and its ecosystems. Millions, if you count those affected by the loss of permafrost. Billions if you look a little more deeply at what the loss of the world's glaciers will mean. The sources of the Indus and the Ganges, the great rivers of the subcontinent, for example, arise in the glaciers of the Himalaya, where precipitation falls as snow during the monsoon season and then is released as meltwater in the dry season. Take away the glaciers, and it's tantamount to turning off the tap to India and Pakistan, one of the most populous regions of the world — and one that's armed to the teeth with nuclear weapons at that.

And if we're not completely anthropocentric about it, there are plenty of other species that face extinction in an ice-free world.

All of this, of course, is quite apart from the unknown and un-quantifiable effect of the loss of ice — a great stabilising influence — on the climate. It's probably safe to say that if there are any surprises attending the loss of the influence of ice on climate, they're unlikely to be nice ones.

Rising tide

Needless to say, if you melt all the water that's presently sitting locked up in permanent land-borne ice masses around the world (including some of the vulnerable ice sheets in Antarctica: see the next chapter) and add it to the sea, you will drastically raise sea levels. It's been estimated that losing the world's glaciers would raise sea levels by half a metre. If the ice sheets of the Antarctic Peninsula follow, you can add another metre. A metre's not so bad, is it? But hold your horses: losing the Greenland ice sheet alone would bring about a sea level rise of six and a half metres. Whoa! Add the West Antarctic ice sheet, another five metres. And finally, if the East Antarctic ice sheet were to follow (unlikely, but the Earth has done without it before), we'd be tipping fully another 57 metres' worth of sea level rise into the ocean. By that point, of course, all the ice on Earth would have been liquidated, and the total ice contribution to sea level rises would be around 70 metres.

And that's not all. Thermal expansion (the simple principle that the volume of a liquid increases when heated) would increase that total further still.

Bummer for anyone who's invested heavily in coastal property, you might think. But think of people who can't just sell up and move inland so easily: many of the island microstates of the world occupy atolls whose entire land area lies just a couple of metres above present-day sea level. A significant proportion of the population of the world lives in the great floodplain of the Ganges delta, and they've a hard enough time of it in workaday floods. A low-to-moderate sea level rise due to global warming will take away their homeland permanently.

And again, those are just the known and predictable effects. It's widely thought that changes in salinity have much to do with the way the ocean circulates, as saline water is denser than fresh and sinks. Thermohaline circulation — that churning, sinking and displacement of water masses — is what drives oceanic currents, which carry heat from the tropics to higher latitudes; and in turn what modulates the climates of most of the world's regions. Change the pattern of circulation, and all bets are off. Again, we can't even begin to speculate about what might happen, but the smart money is on 'something unpleasant'.

Rain, rain, go away

One of the things you can say for certain about even the slightest change in atmospheric, surface or ocean temperatures is that it will have an immediate impact on precipitation patterns — how much water evaporates, how much condenses and where, and how much falls and where. We just don't have much notion of exactly what form this change would take. But it's probably safe to say that many of the drought-affected regions of the world face full-scale desertification, and others can expect increases, damaging increases, in rain and even snowfall. Both have profound implications for patterns of settlement and food production.

All creatures great and small

Mother Nature invented the notion of tough love. Her maternal advice to all her offspring is 'adapt or die'. Thanks to evolution by natural selection, most organisms alive today are finely tuned to the range of conditions that comprise their habitat. Climate is one of the major determinants of habitat. Change climate, and you change habitat. You also likely change the seasonal behaviour of animals, with disastrous effects both for the animals and for anyone who depends on behaviour such as annual migration for food or income.

Plague and pestilence

Warming the Earth will shift geographical barriers to the spread of pest plants and animals that are presently knocked back on an annual basis by cold snaps. Among these are the various vectors (carriers and spreaders) of any number of the world's nastier human diseases, such as malaria, dengue fever and encephalitis in several flavours, to name but a few and to completely ignore those affecting livestock, domestic animals and wildlife.

Summary

So these, then, are the points on which Alarmists and Sceptics can hold hands across the Great Divide. The Earth's climate is hugely variable on the scale of geological time, to such an extent that our own Goldilocks climate can't be considered anything other than a fluke — a fluke of the same order as the coincidence of our planet's chemistry and distance from the sun.

The world is warming. Whether you consider sea surface, the oceans as a whole, the land or the lower atmosphere, you can see an upward trend in the data (although, of course, we should acknowledge that there are some who consider the trend to be an artifact of instrumental or methodological error, statistical chicanery or some combination of all of these). It's the significance of the data, and the period of time over which the data must be considered, that are so hotly contested, as we'll shortly see.

Atmospheric concentrations of CO_2 are rising. There's little or no dispute about this, making it a rock in a sea of contention, surely a tribute to the dedication and ingenuity of one C. D. Keeling. But that's not to say there's no debate about the *significance* of the measured rise. Atmospheric CO_2 and temperature are linked. Even the most diehard Sceptic will concede that the natural greenhouse effect is real. It's over the role of CO_2 in *changing* climate that there is dissension, as we'll see in Chapter 5.

And everyone, Sceptics and Alarmists alike — excluding, as we ought, some whose stake in the carbon economy is so entrenched that their very metabolism seems indexed to coal sales — agrees that the reason we're all getting so heated about whether the world is getting heated is that it doesn't take much in the way of a temperature rise to cause significant, and significantly damaging, changes in the natural world. It's been suggested that all of us could survive a global average rise of around 2°C above the present, with varying levels of discomfort, inconvenience and disruption. Anything beyond that and we're in trouble.

So let's see why we're supposed to start worrying now.

Chapter 4

The Case For Anthropogenic Global Warming

As previously stated, the question that this book seeks to settle — at least as far as it can presently be settled — is whether human activity has been responsible for global warming through the generation of greenhouse gases from industry and agriculture.

There are, accordingly, three propositions that need to be tested.

1. The heat is on

First (and most obviously), is the world warming? For all its little foibles, the instrumental record makes it pretty hard to argue there was no warming throughout the twentieth century. Albeit with a little quibbling over possible distortions of the rate and magnitude of the change (owing to such phenomena as the urban heat island effect, for example, as covered in Chapter 2), even the most dyed-in-the-wool Sceptic will concede that the global average temperature rose between 1900 and 1998, although with a pause between 1940 and 1970 during which a mild cooling trend was visible. But as we will see in Chapter 5, most Sceptics stop short of conceding that the sustained warming trend detectable throughout the twentieth century is a consequence of the anthropogenically enhanced greenhouse effect at work. In Chapter 5, we'll see them disputing that the twentieth-century rise is significant in the context of historical climatic variability — that is, disputing that the rate or the scale of recent warming is unprecedented since the last ice age and somehow indicative of unnatural processes. Indeed, we'll see them arguing the converse: namely that twentieth-century warming was a natural event, and the record global average temperature readings registered in 1998 represented the zenith of a natural warming cycle that has now reversed, and has since given way to a decade of cooling.

If it were simply a matter of looking at post-industrial global average temperature trends, it would indeed be a bit of a struggle to accept that there was something afoot with the climate that nature wasn't capable of doing, and that nature hadn't done bigger and better in the past. But, Alarmists will insist, it's important to understand that the Earth responds dynamically to changes in the climate. Warming means an increase in the retention of heat energy in the Earth system, and this can and does manifest itself in ways other than in a simple increase in sensible (literally: can be sensed) and measurable heat. That's why much of the Fourth IPCC Assessment Report is devoted to documenting changes in the Earth system (apart from world temperature itself) that are indicative of warming. Some of these are fairly intuitive: it's getting warmer, so ice melts . . . Nothing too controversial there. And if lots of ice melts, the sea level rises.

So far, so good.

Others are less obvious without a knowledge of the scientific processes involved, such as the increase in intensity of tropical storms (hurricanes, typhoons, severe tropical cyclones).

Still others are the very opposite of obvious, and have been nominated as indicators of warming only because climate modelling — wherein the 'how' of climate change is studied — has drawn attention to them.

2. No ordinary warming

If we can agree that the Earth is warming, the second part of the hypothesis that requires to be demonstrated is that the present warming is in some way different from the ways in which the Earth has warmed as a matter of course in the distant and not-so-distant past. For it is certain, as the Sceptics urge, that the Earth has experienced significant and rapid warming in ages where there can be no question that natural rather than human agency was the cause. But many climate scientists believe that there are aspects of the present behaviour of the climatic system that have the grubby fingerprints of human activity all over them. We'll have a look at some of these shortly, too.

3. Global warming — it's a gas

Suppose you can adduce evidence that not only is the world warming but it's also warming in a curious and unnatural manner, then it becomes important to know the mechanism. As we saw in Chapter 1, there are good reasons to believe that a rise in the levels of atmospheric greenhouse gases will have a warming effect, so if we can show that human activity has generated the observed increase in the levels of atmospheric greenhouse gases, it will be reasonable to propose that human activity has caused the warming. It turns out that this is the easy bit for today's scientists, and we'll close this chapter by canvassing some of the fascinating techniques used to quantify human carbon emissions and to 'fingerprint' atmospheric carbon.

The earth is getting warmer

1. Cryosphere: deciphering the message from the Earth's ice cubes

One of the most uncontroversial indicators of warming is the loss of ice. After all, the basic physics at work is the same as that in your gin and tonic, writ large. Whether it be permanent ice (land-borne ice sheets, the massive floating ice shelves of the polar regions or the glaciers that bear ice slowly down from alpine basins) or the vast skirt of ice that forms annually on the sea adjacent to Antarctica and the North Pole, if the ice is disappearing, it is indicative of warming.

Ice is a dynamic material, and the quantity and quality of ice in any given region is highly variable. Sea ice comes and goes according to the season, and its extent depends upon a range of factors, of which temperature is only one. The annual disintegration of the fast ice (that is, ice that is 'fast' or fixed to the land) that chokes Antarctica's Ross Sea, for example, depends upon ocean currents and winds as much as it depends upon the warming that arrives with the sun at the end of the long polar night. It's not unheard of for the Ross Sea — and other Antarctic regions — to remain iced-in if anything disturbs the processes that routinely break up and carry away the floes. For a time in 2002, it was feared that a colossal iceberg grounded on Cape Crozier in the Ross Sea would trap the sea ice over the summer, meaning the next year's freeze would add to rather than merely replace it. This looked set to pose a problem not only for the supply of Budweiser and Twinkies to McMurdo Base, but also for the local colony of emperor penguins, which stage an annual 'march' from their inland breeding grounds to the sea in order to feed. More ice, or worst of all, a complete failure of that year's thaw, would see them marching impossibly long distances and not only the foraging birds, but also their mates and their offspring waiting for them to return with food, would surely perish. On the face of it, stories of an overabundance of sea ice do not readily support the global warming hypothesis. But as with everything to do with global climate, it's important to tease long-term, global signals out from regional, short-term noise. The big berg blockade of 2002 to 2005 appears to have significantly restricted the influx of warmer ocean water that usually thins the sea ice from below. But after a succession of unusually icy summers, nature intervened again: a major storm in the North Pacific created a set of swells that fractured Iceberg B15A and wiggled it free from its lodging place.

As it so happens, plenty of recent work has shown that the loss of sea ice has been more pronounced in the Arctic than in the Antarctic, and it has been even more rapid than predicted by Alarmist modelling.[1] Working Group 1 of the IPCC has reported that average Arctic temperatures have increased at almost twice the global average rate over the past 100 years. The thaw of 2008 saw the extent of Arctic sea ice at its second lowest recorded level since the use of satellite-borne microwave measurement began in 1978, with the lowest being the Big Melt of 2007. And before anyone starts popping champagne corks and pointing to the better result for 2008 as a sign of recovery, consider that the rate of ice loss in August 2008 was unprecedented in the era of satellite telemetry; as Figure 22 shows, despite an amount of annual variation, there has been an unmistakable downward trend throughout the satellite era.

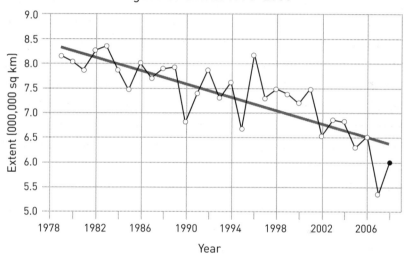

Figure 22. De-icing: the unmistakable decline in August Arctic sea ice extent from 1978 to 2008.

Source: www.nsidc.org/arcticseaicenews/index.html

Nor does it seem that this is an entirely recent trend. A 1997 study of past environmental records (a mixture of anecdotal accounts of ice extent and instrumental measurements) from the Arctic that span 400 years suggests that by the mid-twentieth century the Arctic had warmed to its highest temperature since instrumental records began in 1840.[2] Since that study, temperatures have warmed still further, and you only need to look at Figure 22 to see what that has meant for sea ice.

In contrast to the rapid decline in Arctic sea ice, the Antarctic pack seems relatively unperturbed, but apparently this doesn't mean we can shrug our shoulders and write the Arctic experience off as a regional warming. It's one of the features of the way the climate is currently behaving that the northern hemisphere is warming faster than the southern — we'll have more to say about this shortly — but in any case, Antarctica is a horse of a different colour to the Arctic. Its vastly greater thermal mass (it consists of ice laid on average two kilometres thick over bedrock, rather than the two-metre-thick scum of sea ice that covers the North Pole) means that it has a huge inertia in the face of temperature fluctuations, and keeps the adjacent ocean cool, too, in much the same way as that ice cube chills your gin and tonic. And the Arctic is especially sensitive to fluctuations in albedo, for as ice thins and cracks, it exposes the darker ocean beneath, which absorbs more incident radiation and accelerates warming. In part, this is what makes the present shrinkage of the Arctic ice pack so alarming: every square centimetre of ice lost is another square centimetre of ocean exposed to the warming rays of the sun, heightening the risk of the region entering a vicious feedback loop, especially now the demise of the Greenland ice sheet seems nigh.

This brings us to the other kind of ice you'll find on Earth — everywhere, in fact, from the polar regions to the tropics — namely, glacial ice, which tends to hang around regardless of season in the form of glaciers (ice lying in valleys), ice caps (ice lying over mountain peaks and plateaux) and ice shelves (floating sheets of glacial ice). Ice also lies in sheets on a truly continental scale in the Antarctic and Greenland.

Even these huge slabs of ice are surprisingly dynamic, and quite apart from the monumental pulsing they've staged over the aeons in obeisance to the Milankovic cycles, they're perpetually in motion, flexing and moving in complex ways, as glaciers do. Glaciers and ice sheets advance and retreat in response to a range of factors, most notably temperature and precipitation levels (as it is snowfall, ultimately, that replenishes glaciers and ice sheets at their source). The rate at which they advance or retreat can also be affected by the nature of the bedrock underlying the ice, the vastly complicated nexus of thermodynamics, hydrology and geology that occurs at the interface between moving ice and static rock, and whether anything obstructs its progress or is removed from its path (such as where an ice shelf — the floating terminus of a glacier or ice sheet — comes adrift, pulling the cork on the vast pressure built up behind it and causing a 'surge', the sudden acceleration of ice movement).

While the extent of Antarctic sea ice has stayed within the bounds of natural variation, far more alarming signs of warming have been detected in the behaviour of its vast, permanent ice masses. You don't have to look too hard to see these. Over the course of three weeks in 2002, a vast block of ice 3250 square kilometres in extent and 220 metres thick simply fell apart and floated away. The Larsen B ice shelf was one of three slabs of ice fixed fast along a section of the east coast of the Antarctic Peninsula. The smallest of these, the Larsen A, had fallen to bits in 1995, alerting scientists to the possibility that the other two might go the same way. Nevertheless, the speed with which the Larsen B, the largest of the three ice shelves, did so surprised everyone.

Ice shelves are notoriously crumbly. They're essentially the terminal section of a vast glacier, an ice sheet, floating on the ocean. Not only do they constantly lose ice through surface melting, but they also melt where warmer ocean water circulates around and beneath their submerged section, which accounts for fully 90% of their mass. More spectacular ice loss occurs when they 'calve', and an iceberg splits off and floats away. But you can have all this going on, melting above and below and icebergs calving off the face, without endangering the ice shelf itself. The collapse of an ice shelf is something different and more catastrophic.

The Larsen B ice shelf had been stuck to the bedrock of the Antarctic Peninsula for at least 12,000 years, the entire Holocene and more. But it's surmised that a combination of the declining ice mass on the peninsula and warmer air and sea temperatures over the course of the twentieth century placed it under extreme stress. The great block of ice fractured, and the liquid water that pools on the surface in the warmest parts of Antarctica's margins under the warmth of the 24-hour summer sunlight found its way into the cracks.[3] As this re-froze, it expanded, and the effect of all that expansion was to lever the ice mass apart as effectively as an army of hydraulic-jack-wielding demolition experts.

Another regrettable yet regional and therefore isolated event? Perhaps, but it is one of a growing number, beginning with the tiny Wordie ice shelf in the late 1980s, with the most recent being another peninsula shelf, the Wilkins. Under the lenses of satellite surveillance in March 2008, the Wilkins turned sky blue, the characteristic colour of an ice shelf revealing its deep glacial ice layers as it turns up its toes. And while the collapse of many of its ice shelves, young and old, provides unequivocal evidence that the Antarctic Peninsula is warming, there's similar evidence to suggest the whole ice shelf thing is more than just a regional phenomenon. All in all, 10 major Antarctic ice shelves have collapsed or retreated since 1980. Meanwhile, Canada has five ice shelves left, and it looks like their days are numbered. In September 2008, the Markham ice shelf collapsed, a matter of days after a big crack appeared in another significant Canadian shelf, the Ward Hunt.

Ice shelves, then, are under threat from pole to pole, and one potentially catastrophic consequence of their wholesale demise is that it foreshadows the collapse of the ice sheets behind them. It's long been supposed that water-borne ice shelves play a part in stabilising the mass of ice lying inland. Take away the ice shelf, the theory goes, and you take away a large part of the mechanism holding all that ice in place. The collapse of the Larsen B ice shelf underscored the fragility of regional ice sheets and drew attention to the West Antarctic ice sheet, which is chocked in place by a number of shelves. It has been suggested that the entire ice sheet, a continent-sized chunk of ice, could slide into the oceans (over a few hundred years) if too many more of the ice shelves chocking it in place are removed. This, of course, is quite apart from the loss of mass the world's ice sheets are experiencing due to melting around their edges.

The sheer mass and height of the Antarctic ice sheet tends to protect it from global warming. Not so fortunate is the Greenland ice sheet: a study in 2002 showed that 16% more of its total area had become subject to annual melting since satellite telemetry began in 1978.[4]

The advance or retreat of glaciers depends upon glacier mass balance (whether they're losing or gaining mass overall through snow precipitation up-glacier and melting down-glacier). For this reason, you can't be certain that warming will necessarily cause the retreat of a given region's glaciers, as warming can yield both higher levels of precipitation (as warmer air holds more moisture) and changes in patterns of snowfall. More snowfall in a glacier's névé may produce an advance that will more than offset melting, never mind that both the extra snowfall and the melting are caused by warming. Conversely, the retreat of a glacier may have more to do with local and regional changes than with the global climate.

Still, a general retreat of the world's glaciers would tend to support the notion that the Earth is warming. A recent study reviewed 169 glacier records from around the world, dating from 1600 to 1990. In 2005, the team led by Dutch glaciologist Johannes Oerlemans found they had been retreating on average since 1900, although the retreat paused during the cooler period from 1945 to 1970.[5] This result wouldn't have come as any surprise to Lonnie Thompson, whose team has toured the world drilling ice cores from glaciers at 39 sites, predominantly in the tropical regions, for the last 30 years. It didn't take the painstaking work involved in drilling, recovering and analysing the cores to show that general degradation of the world's glaciers is under way. Each return to sites visited previously on the ice-drilling programme found less glacier to be drilled, as comparisons between photographs taken in the 1960s and others taken more recently attest. Thompson found some glaciers, such as those on Africa's Kilimanjaro, are in danger of disappearing altogether by 2015 to 2020.

Observations of the totality of the world's ice masses confirm that we're losing ice, and fast. A working group for the IPCC surveyed measurements of glaciers and ice caps from 1961 to 2004 and reported in 2007 that the world's combined ice masses had lost 0.50 mm per year ($\pm$ 0.18 mm/yr) sea level equivalent (SLE) during the period. More telling was the change in rate: according to the report, the world had lost ice 50% faster (0.77 ± 0.22 mm/yr SLE) between 1991 and 2004 than in the earlier period. More recent work suggests that ice loss globally is accelerating.[6]

In summary, then, there's enough going on in the cryosphere to indicate that warming is happening, and that it's on a significant scale in historical terms.

2. Aquasphere: a message in a bottle

As we saw in the previous chapter, there is by now plenty of hard evidence that the world's oceans are warming. The significance of this data (and its accuracy, given the uncertainties in the historical record touched on in Chapter 2) is contestable, but the suite of other, empirically detectable effects afflicting the oceans makes it harder to argue that what is being detected are localised or regional phenomena.

Seven seas that run high

Sea levels will rise in a warming world. This is due not only to the obvious effect of adding all that water previously locked up in ice sheets and glaciers (sea ice and ice shelves don't count, as their mass displaces seawater and if they melt it won't raise the volume, in the same way as the ice cube in your gin and tonic doesn't raise the level as it melts), but also to other, less obvious effects. Water expands when warmed, so sea level rises can be expected as a direct result of warming the oceans. Indeed, thermal expansion accounts for as much as half of the total rise in sea levels since measurements began. And then there's the tectonic recovery of the Earth's crust when it is liberated from the burden of ice masses. It's a little-known fact that parts of the Earth are still measurably rebounding from the depressed state they were in under the crushing weight of the ice sheets that covered much of its land area during the last ice age: this slow rebounding needs to be taken into account when attributing the various contributions to measured sea level rises. It also needs to be considered when the possibility of the collapse of the Greenland and West Antarctic ice sheets is contemplated. Both can have a bearing on local and regional sea level trends. The IPCC has also noted that the construction of large dams in the recent past has to some extent (0.5 mm/yr) reduced sea level rise by intercepting fresh water destined for the seas.

Sea levels have been more or less consistently and reliably measured with tide gauges at several points on the globe since the 1800s. The data from these locations can be used to provide a global average value for sea levels. And since 1993, satellite-borne instruments have measured sea surface levels with great precision. The two datasets, when combined, show an unmistakable rising trend, as shown in Figure 23, which represents the latest such compilation by the World Climate Research Programme in February 2008. The grey areas represent error limits, which in turn indicate the reliability of the data (quite reliable in recent years, far less reliable 100 or more years ago).

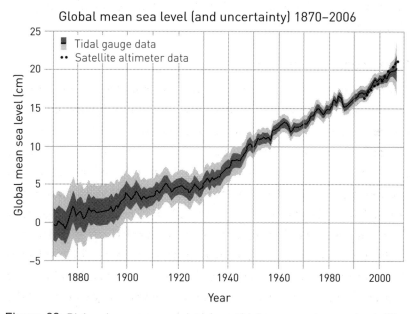

Figure 23. Rising damp: merged data from tidal range meters and satellite telemetry shows a steady rise in sea level between 1870 and 2006. The light and dark grey bands indicate error estimates. Note they're broader as you go back in time, where the data quality and accuracy of tidal gauges cannot be verified.

Source: CSIRO Marine and Atmospheric Research Centre, using tidal gauge data from the Permanent Service for Mean Sea Level and altimeter data from NASA and CNES.

Even the most optimistic reading of this chart indicates a substantial rise in global average sea level since 1880, and both surface and satellite measurement techniques indicate that the rate of the rise is accelerating. In 2007, the IPCC reported that the sea level rose on average 1.8 mm/yr from 1961 to 2003, but at the rate of 3.1 mm/yr between 1993 and 2003. That analysis didn't have the opportunity to consider new information on the apparent accelerated loss of ice in both Greenland and Antarctica, which is likely to make the trend look worse still, and to sharpen our understanding of how much sea level rise is due to ice loss (technically called a 'eustatic' rise) and how much is due to thermal expansion (a 'steric' rise). It's a pretty drastic way of finding out! But quantifying steric sea level rise assumes great importance in verifying the findings of energy balance equations, as we'll shortly discuss.

A grain of salt

You only need to have a swig of seawater to know it's salty (the scientific term is 'saline'). And it stands to reason that if you extract fresh water from seawater, the seawater will become more saline still. Evaporation concentrates the salt content of water; so too does the freezing of seawater, as at the moment it freezes, the salt precipitates out leaving freshwater ice floating on the sea's surface and the seawater more saline. For this reason, you expect the salinity of the oceans to vary according to the processes to which they're subject. Seawater in the polar regions is typically more saline than in the tropics; the vast, deep Pacific Ocean is fresher than the smaller, shallower Indian Ocean.

Studies of salinity levels since 1958 have shown that the saltiness of the oceans is changing in a manner that is consistent with observed changes going on in the distribution of the world's fresh water, in turn consistent with a general warming.[7] The upper ocean in the equatorial regions is becoming saltier, which is consistent with less rainfall and with greater evaporation. The polar regions, by contrast, are becoming less saline, the result of the addition of greater volumes of fresh water through the melting of ice and of a reduction in the scale of freezing.[8]

Plugging the sink

As we've previously noted, one of the major sinks of CO_2 is the world's oceans, and among these the cold Southern Ocean, which comprises 4% of the Earth's total surface area, reigns supreme. But evidence has been produced that indicates the ability of the Southern Ocean to take up the gas has reduced by around 15% since 1981.[9] There are several reasons for this.

Carbon dioxide readily dissolves in water, and the quantity of the gas that will dissolve is determined by the water temperature (any beer drinker worth their salt will confirm that warm beer is fizzier, and releases its dissolved carbon dioxide in larger bubbles when the cap is popped, than a cold one). The colder the water, the more CO_2 it will absorb, and the Southern Ocean is pretty cold, chilled down by the Antarctic ice mass and associated regional climate. What's more, it's constantly perturbed by the great storm systems that charge about the world's nether regions unimpeded by land masses, and the heavy wave action that facilitates the mixing of air and water.

A warmer Southern Ocean will soak up less atmospheric CO_2 as a matter of simple physics, but there are other factors at work, too, that reduce its capacity to soak up atmospheric CO_2. The ocean comprises a number of different layers of different temperatures, and these are liberally mixed by wind and currents. It's been suggested that observed changes in wind patterns (which we'll discuss below) have strengthened the Antarctic Circumpolar Current (ACC), the great gyre of water, the world's largest and longest oceanic current, that sweeps west–east around the ice.[10] This has the effect of bringing water that is already all but saturated with CO_2 to the surface, and submerging masses of water previously available to absorb the gas. It has even been hypothesised that it's this mechanism — the reduction in the Southern Ocean's capacity to act as a CO_2 sink, which in turn increases the global atmospheric concentration of greenhouse gases — that accounts for the rapid warming that marks the Earth's emergence from ice ages in paleoclimate records.[11]

Another process by which the oceans sequester carbon is the so-called 'biological pump', where living organisms take up carbon (whether by photosynthesis or by building their shells out of carbonate) and then die, carrying those compounds of carbon into the deep as they sink. But while seawater can act as a chemical buffer (a solution whose chemistry maintains a balance between acidity and alkalinity), this is so only up to a certain concentration of dissolved carbon. Beyond this, the carbonic acid created in a reaction between water and carbon dioxide predominates, and seawater becomes more acidic. Laboratory experiments have shown that reductions in oceanic pH (that is, increasing acidity) will profoundly impair the ability of hard-bodied plankton to build their calcite shells. There is evidence based on 20 years' worth of records to suggest that the average pH of the oceans is declining, threatening calciferous sea life, particularly the delicate plankton at the bottom of the marine food chain. What's more, while an increase in atmospheric CO_2 has actually supported blooms of plankton in some ocean basins — and each minute organism is extracting carbon dioxide to build its shell, and taking that 'fixed' carbon to the sea floor when it dies — any significant acidification of the ocean will undo all that good work, dissolving the shells and returning the carbon to the ocean and ultimately to the atmosphere.

3. Atmosphere: airy fairy or fiery airy?

Just as the significance of the increasing accumulation of data indicating the seas are warming is disputed, so too is the meaning of the various changes in temperature noted in the different regions of the atmosphere. Since the theory of anthropogenic global warming relies upon the warming effect of greenhouse gases to explain changes in the global climate, the most obvious place to look for the primary consequences is in the atmosphere.

Steaming up

It's a matter of simple physics that the amount of water the atmosphere can hold is determined by its temperature. As the air above the oceans warms, the rate of evaporation increases exponentially (that is, where the rate of growth of a quantity is proportional to its present size, so that the larger the quantity is, the faster it grows. Think, for example, of a series where the next term is reached by doubling the present, so that it goes 1, 2, 4, 8, 16 etc.), which is one of the reasons that atmospheric water vapour functions as such a potent positive feedback mechanism in climate change.

Satellite technology has made it possible to measure the precise water vapour content in the column of air between the spacecraft and the Earth's surface, and records since 1988 have shown that levels of water vapour over the oceans have been increasing by 1.2% (± 0.3%) per decade for the period 1988 to 2004. This has been extrapolated to yield an estimated total increase of around 4% since 1970.[12]

A change in the weather

When the sun shines on the Earth's surface, it warms it. It doesn't warm it uniformly, however, as the quality of the surface that it shines upon differs from spot to spot — land differs from sea, snow differs from grassland, desert sands differ from forests, and so on. This means the air masses adjacent to the ground are warmed differentially, too. Hot air rises, and cooler air slumps into the place it vacates in a process known as convection.

When you look at the weather map in your newspaper or on telly of an evening, you'll notice roughly circular patterns with either an L or an H at their centre. The L stands for an area of low air pressure, while the H stands for an area of high pressure, and these areas of differing pressure have come about through precisely the kind of patchy warming we've just been discussing. An area of high pressure, a 'High', is a mass of cool air pooling on the Earth's surface. An area of low pressure, a 'Low', is a region vacated by a mass of air that has been heated by its proximity to the warm surface and has risen away from it.

You'll notice a series of concentric lines around both Highs and Lows on the map. Like the lines on a topographical map, these represent gradient, in this case a pressure gradient rather than a physical slope. The closer together the lines, the greater the gradient, just as bunched-up lines on a topo map signify something you might fall off. A steep pressure gradient means strong winds. 'Wind' is the movement of air masses from areas of high to low pressure.

The patterns on a weather map are circular due to what's known as 'the Coriolis effect', which is familiar to most of us from the circular movement of bathwater as it runs out the plughole. Just like bathwater, the movement of wind is influenced by the rotation of the Earth, and it goes in circles. A 'cyclone'— the correct technical name for a Low; a High is often called an 'anticyclone', because it rotates in the opposite direction — is a vortex of low pressure that is being filled by air masses that must circle it before they can enter, just like outgoing bathwater.

While air is rising and falling, it's also carrying water vapour around. Warm air is typically moist, as the same surface warming that produced the warm air also causes evaporation, especially over the ocean. Now remember that the temperature of the atmosphere falls the higher you go: as warm air rises it cools, and eventually, the water vapour it bears will condense and precipitate out as rain, snow or hail (often technically called 'precipitation').

In the simplest possible terms, it's the combination of these two effects — convection and precipitation — that produces what we call 'the weather': wind, rain, snow, hail and sunshine (the absence of weather).

The point of all this? Well, since it's the warming of the surface that produces weather, it stands to reason that the warmer the surface, the more the behaviour of weather will change.

With the possible exception of the behaviour of investors in the sharemarket, it's hard to think of any natural phenomenon that rivals the weather for downright, bloody-minded fickleness. It's a function of the interaction of two individually fickle entities — the oceans and the atmosphere — and as a consequence, it's hard enough to predict what it's going to do a couple of days from now, let alone a couple of weeks or, worse, a couple of years out.

Consequently, while there seems to be a growing body of evidence that some weather phenomena are indicating the presence of increased heat energy levels within the climatic system, these datasets are as yet far from unequivocal. It's heat in the surface layers of the oceans that fuels 'tropical cyclones' — hurricanes, typhoons, etc. — which are a supercharged version of the effects described above. Very warm seawater sees masses of very moist air rising very rapidly to great altitude, generating fierce circulation around the area of very low air pressure left behind. The result: lots of very strong wind and rain. Therefore, it's long been expected that global warming will bring about an increase in both the frequency and the intensity of the nastier breed of storm, for example.

After the devastating 2005 North Atlantic hurricane season, which set all kinds of records — from the number of Category 5 storms making landfall on the North American coastline to the sheer scale of the economic damage inflicted — speculation was rife that the season of 2006 would be catastrophic. It was a fizzer, proving that the variables complicating any attempt to explain the chaos of weather in terms of simple heat equations make those attempts vain (and in that case, it appeared to have been a shift in the Southern Oscillation to an El Niño in 2006 that changed wind patterns, cooled ocean temperatures and spared the Gulf of Mexico). Still, at the time of writing, there's evidence to suggest that the stroppier storms have been getting stroppier and lasting longer since the mid-1970s. The proportion of Category 4 and 5 hurricanes has increased since 1970 even though the total number of cyclones and cyclone days overall has decreased slightly in most oceans.[13]

Far less contentious is evidence of changes in the quality and quantity of precipitation. Since the publication of the IPCC's 2007 Assessment Report, intense scrutiny of climate and meteorological records has led to a body of evidence showing increases in extreme precipitation and temperature events.[14] Strange as it may seem in light of this, evidence also seems to be emerging that the number and intensity of droughts is on the rise as well. The apparent contradiction disappears when you consider that both represent a shift in the usual patterns of precipitation, pointing toward a perturbation of weather systems and supporting the notion that warming — which determines atmospheric water vapour content, fuels storm cell convection (the rapid rise of air that creates the intense, local low pressure area at the centre of a severe storm) and dictates wind velocity and direction — is at the bottom of it all. This effect is not confined to land. The aforementioned ocean-wide changes in salinity suggest a global change in the hydrological cycle of evaporation and precipitation, as does the reduction of polar ice.

There has also been a demonstrated widespread reduction in the number of frost days in mid-latitude regions, an increase in the number of warm extremes and a reduction in the number of daily cold extremes observed in the 70–75% of land regions where data are available. Again, since publication of the 2007 IPCC Assessment Report, there have been a number of analyses that indicate regional patterns of warm days and cool nights is changing. One has demonstrated that typical positive trends in daily maximum temperatures of 1–3°C have occurred in Canada and Eurasia since 1950.[15] Another has pointed to a widespread decrease in the annual occurrence of cold nights and a significant increase in the annual occurrence of warm nights for the period 1951 to 2003 for over 70% of the land area sampled, and this, it has been suggested, implies a rise in daily minimum temperature around the globe.[16]

So what? Well, any theory of an enhanced greenhouse effect would predict a change in what's known as the diurnal temperature range (DTR), the difference between daytime and night-time temperatures. That's because whereas the surface doesn't receive any solar radiation at night and ceases to warm, it continues to radiate heat. This results in a net difference between daytime and night-time temperatures. But if some quality of the atmosphere (such as an enhanced greenhouse effect) were to offset the nocturnal loss of heat to space, the difference between night and day temperatures would shrink.

The results from 1950 to 2004 seem to suggest that this is precisely what's happening. The annual trends in minimum and maximum land surface air temperature, averaged over regions for which data were available, were 0.20°C per decade and 0.14°C per decade respectively (that is, nights were warming at a greater rate than days) with DTR decreasing by 0.07°C per decade. Yet it has to be noted that from 1979 to 2004, DTR showed no change, as both maximum and minimum temperatures rose at similar rates.[17]

As fickle as the weather is, certain aspects do, in the long run, emerge from the short-term variability. Certain distinctive patterns of winds, for example, such as the equatorial trade winds and the middle-latitude westerly winds of both hemispheres, have been inferred from records of past climate (as judged by such indicators as the presence in ice cores of dust from great distances upwind, vegetation records that indicate persistent foehn conditions).[18] And although the picture that emerges confirms what we have seen before — namely that the natural world climate is highly variable — in the case of the westerly wind belts, it is believed that these shift their location and intensity on three broad timescales:

1. At the geological snail's pace of the Milankovic cycles. The ice ages see a strengthening and northward expansion of the westerly winds.[19]

2. For time periods measured in centuries, similar but less marked changes are the norm. A study of 50-odd paleoclimate records from around the globe and covering the past 11,000 years identified six such periods of rapid climate change, at 9000–8000, 6000–5000, 4200–3800, 3500–2500, 1200–1000, and 600–150 before present.[20] Most of the changes were accompanied by aridity in the tropics, cooling in the polar regions and intensification of the westerly winds.

3. Finally, there are the climate shifts that occur over short periods of years to decades. The Southern Oscillation, with its colourfully named El Niño ('Little Boy') and La Niña ('Little Girl') modes, is well known. Less familiar, but edging toward centre stage, are the Northern (NAM) and Southern (SAM) Annular Modes — the belts of climate variability encircling the North and South Poles respectively. Presently, SAM is in the positive phase, which is characterised by a cold Antarctica and strong westerly winds in the Southern Ocean. Of course, this reverses in

the negative phase when westerly winds strengthen to the north (around the latitudes of Australia) and the southern polar region enjoys a period of comparative stability.

With all these natural swings and roundabouts, what is so unusual about the present climate patterns? A recent analysis of old meteorological records suggests that the southern mid-latitude westerly belt has migrated polewards in the last few decades.[21] Direct radiosonde (weather balloon) and satellite observations support this finding.[22] It seems that the poleward migration of the wind belts has been going on for over forty years — well in excess of the typical cycles of the Southern Annular Mode and other regular climatic shifts (and inasmuch as we reliably know the length of such cycles from meteorological records).[23]

So what's the significance of this finding? The westerly wind belts that encircle the globe at mid-latitudes basically separate warm tropical air from cold polar air. It's been suggested that warming of the lower atmosphere under the influence of rising amounts of greenhouse gases has increased the temperature contrast between the lower and upper atmosphere, causing the westerly winds to intensify and move towards the poles. This change has been enhanced, incidentally, by the formation of the ozone hole, which favours even colder air over Antarctica. The southern hemisphere westerly belt has strengthened and moved south and now lies directly above the Antarctic Circumpolar Current. As a result, this great flow has been observed to strengthen, raising the possibility that CO_2-rich deep water will rise to the surface at the Antarctic continent, not only reducing the uptake of the gas by the Southern Ocean, but also introducing more heat to the undersides of ice shelves.

Another study has identified a related effect, claiming that satellite data show the region that can be distinguished as 'the tropics' based on a number of characteristics (the regional height of the troposphere, the distinctive tropospheric and stratospheric circulation patterns, the concentration of ozone, regional temperaures and the level of outgoing radiation) has expanded by 5° of latitude since 1979.[24]

4. Biosphere: if we could talk to the animals (and plants)
Poleward bound

The adaptation of plant and animal species is finely attuned to their habitats, and climatic conditions are a significant component of habitat: you can grow coconuts in Florida but not in Virginia. It follows that changes in regional climate that are practically invisible to direct observation will first become obvious in changes in ecology. There's lots of anecdotal evidence of changes in the range of plant and animal species, particularly the poleward migration of critters usually confined to warmer climes.[25] It's important to note that 'poleward' is not the only kind of migration occurring, with some species extending their range up mountainsides to exploit areas that were previously too cold for them, even as other species adapted to higher altitudes or — let's not forget the poor old polar bears — higher latitudes retreat toward a kind of existential Dunkirk.

It just ain't natural

From the above, it's hard to avoid the conclusion that there's evidence that the Earth is measurably responding to the retention of heat. The lower atmosphere is warming, the seas are warming, ice is melting, weather patterns are changing, and globally flora and fauna are being affected. And it's important to remember that according to conventional wisdom, a large proportion of the heat energy that has been retained within the climate system is currently being stored in the oceans. Warming of the uppermost layers of the ocean comes and goes and is par for the course, and little can be deduced from evidence that the sea's surface is heating up. But evidence of warming in deeper ocean formations is another matter. This is where the climate system stores its heat, and any increase in temperatures measured down here is indicative of far greater 'committed' warming in the pipeline.

But you can concede that the Earth is warming without for a minute entertaining the notion that human beings have anything to do with it, as we shall see in the following chapter. After all, it's irrefutable that the Earth was warming and cooling in its own time long before humans were around to observe any of it, let alone drive their Hummers or ride their mountain bikes to lectures on climate change.

So let's move on to the second of the three points this chapter is concerned about. If we accept the evidence for global warming, what is there to indicate that there's anything different about the way the Earth is warming this time?

The way it warms

Certain aspects of the phenomena cited above are unusual in the context of climatic records. The rate of Arctic sea ice loss seems unprecedented. One piece of signally lateral thinking saw a team of Canadian researchers looking at the remains of bowhead whales recovered from Arctic seabed cores.[26] Since bowhead whales live at or near the edges of pack ice, the presence of their remains in any given sediment sample is a reasonable indicator of the extent of the pack. On the basis of 400 sets of whale remains, dated using radiocarbon techniques, the authors reconstructed the last 10,000 years in 1000-year time periods. Their data, albeit interpolated between points, reveal fairly persistent sea ice for the last 8000 years in the vicinity of the Canadian Arctic islands, in contrast with the last few years, when passages between some of these islands have been ice-free in summer.

And you don't need to go messing about with old whale bones to know that we've seen persistently unusual ice conditions in the frozen north, compared with 150 years ago. One of the holy grails for Victorian explorers was the so-called 'north-west passage', a channel of open water thought to exist between the northern extremities of North America and the Arctic ice pack. The passage proved elusive, and the search for it often fatal, until a navigable route was finally identified in 1905 by none other than the gritty Norwegian explorer and over-achiever Roald Amundsen, the man who famously pipped Robert Falcon Scott to the post in the infamous race for the South Pole. Several routes were subsequently identified, all fickle, all mostly iced up and all perilous. Soon, however, if current trends continue, the north-west passage may well be ice-free year-round, and it's under serious consideration by shipping companies as a shortcut from the Pacific to the Atlantic.

Worse still, the north-*east* passage along the northern coast of Siberia (often called the Northern Sea Route) is now open for a couple of months of the year, too, and a German shipping company now plans to use it as a shortcut to Japan, using icebreakers only when the dregs of the Arctic pack get in the way.[27] August 2008 is believed to have been the first time in 125,000 years that both the north-west and the north-east passages were ice-free.

The rapid warming of the Arctic and of the Antarctic Peninsula — more rapid than in the temperate and tropical zones — is alleged to be consistent with predictions of warming due to the enhanced greenhouse effect: the capacity of gases to absorb infrared radiation is greater in the drier atmosphere of the polar regions, and the frozen regions are susceptible to the albedo feedback loop, whereby melting exposes dark earth which warms faster, accelerating melting (and so on). The rate of atmospheric warming in the north polar region is about double the global average, although it is still significant in the south (more than 30% higher than the average). The effects are less dramatic in the Antarctic interior, which (as previously stated) is protected by altitude and sheer thermal mass from the worst of atmospheric warming. But it's a different story around the edges. Environmental data indicate that the breakout of the Larsen ice shelf has left open water there for the first time in at least 10,000 years and perhaps far longer. The Peninsula is the fastest-warming area in the southern hemisphere, with air temperatures increasing by approximately 2.8°C over the last 50 years. Outside the Peninsula, the greatest warming has been at Scott Base in the Ross Sea, with an increase of approximately 1.45°C, and at a Russian station, Novolazerevskaya, with around 1.0°C over the same period.[28]

The sheer rate of the warming that began in the twentieth century seems without precedent. Ice cores recovered from glaciers in tropical to subtropical latitudes don't show anything quite like it for the past two to five millennia. Results yielded by measuring oxygen isotopes in ice cores from the Tibetan Plateau and Andes mountains record an irregular but pronounced rise in temperature, beginning in about 1850, that is consistent with temperature reconstructions and meteorological records for the past 1800 years, and which is unprecedented for that period.[29]

Ice-core work undertaken in the Peruvian Andes also provides evidence of an abrupt change in Holocene climate about 5100 years ago, when cooler conditions prevailed and glaciers expanded. More recently, however, warming has forced Peruvian glaciers into retreat, pushing them back to 5000-year-old limits and exposing the remains of soft-bodied plants that have been dated to 5100 years before the present using radiocarbon techniques.[30]

Reconstructions of the way in which global warming has happened before — that is, natural global warming — tend to indicate that the southern hemisphere has typically warmed first, followed by the north. As better dated, higher-resolution records of past climate change are developed, they confirm that the present phase of global warming is unusual.

In the natural order of things, marked changes in atmospheric circulation, indicative of warming or cooling, commonly begin in the southern hemisphere and then are followed by similar changes in the northern hemisphere. Data produced using dust traces trapped in ice cores as a proxy measurement for atmospheric circulation show a period of warmer, calmer weather in the southern hemisphere (circa AD 500–1000) preceding similar conditions in the northern hemisphere by approximately 300 years.[31] From around 1000 years ago to the near-present, the southern hemisphere cooled and the atmospheric circulation became more intense — a state that was reached in the northern hemisphere around 400 years later.

In contrast to this familiar, natural pattern, however, the northern hemisphere has warmed and winds appear to have decreased over the last century ahead of any clear signal in the south. Nor are such changes restricted to recent geological time. Similar southern hemisphere leads for the period 57,000 to 9000 years ago have been noted in work using ice-core oxygen isotope measurements to construct temperatures in Antarctica and in Greenland.[32] Abrupt warmings in Antarctica, together with increases in sea surface temperature in the Southern Ocean, appear to precede abrupt warmings in the northern hemisphere.[33] The reasons for this are unclear. It has been speculated that the density of intermediate-depth waters near Antarctica may change, and when these water masses reach the North Atlantic they may stimulate the so-called 'Ocean Conveyor' (the pattern of North Atlantic oceanic currents) to transport more heat from the equator to the North Atlantic and Europe.[34] The pattern this time around is different, with warming in the northern hemisphere leading warming in the south, which suggests different processes at work. It has been postulated that the reason for the difference is that the southern hemisphere's response to global warming has either been buffered by the Southern Ocean's ability to absorb temperature rises or masked by its natural variability.[35]

The sun don't shine

The thing that drives the climate is the amount of energy coming in from the sun. The sun's radiation is subject to cyclical variations: from wobbles as it spins on its axis and from sunspot activity — pairs of dark spots visible on the solar surface that indicate massive looping eruptions of superheated material. This activity comes and goes, with periods when there is virtually none to periods where the entire solar surface is pocked with sunspots. Periods of heightened or lesser sunspot activity are termed solar maxima and minima respectively, with more sunspots signifying more radiation reaching Earth from the sun. The last solar maximum was in 2001, and another is expected in 2012. Over the last 30 years, satellites have made possible high-precision measurements of the amount of energy received by the Earth from the sun, a value referred to as total solar irradiance (TSI). These records (graphically represented in Figure 24) show TSI varying according to what the sun's doing at the time — how many sunspots there are on the surface, and what point the sun has reached on its

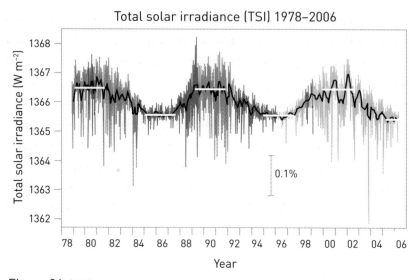

Figure 24. Little ray of sunshine: precise measurements of total solar irradiance (TSI) show a steady, rhythmic variation since records began in the late 1970s, with no rising trend to account for the increased energy detectable in the Earth system.

Source: Data from the World Radiation Center, VIRGO Experiment on the cooperative ESA/NASA Mission SoHO.

rotation — and while there is little obvious trend, such variation as there is suggests that the Earth ought to have been cooling rather than warming since 1978.

Blowing hot and cold

If you accept the physics underpinning the theory of anthropogenic global warming, then the different temperature trends that have been observed in the stratosphere and the troposphere suggest that the effects of human-generated greenhouse gases are making themselves felt.

The theory is compelling but complicated, so bear with it.

Carbon dioxide is present in both the troposphere and the stratosphere: so far, so good, we know it's a good mixer. We're pretty familiar with the role of carbon dioxide in the troposphere. It absorbs infrared radiation, right?

Well, we need to think about carbon dioxide in a whole new light when we consider the stratosphere. Because while CO_2 does exactly the same thing in the stratosphere — it absorbs infrared radiation — it's the ability of CO_2 molecules to re-radiate infrared that is the more significant effect way up there. Tropospheric CO_2 is absorbing and re-radiating all the time, too, but we emphasise the absorption when we're discussing the troposphere (you'll often hear it said, inaccurately, that tropospheric CO_2 'traps' infrared) because the infrared that is re-radiated tends to be reabsorbed by the Earth's surface, by the ocean, by other greenhouse gases (especially water vapour) and by other molecules of CO_2. The salient point is that it is being passed around between molecules in the system comprising sea, land and lower troposphere, which are in (or are closely approaching) a state of equilibrium.

Above the troposphere, at the altitude of approximately 20 km, things change. The principal source of infrared radiation is no longer the Earth's surface, with much of it having been detained by the greenhouse gases in the troposphere, being passed around in the aforementioned state of equilibrium. The principal source of heat in the stratosphere is ozone, which absorbs incoming ultraviolet radiation from the sun and emits the extra energy as infrared radiation. This is readily absorbed by stratospheric carbon dioxide.

We saw in Chapter 1 that the effect of infrared on a carbon dioxide molecule was to set it wobbling and flexing in eccentric ways that depend upon which frequency of infrared was responsible. When CO_2 molecules in this state collide with other molecules — either further CO_2 or O_3 molecules — this energy is released. Some of the collisions (and all of the collisions with O_3) mean that the energy is radiated. The rest is transferred from one molecule to another.

Much of the energy that is radiated in the stratosphere is lost to space, such that the CO_2 that is absorbing and re-radiating infrared from O_3 never reaches equilibrium. Instead, the function of CO_2 in the stratosphere is to lose to space the heat that has been generated by sunlight acting on O_3. Its net effect is to cool the stratosphere.

Since the re-radiation of energy absorbed by stratospheric CO_2 depends upon collisions between molecules, the more molecules, the greater the number of collisions and the greater the re-radiation. So in simple terms, that means the more CO_2 in the stratosphere, the more efficient it is at cooling.

Thus, when scientists find clear evidence that the stratosphere is cooling at the same time as the troposphere is warming, they get a bit excited themselves, and they too fizz about seeking other, less excited bodies to communicate the news to. So strongly do they believe it attests to anthropogenic carbon dioxide's effect on the atmosphere that it has been called 'fingerprint' evidence of anthropogenic global warming — the grubby, sooty traces of carbon released by human activity all over the data.

Trouble is, there are a couple of other factors that could account for stratospheric cooling, too. Since the heat up there is produced in the first instance by the reaction of ozone with sunlight, the depletion of stratospheric ozone or a reduction in the amount of sunlight would have the same effect. It then becomes a matter of attributing cooling. Work is ongoing on this, but scientists are confident they can identify a stratospheric cooling trend that can't be sheeted home to ozone depletion or to (precisely measured) variations in sunlight. Looking at the pair of graphs in Figure 25, they can still see the fingerprints.

The additional significance is that this renders dubious any claim that an increase in solar radiation is responsible for the measured warming of the troposphere. If it were a matter of more sunlight, both the troposphere and the stratosphere would be warming.

Together with the fundamental physics of the greenhouse gases interacting with infrared radiation, the stratospheric/tropospheric temperature trend differential is another piece in the jigsaw (although it will fail to convince anyone who believes that the greenhouse gases are an insignificant contributor to climate: we'll meet them in the following chapter).

The hot spot

One of the predicted effects of an excess of greenhouse gases in the atmosphere is the appearance of a 'hot spot' in the mid to upper

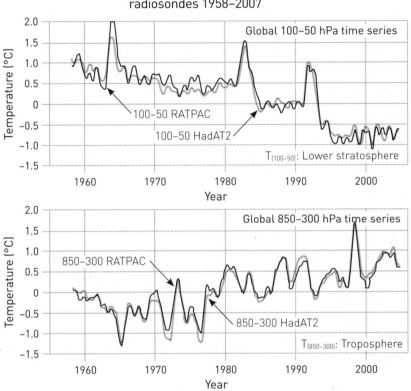

Figure 25. Blowing hot and cold: radiosonde measurements of the temperature of the stratosphere (upper panel) and the troposphere (lower panel) show a cooling and a warming trend respectively, both thought to be the effect of increased concentrations of carbon dioxide. The original data were monthly measurements, but here they have been 'smoothed' by using a seven-month running average and have been expressed as a departure in degrees Celsius from the 1979–97 average.

Source: UK Meteorological Office, Hadley Centre, www.hadobs.org

troposphere above the tropics, where the energy re-radiated is at its most intense. The idea is that the tropics, being subjected to more and more direct sunlight than the higher latitudes, will warm faster at the surface, in turn re-radiating more energy into adjacent regions of the atmosphere. So what's been observed?

Work studying the so-called 'thermal winds' of the upper atmosphere (the different movement of layers of air caused by temperature differentials) with radiosonde readings has inferred the existence of just such a spot, as shown in Figure ii in the first colour section.[36]

Note, though, that thermal winds are a second-order effect of heat; these findings have not been corroborated by other direct measurement techniques, including by satellite telemetry, so this piece of evidence remains contentious.

Do the math

The first attempt to quantify the energy that the Earth receives and the re-radiated energy that escapes the system into space was the set of calculations by English meteorologist William Henry Dines, one of the pioneers of the construction of instrumentation for upper atmosphere measurements. Based on the observations he personally collected by making balloon ascents with his gadgets, he developed a figure for the quantity that is known these days as 'terrestrial radiation', or 'outgoing longwave radiation' (OLR) in 1917.

Now, of course, satellites do much of the work that the intrepid Dines did fumbling about with brass instruments in wooden cases as he squatted, half-frozen and gasping for breath, in the gondola of his balloon. And the brainwork that would have taken him and his pencil weeks can now be performed in a flash on a laptop. The modern versions of terrestrial radiative budget calculations are done by climate models.

Alarmists will tell you that those much-maligned tools known as AOGCMs (Atmosphere–Ocean General Circulation Models) operate on such basic principles as Newton's laws of motion and the fundamental laws of thermodynamics — stuff that's sat uncontroversially in the pages of textbooks for over a century. Besides these basic operating parameters, other qualifiers are built in to approximate the geography of the Earth, the brightness of the sun, details of the Earth's orbit and the tilt of the Earth's axis, plus the planet's rate of rotation. Their handlers insist that little manipulation or 'tweaking' of these parameters goes on: little more than the conditioning variables are entered, and after that, the programs are allowed to run their course based on the data they're fed. Those who work with them are reassured by the fact that, run forward in time for a few decades from the data used to initialise them, they can faithfully reproduce later mean states of the global climate (overall temperature structure, winds, pressure, moisture distribution, cloud distribution, sea-ice extent, snow cover, etc.), the seasonal cycle of these phenomena, and even components of the inter-annual variability of the climate, such as El Niño/La Niña events, the Southern Annular Mode, the North Atlantic Oscillation, the Pacific-North American pattern, Pacific Decadal Oscillation and the Atlantic Multi-decadal Oscillation.

And represented in Figure 26, you can see what results they give you if you tell them to reproduce the last 50 years' worth of climate with and without taking the enhanced greenhouse effect into account. The lightly shaded area gives the range of responses generated for the oceans, the land and a combination of both for the entire globe taking the climate effects of human-generated greenhouse gases into account,

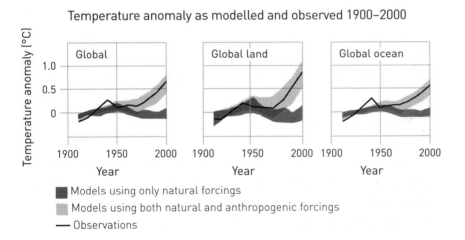

Figure 26. Model answers: the results of model runs taking into account natural climate forcings only (dark grey band) and taking into account natural forcings and the effect of greenhouse gases (light grey band) for the hundred years from 1900 to 2000. Observed temperatures for the same period are represented by the solid line. As you can readily see, climate models are unable to replicate the behaviour of the global climate over the last 100 years without taking anthropogenic greenhouse gases into account.

Source: IPCC 2007 WG-1 AR4. http://www.ipcc.ch/graphics/graphics/ar4-wg1/jpg/spm4.jpg

which matches the black line — actual observations — pretty well. The darkly shaded line, by contrast, which is the range of simulations taking only natural 'forcings' into account, suggests that we should have been experiencing 50 years' worth of mild cooling.

The reason the disparity exists, it has been argued, is that there has been, and is, a net and growing imbalance in the energy the Earth is receiving and the energy it's re-radiating. To explain the increase and variability in global mean surface temperature records and ocean temperature records over the last century, extra energy has to be found somewhere in the Earth system. The amounts that might be journalled in on Nature's side of the ledger — due to such factors as solar variations, the incidence of cosmic rays (we'll have more to say about these in Chapter 5) and the climate effects of volcanic eruptions — aren't sufficient to balance the energy books. Climate modelling only really begins to produce results consistent with the warming in the latter half of the twentieth century when the enhanced greenhouse effect is factored in.

So where's that extra energy now, then?

Most of it is in the oceans, which are both slow to absorb heat and slow to release it — a quality we've referred to as thermal inertia. The oceans account for 71% of the Earth's surface area, and they have a vast capacity to store heat in the deeps.

It's been calculated, both by direct measurement (those tricky instrumental records again) and by deduction from satellite altimetry (from a rise in sea level, the thermal expansion of the oceans can be calculated), that the oceans absorbed 89% of the energy that the Earth system soaked up between 1961 and 2003.[37] That's an annual average rise of 0.35 watts per square metre (W/m^2) over the period. Alarmingly, the authors of this study, led by climate change pioneer and crusader Jim Hansen, performed model runs that estimated the average annual imbalance between 1993 and 2003 to be to the order of 0.85 W/m^2 (± 0.15 W/m^2), meaning the net deficit of energy-out to energy-in is growing. To put it into some kind of perspective (and presumably to scare the pants off us), they calculated that if the Earth had run that kind of energy imbalance for the entirety of the Holocene (10,000 years) the upper layer of the oceans would be reaching boiling point right about now.

The extra energy that the oceans have retained stays there, cycling through the various currents, upwellings and downwellings that the ocean goes in for, and only slowly releasing it into the lower troposphere in a process that is reckoned to take between 25 and 50 years to reach 60% of its equilibrium. Based on their calculations, Hansen et al. estimated that there was 0.6°C's worth of 'committed' warming in the oceans that must play out over the next half-century, even if we arrested all emissions at today's levels.

It should be noted that Hansen et al. based their findings on modelling exercises, and that one of the parameters in this was a climate 'sensitivity' of approximately 2.8°C (that is, the presumption that if CO_2 concentrations were doubled from pre-industrial levels, it would result in a net warming of 2.8°C). This is a contestable value, as we'll see in Chapter 6. Other parameters included the various 'feedbacks' involved in the climate system, and among these Hansen judged the effect of aerosols (both human-generated and volcanic) to be the greatest uncertainty. He does not explicitly mention the gnarliest feedback of them all, namely clouds and cloudiness. It's unclear whether his modelling allowed for clouds at all, and if so, what value he assigned them.

Still, his results accorded well with observations of the temperature of the first 750 metres of ocean — observations that his models couldn't replicate using natural climate forcings alone — which gives a reasonable degree of confidence in the findings.

So why are we stuck with modelled estimates of outgoing longwave radiation, given we've had all those radiometers floating about in orbit for the best part of thirty years?

The trouble is, most — if not all — of the satellites watching the climate are primarily there to assist weather research. No one has yet thought to launch the type of satellite that could enter the kind of distant geostationary orbit and make the kind of measurements that would be necessary to generate a meaningful series of data for outgoing longwave radiation at the top of the atmosphere. While the amount of incoming energy from the sun has been well documented (it's averaged 1367.4 watts per square metre per annum over the 30-year period and ranged between 1366.5 and 1368.3 during solar minima and maxima), no equivalent number for the energy re-radiated by the Earth at the top of the atmosphere (usually referred to as outgoing longwave radiation, or OLR) is available. There simply aren't enough overlaps between the various instruments that have come and gone in the job to compile meaningful time series (as an overlap allows you to compare the results of the new instrument with the old and calibrate their respective readings to one another).

Unnatural global warming — it's a gas

Having established (as the Alarmists see it) that the warming the globe has been undergoing since the beginning of the twentieth century is atypical of natural patterns of warming, we have dealt to two of the three challenges of this chapter — global warming is occurring and it's all a bit odd, with greenhouse gases being at the centre of the Alarmists' explanation. Our third and final hurdle is to identify whose greenhouse gases they are. How sure can we be that human beings are responsible for this excess?

It turns out that it's easy enough to demonstrate that human activity has increased atmospheric levels of greenhouse gases, especially carbon dioxide.

Burn, baby, burn

The simple chemistry of combustion means that during the burning of fossil fuels, oxygen is removed from the atmosphere while atmospheric CO_2 proportionately increases. The levels of both gases can be measured with great precision, and as the graph in Figure 27 illustrates, recent measurements in both hemispheres show the strong linkages between increases in atmospheric CO_2 concentrations and

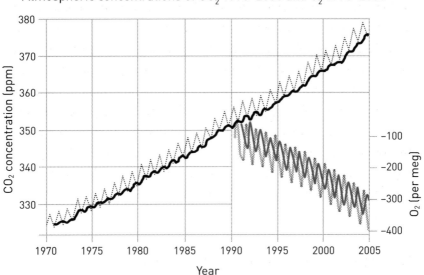

Figure 27. Burn it up: rising northern and southern hemisphere atmospheric CO_2 concentrations, overlaid with curves for falling atmospheric oxygen concentrations in both hemispheres since O_2 measurements began in 1990. The correlation points to combustion as the likely source of atmospheric CO_2.

Source: Keeling and Whorf (2005) and Manning and Keeling (2006).

decreases in those of O_2. The dotted and solid black traces on the left represent (respectively) the same data from Mauna Loa on Hawai'i and from Baring Head in New Zealand that we saw in Chapter 2, with the greater seasonal variation associated with the 'land' hemisphere's annual uptake of carbon visible compared to the relatively flat trace of the 'ocean' hemisphere. The dashed and solid grey traces in the lower right panel represent data from two stations monitoring atmospheric concentrations of oxygen since 1996, namely Alert in Canada's far north and Cape Grim in Australia.

What goes up must come down

The quantity of fossil fuels used since the industrial revolution have long been estimated. Since 1958, accurate data have been available on total annual world consumption of fossil fuels, making it possible to calculate the quantity of carbon released annually into the atmosphere by combustion (although it has been suggested darkly that the oil companies that prepare these figures have lately been inflating them to give themselves some headroom once formal limits on consumption become a reality). As we've seen, much of this carbon is taken up by the oceans and by the biosphere, leaving an amount commonly referred to as the 'airborne fraction' floating around. The mean airborne fraction since 1958 has been roughly 0.55: in other words, 55% on average of the CO_2 derived from the consumption of fossil fuels has remained in the atmosphere, year by year. The remainder has gone into the oceans and the terrestrial biosphere.

Fossil fuels and their carbon fingerprint

It stands to reason that if 55% of the carbon arising from the burning of hydrocarbons each year stays in the atmosphere, then human activity is increasing atmospheric concentrations of carbon dioxide. But it turns out there's a method of going one step further and *proving* that carbon dioxide from anthropogenic sources is increasing, without relying on any such chain of deduction. So unequivocal are these data supposed to be that they're often referred to as 'fingerprint' evidence.

The carbon contained in CO_2 can be one of three naturally occurring isotopes. Two of these, denoted ^{12}C and ^{13}C (the number reflecting their atomic mass), are stable. The third isotope, ^{14}C, is produced when cosmic rays interact with nitrogen in the upper atmosphere. A neutron of cosmic origin displaces a proton from the nitrogen nucleus, creating a nucleus with six protons and eight neutrons — ^{14}C, often known as 'radiocarbon' because it's radioactive. Carbon 14 is famous for its usefulness in 'carbon dating' of ancient organic materials, although a big spike in atmospheric concentrations of ^{14}C in the late 1950s due to the atmospheric testing of nuclear weapons has complicated the task. (The research that detected this effect galvanised the nuclear powers, and atmospheric testing was soon abandoned in favour of underground explosions. Still, you, dear reader, are more radioactive than you would have been thanks to the radiocarbon from nuclear testing incorporated in your living tissue.)

Carbon 14 would have been useful in tracing the origins of atmospheric carbon, too, but nuclear testing put paid to that. Luckily, the ratio of the far more abundant stable isotopes of carbon (^{12}C and ^{13}C) can yield useful information about the natural world. The isotopes of carbon in any given sample can be quantified in an instrument named an isotope ratio mass spectrometer. An arbitrary standard was adopted in the 1950s (a big decade for carbon), whereby unknown samples of air are compared to the ratio of ^{13}C to ^{12}C in a mineral named Pee Dee belemnite (named after the fossilised, rod-shaped remains of an ancient squid in the Pee Dee formation in South Carolina). The ^{13}C:^{12}C ratio in this mineral is assigned a value of zero, and other samples are described in terms of the difference in their ^{13}C:^{12}C ratio from this reference point. The ^{13}C:^{12}C ratio of pre-industrial CO_2 is known from a comparison of accurately dated reservoirs of carbon such as ice cores, tree rings, and speleotherms (stalagmites and stalactites), and is described as having a δ^{13}C (pronounced 'delta-^{13}C') ratio of around -7 parts per 1000 (that is, the pre-industrial atmosphere had 7 parts per 1000 less ^{13}C than the Pee Dee belemnite. Fossil fuels, by contrast, have a very much larger negative δ^{13}C score of -20).

The point of all this? Well, if you go burning fossil fuels, you are putting carbon products into the air that have a lesser δ^{13}C score than the carbon from the pre-industrial atmosphere had — in effect, you're diluting atmospheric concentrations of ^{13}C. It's like adding clear water to a bathful of dyed water, and even though some proportion of the dyed water is disappearing down the plughole (into natural sinks such as the oceans and biota), the rate of ingress is exceeding the rate of outflow. The bath level is rising, and the hue of the dye is getting paler. If it can be shown that concentrations of atmospheric ^{13}C have been declining in recent years (it's accepted that the overall atmospheric concentration of all forms of carbon dioxide is increasing), it's a foolproof indicator that fossil carbon is increasing in concentration. And, of course, the point is that scientists can show it. The results gleaned from isotope ratio mass spectrometers are depicted in Figure 28, which shows that since the industrial revolution the CO_2 released from fossil sources has reduced the average $\delta^{13}C$ of atmospheric CO_2 to about -8 parts per thousand.

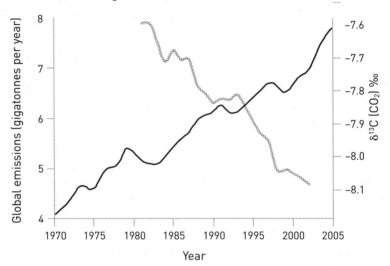

Annual global emissions and $\delta^{13}C$ 1970–2005

Figure 28. Lightening up: the ratio of carbon 13 to carbon 12 (grey line) has been declining since 1981, when it began to be measured, at a rate that is elegantly correlated with the rising rate of greenhouse gas emissions (black line) from human activity (fossil fuel consumption and cement manufacture).

Source: Data from http://cdiac.ornl.gov

As you will have noticed, the graph goes further, correlating this dilution with rising annual fossil fuel consumption (and cement manufacture) over the same period.

Once again, there is a proxy record available that agrees well with this more modern effect. A clear record of the change in isotopic composition of atmospheric carbon from fossil carbon dilution can be seen in the ratio of $^{13}C:^{12}C$ in a 300-year-old record yielded by measurement of corals from the Pacific and Caribbean.[38] Corals, of course, are squishy little critters that engage in fantastic housing developments, building themselves great protective tenements out of limestone made from the carbon (and the calcium) dissolved in seawater. Figure 29 shows how this ratio decreases in response to

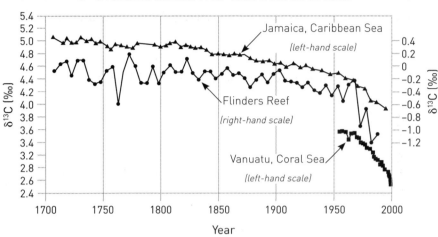

Figure 29. Coral-lation: the decline in the ratio of carbon 13 to carbon 12 is corroborated by the evidence of coral cores drilled at three sites around the world. The variability in the results for Flinders Reef in Australia is thought to be related to the way water moves on and around the reef during different phases of the Pacific Interdecadal Oscillation.

Source: Pelejero et al. 'Preindustrial to Modern Interdecadal Variability in Coral Reef pH.' *Science*, 309, 2005, 2204–2207.

increasing concentrations of light carbon in the atmosphere. This change is much larger than any natural variability for that period. Furthermore, it tends to confirm the uptake of anthropogenic gases by the oceans.

Summary

There is a suite of evidence for anthropogenic global warming, which reflects the way scientists have scrutinised the Earth system for signs that energy has been retained that would otherwise (in the absence of an excess of greenhouse gases resulting from human activity) have been re-radiated to space.

Excess energy is retained in the first instance in the oceans, which cycle it through the depths and only slowly release it to the atmosphere. Thus, the measurable warming (and thermal expansion) of the world's oceans is powerful evidence of just such a retention. So, too, is the acceleration of ice loss, and observed change in weather patterns, and changes in the range and behaviour of plants and animals.

It could be objected (and is, as we'll shortly see) that natural warming would have exactly the same effects. In order to head off this argument, evidence has been compiled that shows ways in which the rate, scale and pattern of the warming the Earth is presently experiencing are unlike other warm spells that have been reconstructed from records of the paleoclimate. We seem to be losing ice faster than at any time since the last ice age, and in some parts of the world the extent of ice loss is greater than at any period in a very long time. Whereas other instances of warming have seen the southern hemisphere affected first, followed by the northern, this time that pattern has been inverted. What's more, the observed combination of a cooling trend in the stratosphere and a warming trend in the troposphere indicates the effects of an excess of greenhouse gases.

And speaking of greenhouse gases, the clever stuff that can be done with isotopes of carbon makes it virtually certain that the measured increases in atmospheric carbon dioxide are due to the combustion of fossil fuel, which has been altering the isotopic ratio of the atmosphere and diluting concentrations of radiocarbon. This tends to confirm the implications of the measurements of oxygen and carbon dioxide, which show a straightforward depletion of oxygen corresponding to the rise in CO_2, in turn suggesting that all that CO_2 arises from a whole bunch of combustion going on.

What all this means for Alarmists is that there's evidence to support the theory of anthropogenic global warming. Why, then, are there still people out there willing to take issue with it?

Chapter 5

The Case Against Anthropogenic Global Warming

As we have seen, the theory of anthropogenic global warming states that human activity has led to a rise in emission of 'greenhouse gases', which will in turn enhance the greenhouse effect and lead to global warming with deleterious, even catastrophic, effects.

The theory of anthropogenic global warming has been under concerted attack since it began to be promoted as an issue worthy of serious concern in the 1970s. Much of this attack was mounted and is sustained in the true spirit of scientific scepticism, where it is de rigueur to test your assumptions, the empirical method you employ and the conclusions you reach equally stringently. But in more recent times, much of the effort expended under the aegis of climate scepticism has been directed toward raising doubt rather than testing veracity — a different enterprise, as anyone who has ever criticised the failings of the criminal justice system will agree. In this category, Sceptics can be divided into those who sincerely believe that the climate cannot or will not change in any detrimental manner due to human activity, and those who have a vested interest in ensuring that *others* believe the climate is immune or indifferent to human activity.

As a consequence, climate change Sceptics come in many flavours. Some accept some aspects of the anthropogenic global warming theory, but dispute others. Some deny everything. And as with any position on any question of polemics, there are extremes: some attack the unassailable; others defend the indefensible. Some deny that human activity is the principal source of measurable increases in atmospheric carbon dioxide. Some deny that the significant increase in atmospheric concentrations of carbon dioxide (and other greenhouse gases) that has occurred since the industrial revolution can have anything other than a trifling effect on climate, and accordingly dismiss any attempt to match increased levels of greenhouse gases to rising temperatures. Some deny that measurements indicate any clear increase in global average temperatures, or assert that if they do, those measurements are faulty. Some deny that the prospect of climate change — and in particular, an increase in global average temperatures — is a bad thing.

Science consists only of theories, and the validity of theories is judged by their consistency with empirical evidence. A substantial body of anomalous data will eventually force a reconsideration of a theory; on the other hand, a theory will be considered valid where the empirical data tend to vindicate its predictions over time. To some extent, climate change Sceptics are correct to argue that the burden of proof is on the proponents of the anthropogenic global warming theory, because it is the latter who are arguing for policy change. But the Alarmists are also correct to say that 'proof' is too high a standard. Given the rate at which human activity is contributing greenhouse gases to the atmosphere — and given the rate at which that rate is increasing — the Alarmists argue we simply cannot afford to wait until all remaining doubt has been dispelled. So there is a fine line to be trod between the radical doubt that is essential to the scientific method, and irresponsible quibbling.

This chapter does not propose to canvass all possible doubts, niggles and prevarications raised by the population of climate Sceptics. It is proposed, instead, to describe only those objections to the theory of anthropogenic global warming that seem to have some scientific merit. These boil down to three.

First, there is what might be called the default sceptical position, which takes two uncontroversial claims — that the Earth's climate is naturally widely variable, and that the climate system is immensely complicated and only partially understood — and makes of them a new and highly controversial assertion: that any warming trend discernible is due to poorly understood natural processes.

Then there is the vigorous and multifaceted querying of the relationship between atmospheric concentrations of CO_2 and temperature. We'll have more to say on this in the following chapter, because it's possible (and relatively common) to accept the theory of anthropogenic global warming but to contest the IPCC's predictions of the extent and the effect of any human-induced warming. Here, we'll confine ourselves to the attempt to refute the link between anthropogenic greenhouse gases and climate.

And lastly, there's the contention that the Earth system is capable of responding to and mitigating any climate forcing for which human beings are responsible.

CO_2 is innocent!

It goes without saying that if you can show that a rise in atmospheric concentrations of carbon dioxide (and other greenhouse gases) does not lead to a rise in temperature, then you've gone a long way toward discrediting the theory of anthropogenic global warming. The rise in atmospheric carbon dioxide, as documented by Keeling et al. since 1958, is pretty much incontrovertible, so naturally most attention has been directed at temperature records and their correlation with the CO_2 curve. We've already covered the various concerns raised over the instrumental temperature record — both over how the data have been gathered, and how those data have subsequently been handled. But it will come as no surprise to learn that reconstructions of both the paleoclimate and the prehistoric atmosphere are significant bones of contention in their own right. The reliability and the significance of both temperature and atmospheric gas records as derived from the so-called 'climate museum' — the ice cores — have been challenged.

1. Stomata trouble

It's a key claim of the proponents of anthropogenic global warming that present-day carbon dioxide levels are without precedent in the last 650,000 years. The usual basis for this claim is the analysis of gas samples taken from ice cores, extending back as far as 800,000 years. As we've seen, these are regarded as a direct rather than a proxy measurement of the prehistoric atmosphere, as the firn actually traps air as it forms.

Ice cores, however, are not the only game in town when it comes to measuring the mixing ratios of prehistoric atmospheric gases — or at least, not for the Sceptics. Research has suggested that the number of stomata on the needle-like leaves of certain species of conifer vary according to atmospheric levels of CO_2 (stomata are the 'pores' in the leaves of green plants through which they absorb carbon dioxide from the air, and through which they release oxygen and transpire water vapour).[1] This is presumed to be true not only of the needles on trees growing in the present atmosphere, but also of examples of the same species which died long ago and which, thanks to their resilience, have survived intact in swampy ground to be exhumed by climate researchers. Counting the stomata on the preserved remains of these species of tree, it is suggested, provides an accurate proxy measurement of prehistoric CO_2 levels. The most-studied species in this context is *Tsuga heterophylla*, or the western hemlock, a tall (growing as high as 70 metres) and long-lived (as much as 1200 years) conifer native to the west coast of North America.

Figure 30 shows the atmospheric mixing volume of carbon dioxide as reconstructed from preserved western hemlock needles reaching back for the last 1800 years, overlaid with the reconstruction from two ice cores from the same period.

The graph shows a couple of things. First, the atmospheric carbon dioxide story as told by western hemlock is very different to that told by the ice cores. Whereas the ice-core data for the same period (or at least, from two highly regarded cores, represented by black dots and white squares respectively) show a relatively steady concentration level, rising dramatically in the post-industrial era, the hemlock data

Atmospheric CO₂ concentration reconstruction based on western hemlock stomatal count AD 300–2000

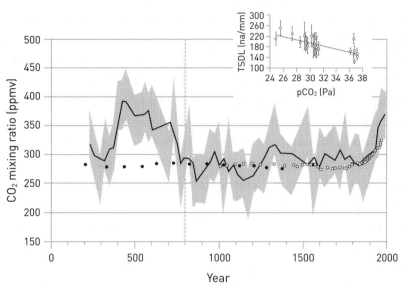

Figure 30. Stomata data: 1800 years of atmospheric carbon dioxide concentrations as reconstructed by counting the stomata on western hemlock needles (black line; the grey shaded area represents the uncertainty range). The circles are CO_2 measurements from the Law Dome ice core. If the western hemlock data are valid, they show that ice cores do not reflect the variability in atmospheric CO_2 concentrations.

Source: Kouwenberg et al (2005).

show a high degree of variability, with levels oscillating between 200 and 400 parts per million. Second, it shows the CO_2 level matching and even exceeding the 387 parts per million of the present-day atmosphere twice in the recent past. At the start of the 150-year-long Medieval Warm Period (MWP) from AD 950–1100, for example, when temperatures are often alleged to have been higher than today's, it closely approached present-day levels. Five hundred years earlier still, the hemlock would have us believe the CO_2 level nudged 400 ppm. The significance of this? Well, if they are to be believed, the trees show that atmospheric carbon dioxide levels are capable of ramping up through natural processes that don't need any help from us, since apart from the odd burning tarpit or sputtering pitch torch, there wasn't much in the way of fossil fuel consumption going on in the Dark or Middle Ages. Interestingly, too (although less relevant to the present enquiry), it has been claimed that the variation in stomata correlates neatly with sea surface temperatures, which would support the view that the oceans function as a sink for carbon dioxide.[2] At the very least, if they can be trusted, the western hemlock data suggest that the straightforward relationship between rising CO_2 levels and rising temperatures is not quite so simple as all that.

So can these trees be trusted?

There are two main reasons why the data generated from studying stomata are considered to be inferior to ice-core data.

First, they're a proxy measurement of CO_2 relying upon a relatively precarious interpretation process to translate direct measurement (counting stomata) into CO_2 concentration data. Worse, as conceded by one of the leading researchers in this field, it's virtually certain that the number of stomata varies because of several factors, not just because of CO_2 concentrations, and it's far from certain that the procedures for correcting for these potential sources of error are reliable.[3] The analysis of gases trapped by ice, by contrast, is regarded as the next best thing to directly measuring gas levels in the air through which the snowflakes fell.

Second, they're a local (or at best, regional) measurement, owing to the limited range of the target species, and while the same objection can be (and is) raised to ice-core data, the remote sites from which ice cores are retrieved are more likely to be representative of the global average concentration of CO_2. What's more, the tight agreement and sheer number of ice cores from a variety of drilling sites distributed around the globe tend to command greater respect than the isolated, regional proxy that the hemlock data represent. And even the contention that the variability shown up in the stomata data is a function of its greater resolution is contested: Kouwenberg's entire dataset relied upon a single sediment core which was relatively poor in stratigraphy suitable for assigning ages through radiocarbon dating.

Even if you were to set aside the contradictory evidence of the ice cores and accept the variable CO_2 picture as painted by the western hemlock data, it's going to be of limited value in determining what the climate effects of present-day levels of CO_2 will be. Nor will it be of any value in working out what the world will be like at the middle of this century, when atmospheric concentrations of CO_2 are predicted to reach 560 ppm — well beyond anything the oldest known western hemlock ever lived through.

2. It just won't fit my curves

It's commonly noted that CO_2 concentrations have been inexorably and monotonously rising year by year ever since direct measurement began in 1958, and yet the global temperature record has failed to mirror its stately progress (see Figure 21 in Chapter 3). Instead, global average temperatures have been all over the shop, rising, falling or remaining steady in a way that bears little immediately apparent relation to carbon dioxide levels.

The Alarmists retort — much as those who play the financial markets do — that you must ignore the stochastic (random or chaotic) events and focus on the underlying trend. That's why temperature data are often 'smoothed' in order to tease the signal from the noise. The climate system is complex and features the intricate interplay of a vast array of elements; the signal from any given forcing, be it solar irradiance, greenhouse gases, chaotic events such as the injection of volcanic aerosols and so on, is often blurred by lags (as where a proportion of CO_2 is absorbed by the oceans before being released as the oceans warm), or masked by counter-effects and muddled by the strong, rhythmical signals of the North Atlantic and Southern Oscillations and the even deeper pulse of the Milankovic cycles. In the context of the slow and complex response of the Earth system, 50 years (the period over which direct measurement of atmospheric gases has been undertaken) isn't a long time. Notwithstanding all this noise, the argument goes, and never mind the decade-long, slight cooling that global average temperatures have exhibited since 1998, the trend has been the same for temperature as for carbon dioxide: it's on the rise.

3. The horse and the cart

Both sides of the climate change debate accept that reconstructions of the paleoclimate indicate that on every previous occasion where the Earth has warmed and atmospheric concentrations of carbon dioxide have risen, temperature has gone first, followed by carbon dioxide. And there can be no question of human agency in these events, because many of them long predate the rise of civilisation, let alone the oil companies. Rather, what seems to be at work is a small shift in a solar or Milankovic cycle that forces a correspondingly small rise in temperature. This is enough to trigger the various feedback mechanisms involved in global warming including, notably, an increase in the atmospheric concentration of greenhouse gases as the oceans warm and dissolved carbon dioxide (especially) leaves solution. There seems from the records to be a time lag of between 200 and 800 years between the initial solar forcing and the initiation of a rise in carbon dioxide levels, and each such warming period seems to last around 5000 years. It's thought that the 800-year lag represents the time that it takes for warming of the oceans to percolate through the deep layers, flushing out the carbon-dioxide-rich water that has languished there since the last glacial period.

It has been argued, on the basis of this, that there has never been a single instance where carbon dioxide has initiated a period of global warming. Yet it's a simple error in logic to conclude that this means an increase in atmospheric CO_2 *cannot* force the climate. Indeed, the same historical record tends to reinforce rather than undermine the warming effect of atmospheric CO_2 (and other greenhouse gases). It's surmised that during past glacial periods, global temperature has dropped for two reasons:

1. The atmosphere was actually comparatively depleted of greenhouse gases — there was only about 190 ppm CO_2 in the atmosphere, and other major greenhouse gases such as methane and nitrous oxide were also lower — and thus less outgoing heat was trapped close to the surface.

2. Generally cooler temperatures sparked a negative feedback loop, where the Earth's surface became more reflective due to the persistence of ice and snow on land and to a greater sea ice extent than today's. The combined effect of both was to increase the Earth's albedo, such that incoming solar radiation was efficiently reflected into space without causing warming.

Now the second of these two influences is reckoned to be the larger, accounting for about two-thirds of the total radiative forcing. The effect of CO_2 and other greenhouse gases is supposed to account for the other third. The contribution of greenhouse gases to the glacial–interglacial coolings and warmings amounts to about half of the full amplitude (the height of the curve) if you include methane and nitrous oxide. So as the Alarmists read the record, the glacial–interglacial cycle is triggered by slight variations in insolation that are then amplified by changes in albedo and rises or falls in the concentration of greenhouse gases. The potential of the greenhouse gases to affect the climate regardless of fluctuations in insolation — the amount of radiation energy reaching a given surface area (and so lessened by atmospheric absorption) — is considerable. The fact that they have not been solely responsible for any of the prehistoric climatic fluctuations is understandable, because outside the kind of temperature change brought about by Milankovic or solar cycles, nature has no mechanism for releasing greenhouse gases on the scale of which post-industrial human activity is capable.

We'll have more to say on this subject, and the extent to which it is thought CO_2 can force climate and raise temperatures, in the following chapter.

Whodunnit?

In the previous chapter, we outlined what might be called the circumstantial evidence of anthropogenic global warming — the natural phenomena that fit with the predictions of the theory. At the very least, many of the observations listed there serve to support the thesis that the Earth is getting warmer, and it's hardly surprising that many Sceptics accept that a rise in global average temperatures underlies much of what has been observed in the Earth system. And it's reassuring that most of the scientific community's serious sceptics do acknowledge that it's not enough simply to deny that human activity has caused this warming. It's incumbent upon them to show either that something other than human activity is responsible, or that there's some feature of climate that offsets or mitigates the impact of anthropogenically produced greenhouse gases.

We've already touched upon the weakness of the correlation between topsy-turvy global average temperatures and the disturbing, inexorable rise of atmospheric greenhouse gas levels, and noted what a happy hunting ground it is for climate gainsayers. But such are the stakes in this debate that if they are to deny that the global temperature record is influenced by greenhouse gases, then they must provide an alternative theory of climate change, showing what causes the Earth to warm and cool or, at the very least, what prevents the mechanism as described by the theory of anthropogenic global warming from operating as predicted.

Here, too, there's an amount of wiggle room. Regardless of what the very best climate scientists will tell you, and regardless of the boldest claims made by the boffins who build and tinker with AOGCMs, the Earth's climate in all its myriad details remains at best only partially understood. It's all very well to argue, as Alarmists do (like a stuck record), that the climate models are constructed with respect only to basic, uncontroversial laws of physics. The even more advanced state of biochemistry hasn't yet given us a complete understanding of the human brain, and while it's possible to map and model the brain in a way that gives us a working knowledge of its processes, we nevertheless fall far short of explaining its deeper mysteries. We're about as close to a complete understanding of the Earth's climate as we are to explaining consciousness, or the more outlandish reaches of human behaviour. Indeed, our understanding of a cardinal climate event such as the last ice age is about as complete as our understanding of how it was that George W. Bush got a second term in office.

Of course, it doesn't help that climate science is, comparatively speaking, in its infancy. Few would have heard of it 30 years ago, let alone considered majoring in it at a university or making a career in it. As we've seen, the tools and techniques we possess to generate the datasets upon which our current understanding of climate is based are comparatively new.

For these reasons, and quite apart from the aversion of scientists to making absolute statements, there's a place in the sun for sceptical argument, even if it's only the crudest form of destructive hypothesis: 'We don't know for sure, so let's just say it isn't so.' That's why you'll find so much space and cyberspace in books, magazine articles, blogs and websites devoted to nitpicking the findings of the IPCC.

But again, finding a few errors in what's been produced as evidence for anthropogenic global warming isn't enough to reassure us that all danger from that quarter has passed, unless a highly plausible alternative theory of how climate shifts or how it resists forcing is put forward.

I can explain everything

So what do the Sceptics have for us in this department? It turns out that they have come up with two plausible candidates.

The leading alternative hypothesis for climate change is that solar forcing determines all but the most trifling degree of climate on Earth, and that anything human beings do, whether it's considered bad — releasing greenhouse gases into the atmosphere — or good — cutting fossil fuel use, capturing and sequestering carbon, et cetera — can't affect climate trends one iota.

And the other, broadly similar line of argument is that the Earth system possesses a kind of built-in thermostat (in the form of weather) that will resist any climate forcing arising from human activity.

Let's have a look at these in a little more depth.

1. Here comes the sun

There's no doubt that the sun is ultimately the determinant of the Earth's climate. As we've noted, the Earth's orientation with respect to the sun — whether it be the planet's rotation, wobble, tilt, or the elongation of its elliptical orbit — has an effect, and these effects are visible in the ice cores and other proxy measurements of the Earth's past climate. Around half of the total solar irradiance (TSI) measured just outside our atmosphere comprises radiation in the visible electromagnetic spectrum. The other, invisible half is itself mostly made up from the infrared part of the spectrum, although anyone who has ever smeared sunscreen on themselves has tacitly acknowledged that there is also a component from the ultraviolet band of the spectrum. Insolation is greatest at those surfaces that directly face the sun, less at those at an angle. The poles therefore receive far less than the equator and, consequently, it's warmer at the equator than it is at the poles. TSI has been precisely measured ever since the satellite-borne technology became available in 1978: it's roughly 1367 watts per square metre, give or take the rises and falls that occur during the solar maxima and minima that chase each other through an 11-year cycle. It can be shown that there is little or no significant correlation between TSI and temperature trends as measured over the same period — even though there is an entire school of climate change denial that believes variations in the sunspot cycle completely describe the Earth's climate, and whose adherents are now confidently expecting a phase of global cooling as a consequence of the decline from the 2001 solar maximum.

But there are other sources of incident energy that are not quantified by measurements of TSI. It seems likely that other solar fluctuations such as solar flares, which produce bursts of energy and subject the Earth and its atmosphere to colossal amounts of radiation, have an effect on climate, but the nature and scale of that effect is uncertain. Meanwhile, too, the Earth is bathed in various fluxes of high-energy particles, such as the solar wind (the unceasing flow of superheated material that emanates from the solar corona and that, among other things, causes comets' tails to stream away from the sun) and the shower of extremely high-energy particles which are misleadingly called cosmic rays. The name is misleading because they are neither rays (they are particles, mostly protons, but also including the nuclei of helium and other, heavier elements, too — although some of the behaviours of these particles as they move resemble those of rays, quantum physics being what it is), and nor for the most part are they strictly cosmic (as most originate from within our galaxy, many of the rest from within the solar system and only a vanishingly small proportion from the cosmos at large). So what, if any, are the climate effects of all this other incoming radiation?

It turns out there is an eye-catching correlation between cosmic ray activity and global temperatures — they're a better fit, at any rate, than the curves for CO_2 levels and global average temperature, as Figure 31 shows.

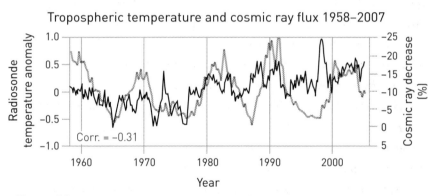

Figure 31. Cosmic coincidence: the correlation between cosmic ray flux (black line) and the variation in tropospheric temperature anomaly is eye-catching.

Source: Svensmark et al (2007).

Looks good. But how does it work, you may well ask? When the charged particles that comprise cosmic rays encounter the particles comprising the atmosphere, collisions take place, and a whole range of new electrically charged particles are formed in a process known as spallation. These particles descend through the atmosphere in 'showers', and a Danish physicist Henrik Svensmark has suggested that many are capable of forming the kind of nuclei that are needed for the condensation of water vapour (that is, the return of water from its gaseous to its liquid or solid states — water or ice respectively — depending where in the atmosphere condensation occurs).[4] Agglomerations of ice crystals or water droplets hanging around in the atmosphere are better known as clouds, and clouds are capable not only of trapping heat radiated from the Earth's surface, but also of increasing the atmosphere's albedo to solar radiation and reducing the amount of radiation that reaches the surface to produce warming. That is, an increased incidence of cosmic rays can cause an increase in cloudiness, which might trap heat close to the Earth's surface but might also dim sunlight and cause a net decrease in insolation. No prizes for guessing which effect the sceptical analysts of this process consider to be dominant.

Intriguingly, the amount of cosmic rays that reach the Earth's atmosphere is modulated principally by solar influences. During periods of heightened sunspot activity, fewer particles get through. As sunspot activity declines, the deflector shield that the sun casts over us weakens and we are subjected to greater concentrations of cosmic rays. If Svensmark and his crew are correct in their description of the cloud-forming effect of spallation products, you'd expect to see an ebb and flow in cloudiness that corresponds with rises and falls in solar activity. So how does it look?

The short answer is that the correlation is near-perfect. Based on the graph shown in Figure 32, you'd be justified in concluding that fluctuations in cosmic ray flux determine low-level cloudiness. Low-level clouds are significant because it's believed that whereas high, thin cirrus clouds trap more infrared than they reflect incoming solar radiation, the opposite is believed to be true of lower clouds, and must therefore affect insolation and, ultimately, temperatures. What's more, the mechanism that is supposed to underlie this process has been shown to have some validity in laboratory experiments, as Svensmark et al. have shown that ultraviolet radiation can produce ions that can in turn function as nuclei for condensation.[5] Perhaps the sect of sunspot worshippers are onto something, after all.

This theory has received critical attention from the Alarmists (although perhaps not so much as it merits) on two main grounds.

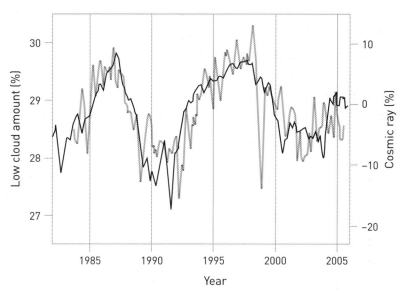

Figure 32. We really do know clouds: the correlation between cosmic ray flux (black line) and low cloud records is remarkable.

Source: Svensmark et al (2007).

The first has to do with the comparatively short period covered by the data: what a pity the Victorians didn't get onto rocket propulsion! The second is over the detrending of the tropospheric temperature data in Figure 31. Anthropogenic global warming theory predicts time lags, often substantial, between stimulus from forcing and response from temperature, whereas the work on cosmic ray flux has tended to focus on a correlation with the volatility of global temperature, and has not addressed the trend in temperature.

What's more, the laboratory demonstration of ion production by ultraviolet radiation is not quite the same thing as showing that spallation products function as condensation nuclei in low-level cloud formation, so the precise mechanism by which cosmic ray flux influences cloudiness, hence insolation, hence temperature 'remains speculative', as an authoritative critique has put it. Still, if it can be shown that cosmic ray flux makes a significant contribution to short-term climatic variation, that's a worthy addition to our understanding.

2. Raining on the IPCC parade

We've had a number of occasions to remark upon the positive aspect of the natural greenhouse effect, namely that it traps enough of the outgoing infrared radiation to keep the Earth sufficiently warm to support life. But there's a flipside to the presence of the greenhouse gases as well — or at least there would be if another natural mechanism didn't intervene to offset it. The greenhouse gases in the troposphere are efficient enough to make the Earth's surface intolerably hot if there were not some means by which heat was dissipated; luckily, we have the weather — the mechanism that transports heat from the lower regions of the troposphere to the higher. Between the two of them — the tendency of greenhouse gases to trap heat and keep the Earth warm and the tendency of the weather to transfer heat from lower to higher in the atmosphere — they maintain a Goldilocks climate — not too hot, not too cold: just right.

Weather is an expression of the second principle of thermodynamics, which states that energy moves from where it is greatest to where it is least. The Earth's surface — land and sea — heats up as a result of absorbing incoming sunlight. Of course, and as we've lately reminded ourselves, the extent of the heating isn't uniform: some parts of the Earth (the tropics) receive more radiation from the sun, the land heats up more quickly than the oceans, and if there are clouds about, then those parts that aren't under cloud heat more quickly — all quite apart from the fact that heat from the Earth's surface is transmitted both by convection and by radiation into the atmosphere. Given the patchiness of the way solar radiation interacts with the Earth's surface and the way heat re-radiated by the surface interacts with the blanketing gases of the atmosphere, there's plenty of scope for heat transfer.

The weather involves two heat effects. First, the movement of air masses differently affected by adjacent surfaces — hotter areas of the Earth's surface heat the air immediately above them, and air masses so heated rise (in a movement called convection) to be replaced by cooler air masses. Second, heat energy is transferred through what's called the latent heat capacity of water. Everyone knows that to boil water, you must add energy to it: you flick a switch, electricity flows through a kettle's ceramic element and is converted to heat energy, which is absorbed by the water adjacent to it. The water molecules, perpetually in motion, move faster and further thanks to this additional energy — latent heat — until, at a certain point, they move fast and far enough for the water to change states, and for bubbles of water vapour to begin to rise through the liquid and dissipate into the surrounding air. The water is boiling, and evaporating (literally, emitting vapour). Water vapour will rise through cooler gases until it condenses and changes state from gas to liquid again, whereupon all that extra energy that was added to cause it to evaporate is released again into the surrounding, cooler air masses. Heat has been transferred from the source (in this case, the kettle's element) to the medium surrounding the condensing vapour somewhere up there in the atmosphere. The process is identical when incoming solar radiation evaporates water from the ocean, which then condenses high in the troposphere: heat energy has been transferred from the ocean to the atmosphere. Similarly, the effect of plants evapotranspiring water from their stomata draws heat from the air adjacent to the Earth's surface and redistributes it to the atmosphere; and when you sweat, the perspiration evaporating draws heat from the blood vessels just under your skin and cools you down.

The rise of heated air masses (and their replacement by cooler air) as complicated by the rotation of the Earth (the Coriolis effect), together with the evaporation of water from the surface and its condensation in the middle and upper reaches of the troposphere (as clouds of water droplets or ice crystals, depending upon the altitude), is what makes weather — wind, clouds, rain, hail and snow. And in the process, heat is transferred from the surface into the air, and from the hotter regions (the tropics) to the cooler (the poles).

So while we've previously encountered water vapour as a villain — as a potent greenhouse gas — it's also something of a hero, as it cools the Earth's surface via the process of evaporation. It's a complex character, and a bit of a wild card in energy budget equations.

Evaporation cools the Earth's surface by transferring heat from the surface into the atmosphere (where it stands a greater chance of dissipating to space), but water vapour is a greenhouse gas, and can trap outgoing infrared radiation. Precipitation (rain, hail or snowfall) removes water vapour from the atmosphere and reduces its greenhouse potential. Clouds both trap outgoing infrared radiation (and warm the lower troposphere) and increase atmospheric albedo (dimming sunlight and reducing the incidence of solar radiation that warms the surface). What, then, is the net effect of weather? This is a point, perhaps more than any other, where Alarmists and Sceptics truly are poles apart.

A major component of the theory of anthropogenic global warming is that CO_2 alone is not capable of raising temperature by a significant amount. Instead, the danger is that the small rise initiated by CO_2 will increase the rate of evaporation, which will load the atmosphere with more water vapour which will, in turn, trap far more outgoing infrared radiation than CO_2. This implies a statement about precipitation — the means by which the atmosphere unburdens itself of water vapour — namely that it will not change significantly. Sceptics note that tropical weather systems are more efficient precipitation systems than the weather in the cooler, higher latitudes, suggesting that weather systems in a generally warmer world will increase in precipitation efficiency and become concomitantly more efficient at cooling. The most efficient weather systems of them all in terms of removing water vapour from the atmosphere are thought to be hurricanes, and the IPCC itself predicts an increase in the number and intensity of severe tropical storms — a cranking-up of the Earth's own air conditioner as a response to warming.

So who's right? While the precise equations aren't known, research by Gettleman et al. (2000) showed that the atmospheric water vapour content was growing, as could be expected from an increase in evaporation that was not offset — or not totally offset — by more efficient precipitation.[6]

3. The eyes have it

Besides the efficiency of precipitation systems, another elegant mechanism by which the Earth responds to climate shocks has been proposed, namely the 'iris hypothesis'. The iris is the coloured ring in the human eye that surrounds the pupil, which is the aperture through which light is admitted to the light-sensing retina behind it. The iris comprises muscles that can dilate or contract the pupil in response to the amount of light striking the eye. In bright lights, the iris narrows the aperture of the pupil; in dim light, it pulls the pupil open.

In a celebrated piece of work by one of the most respected climate change Sceptics, Richard Lindzen, it was postulated in 2001 that the Earth possessed an analogous mechanism, based on the behaviour of water vapour.[7] According to the hypothesis, as the atmosphere above the tropics warmed, the efficiency of the rain-making system would increase, drying the air and leading to a reduction in cloud formation. The veil of high cirrus in those regions would diminish, allowing more infrared radiation to escape into space in the night. Cooler temperatures would have the opposite effect, with a thickening cirrus presence trapping fugitive infrared at night, so the mechanism resembled the opening and closing of the iris of the eye. Lindzen et al. calculated that each degree of warming at the surface would lead to a 20% reduction in cirrus, enough to offset any forcing from increased evaporation. That's the hypothesis, and part of its charm is that it didn't rely upon a denial of anthropogenic global warming at all. Rather, the two effects could be running simultaneously, with the iris effect offsetting the forcing from the enhanced greenhouse effect.

The iris hypothesis was, of course, immediately controversial, and in 2002 a satellite-based measurement system was directed to examine the effects of tropical cirrus. The results of this survey seemed to indicate that the high cloud layer had the opposite effect to that predicted by Lindzen.[8] The notion that cirrus cloud actually plays a part in global dimming and cools rather than warms the Earth's surface had first been postulated way back in the 1960s. Indeed, and if only to prove that the blackest cloud has a silver lining, data collected while the US civil aviation fleet was grounded for three days following the September 11, 2001 terrorist attacks on the World Trade Center showed that the absence of contrails (the trail of ice crystals left by airliners plying the stratosphere) had actually warmed the surface beneath, suggesting that cirrus cloud does reflect incoming solar radiation and exerts a net cooling effect.[9] Since then, further observations have served only to make the whole issue foggier, with some measurements showing little or no change in cloud formation, duration and dissipation, and others showing that such changes are occurring. Figure 33 shows the lack of an obvious trend upwards or downwards in cloudiness anomaly.

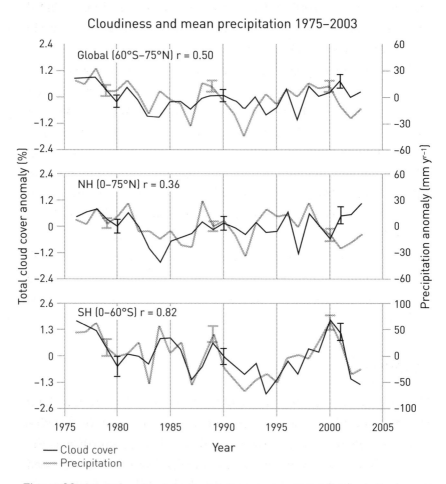

Figure 33. I can't see clearly now: charting average global (top), northern hemisphere (middle) and southern hemisphere (bottom) anomalies in cloud cover and precipitation doesn't tell us much. There is no trend, and little obvious pattern beyond the suspicion of a cycle, probably related to the Southern and North Atlantic Oscillations.

Source: IPCC 2007 WG-1 AR4,
http://www.ipcc.ch/graphics/graphics/ar4-wg1/jpg/fig-3-22.jpg

Meanwhile, of course, the debate over whether clouds and cloudiness represent a net positive or negative climate forcing has raged unabated, and seems no nearer to resolution. So water, like girls, can do anything, and its role in climate change depends on whom you ask about it. The Earth's climate is cooler than it would be if there were no clouds. Thus the principal effect of clouds is albedo. Fewer clouds will mean more warming. But models simulate the climate best if they assume clouds also *trap* heat. The uncertainty is which effect will predominate in a warmer world.

Some Sceptics agree that albedo is the dominant characteristic of clouds, but conclude that more evaporation (and thus more water vapour in the atmosphere) will mean more clouds, more albedo and a net cooling. Others (like Lindzen) prefer to regard clouds as barriers to nocturnal heat loss, so more clouds will cause net warming. Still others believe that warming will increase the efficiency of precipitation systems, meaning more heat is carried aloft in the cycle of evaporation and condensation, allowing a greater proportion of surface heat to be radiated into space.

On one thing, and one thing only, everyone on both sides is agreed. No one really knows for sure what the significance of water is for the theory of anthropogenic global warming.

Summary

Get past the distractions (that is, the spurious, frivolous or nitpicking objections to the theory of anthropogenic warming) and the Sceptics' arguments fall into two broad groups. There are those who dispute the theory of anthropogenic warming, arguing that any warming witnessed by post-industrial humankind is within the bounds of natural climatic variation, and that there is no causal link between atmospheric carbon dioxide concentrations and surface temperature variations. Some alternative mechanisms have been proposed: since it's fluctuations in solar radiation that have indisputably driven the major climate events of the remote past, it's argued that compared to solar irradiance, other climate influences are insignificant (this is what you might call the default sceptical position). And the correlation of cosmic ray flux and global average temperatures has been investigated, and a possible link between cosmic rays and cloudiness has been proposed.

The other broad group of climate Sceptics actually accept the theory of anthropogenic global warming, but argue that there are mechanisms by which the climate self-regulates, making the IPCC's predictions of the rate and scale of temperature rises inaccurate and exaggerated. These mechanisms, it is suggested, are weather-related. Either convection (the evaporation of water from the surface and its condensation in the upper troposphere) transports heat away from the surface, and the efficiency of this effect increases with greater surface temperatures, or cloudiness increases with increased water vapour, increasing albedo and cooling the surface.

As we went along, we assessed these arguments for merit. We find what we're left with is a handful of weak objections to the theory of anthropogenic warming, but a set of valid doubts about the IPCC's numbers, especially the IPCC's projections of how much warming we should expect from how much more atmospheric CO_2. It's those numbers we'll now proceed to examine.

Chapter 6

How Much CO$_2$ Leads to How Much Warming?

The Earth's average atmospheric temperature routinely varies. A difference of half a degree Celsius, plus or minus, is common between years. In years when a major volcanic event takes place, injecting vast quantities of aerosol material into the upper reaches of the atmosphere and dimming incoming solar radiation, global temperatures can dip by as much as a full degree. But temperature tends to be 'mean-reverting' — that is, once whatever cause of short-term perturbation has passed, it returns to its previous track — and the long-term trends in the world average temperature due to natural forcings, whether their net effect is cooling or warming, are very slow-moving. A difference of 0.2˚C between the averages of successive 50-year periods would be typical.

There has been so much focus on the debate over trends (past, present and future) in the world's average surface temperature that attention has been diverted from other elements of the evidence that supports the theory of anthropogenic global warming. Because as we saw in Chapter 4, it's not just the fact that there's an upward trend discernible in multi-decadal global average temperatures that is causing concern. More worrying is the accumulation of evidence that suggests human agency has created an energy imbalance in the Earth system that must cause warming, whether that warming has been fully realised or not.

If we were to accept that the accumulated evidence supports the case for anthropogenic global warming, the question then becomes, how serious an issue is it? Does it matter a hoot how much carbon we unlock from prehistoric sources and add to the atmosphere? Does it all stay up there? How much extra carbon dioxide (and its equivalent in other greenhouse gases) causes what rise in global temperatures, and are these rises anything to worry about?

Let's put it in perspective. We know that CO_2 concentrations have risen from 280 ppm in pre-industrial times to over 380 ppm at the time of writing. There's precious little convincing evidence that this concentration has been exceeded during the Holocene. That means civilisation as we know it has never experienced the kind of climate you get when the atmospheric greenhouse gases reach those levels. Nor is there much convincing evidence that CO_2 concentrations have been substantially higher than present-day levels in 200,000 years, the entire *Homo sapiens* epoch. If we accept the theory of anthropogenic global warming, we must confront the prospect that we may soon be inhabiting a world whose climate is different to that to which our species has adapted. After all, greenhouse gas concentrations seem set to keep rising at the equivalent of 1.5 ppm of carbon dioxide per year.

Let's put it another way. *Homo sapiens* is thought to have been around for 200,000 years. Agriculture, the development of metal tools and the domestication of animals — in other words, the rise of civilisation — are more recent, and are only as old as the Holocene (around 10,000 years before the present). Over the entire history of the species, temperatures have plunged to 9°C below present averages, and risen to 2°C higher. Over the entire history of civilisation, on the other hand, temperatures have only ever ranged in a much narrower band: between 0.5°C above and 0.5°C below. Civilisation itself may well be a product of a flukey spell of clement weather the planet's enjoyed these last few millennia. It stands to reason that if temperatures test the +2°C boundary, we will find ourselves 'boldly going where no man has gone before', to paraphrase noted climate scientist Captain James T. Kirk.

Suppose the theory of anthropogenic global warming is correct, how much warming can we expect from the forecast rise in greenhouse gas concentrations? We'll briefly pre-empt the following discussion and say that the answer to this question varies widely, and depends upon how much (and which parts) of the anthropogenic global warming hypothesis you accept. To Alarmists, who believe the whole shebang and shooting match, elevated carbon dioxide instigates a warming and concomitantly an increase in that most potent of all greenhouse gases, water vapour, which causes further warming, which triggers loss of albedo, reduces the capacity of the oceans to act as a sink for CO_2 to the extent that they become a net emitter of CO_2, ditto the rainforests, ditto the vast methane deposits of the clathrates and in the permafrost . . . Your answer, based on these beliefs, will be high.

If, however, you accept that CO_2 has played an amplification role in the whole natural warming cycle in the past, but that the effect of increased water vapour on climate is weak or even negative (due to increased cloudiness, say, or the cooling effect of increased precipitation, as discussed in the previous chapter), then you're likely to be talking smaller numbers and to be of a less nervous disposition altogether.

Numbers! Quick, gimme numbers! We need to know what rise in global average temperatures we can expect with the forecast rise in greenhouse gas concentrations and (for peace of mind's sake) how that figure is arrived at.

The IPCC estimates that if atmospheric CO_2 was doubled, a rise of between 2 and 4.5°C could be expected, with a best estimate of 3°C. Typically of the IPCC, they attempt to assign a probability to the chances of the impact falling within this range. They reckon there's a 67% chance that doubling CO_2 will cause a rise of between 2 and 4.5°C (and in plain English describe it as 'likely').

Faced with numbers like this, you've got to ask yourself one question. Do you feel lucky? Well, do you?

And before the gamblers out there relax too much, we'll pre-empt another aspect of the following discussion, and reveal that the bulk of the remaining probability lies on the high side of the range. Put simply, the IPCC is very confident that the warming resulting from doubling CO_2 will not be less than 2°C. But the IPCC is not at all confident that it won't be higher than 4.5°C.

You'll note that it's a range, and that the figure of 3°C is only an estimate. This reflects the many uncertainties that the IPCC acknowledges are in the string of calculations required to reach this point. Why is there so much doubt? As a roundabout way of answering that question, let's have a brief look at the history of computations on the subject.

A short history of climate change number crunching

The relationship between carbon dioxide concentrations and atmo-spheric temperature has puzzled scientists for over 100 years now. Successive attempts to quantify the relationship have served to highlight not only the physical principles that are most important to the estimates, but also where the uncertainties are greatest. This also gives us a sense of how robust the current answer to the question might happen to be.

As we've seen, the greenhouse effect was proposed in 1824 by Joseph Fourier. He recognised that the atmosphere was largely transparent to incoming shortwave solar radiation, but that the Earth's surface was warmed by solar radiation and re-radiated long-wave infrared radiation (heat), which was partially intercepted by some constituent of the atmosphere. Fourier recognised that the amount of radiation given off by a body is in some way proportional to the temperature of the body. The implication of this is that if the Earth (by which is meant the planet and its atmosphere) is radiating the same amount of energy to space as it is receiving, it will maintain a roughly even temperature. Any change in the balance, whether it's on the incomings or outgoings side of the ledger, will mean the temperature of the Earth and its atmosphere will need to adjust to restore the radiative equilibrium.

In 1859, John Tyndall put names to the faces of Fourier's greenhouse gases. He used a spectrometer to study the absorptive powers of various gases and demonstrated that certain molecules (notably water vapour and carbon dioxide) absorb infrared radiation in bands of the spectrum that are distinctive to each species. Noting the number of bands in which water vapour absorbed, he argued that variation in humidity probably accounted for most of the world's climate variations through time.

In 1879, the relationship between the temperature of a body and the level of heat it radiated was quantified in the so-called Stefan–Boltzmann law. Jozef Stefan, a Slovenian chemist, derived the principle from a combination of Tyndall's observations and the theoretical work in thermodynamics done by his promising young Austrian student, Ludwig Boltzmann (who went on to teach Svante Arrhenius: the brave new world of nineteenth-century thermodynamics was a small one). Basically, for those who are interested, Stefan's law states that the amount of radiation a blackbody (a theoretical body that absorbs all the electromagnetic radiation that falls on it) will emit is directly proportional to the fourth power of the blackbody's thermodynamic (or absolute) temperature (that is, measured on the absolute or thermodynamic scale, which takes the point at which the atoms in matter are completely motionless as zero).

As we've seen, Svante Arrhenius had a crack at sheeting home the ice ages to reductions in atmospheric CO_2 concentrations. Arrhenius was dubious about Tyndall's claims for water vapour, although he accepted water probably played an amplifying role in warming induced by other causes. He had made measurements of the infrared radiation reaching Earth from the moon, and by applying the Stefan-Boltzmann law to these data, he was able to derive the relationship between atmospheric CO_2 and infrared radiation (and thus, temperature).

For fans of algebra, this is what Arrhenius's CO_2–temperature relationship looks like written down:

$$\Delta T = \alpha \ln (C/C_o)$$

where ΔT is change in temperature, C is the new concentration of carbon dioxide, C_o is the original concentration of carbon dioxide, and α is a quantity known as the Boltzmann Constant, which Arrhenius derived from the Stefan-Boltzmann law.

And for algebraphobics, this is how he described it:

> if the quantity of carbonic acid [carbon dioxide] increases in geometric progression, the augmentation of the temperature will increase nearly in arithmetic progression.[1]

Cutting to the chase, for anyone who's allergic to progressions of any kind, Arrhenius calculated on the basis of his sexy new rule that a doubling of CO_2 concentration would raise atmospheric temperature by between 5 and 6°C. This was the first estimate of what the climate would do if carbon dioxide levels were doubled (a value that is generally talked about as the climate's 'sensitivity' to carbon dioxide), and Arrhenius thought — understandably, based on the energy scene at that time — that it would take thousands of years to get there.

In 1900, another Swede muddied the waters somewhat. Knut Angstrom's work on the absorption coefficients of CO_2 and water vapour indicated that they absorbed infrared in the same regions of the infrared spectrum. Angstrom concluded that any rise in CO_2 would have no net effect, as water vapour would already have absorbed any radiation that additional CO_2 otherwise might have absorbed. Arrhenius protested, and urged his contemporaries to keep burning lots of coal in order to avert the risk of another ice age — history's first link between fossil fuel consumption and global warming. Nevertheless, reassured by Angstrom, attention wandered away from the climatic significance of CO_2 for the best part of fifty years, and in the meantime, people did indeed burn lots of coal.

In 1938, British steam engineer and amateur meteorologist Guy Stewart Callendar presented figures to the Royal Meteorological Office that suggested global average temperatures were rising. He even had an explanation. Whereas Angstrom had thought that water vapour took care of any infrared radiation that extra CO_2 might otherwise hope to have absorbed, Callendar's theory of the matter had a role for the effects of pressure on the absorption profiles of the greenhouse gases. Change the pressure, he reckoned, and the gases that are around to do the absorbing change. Rather than thinking of the atmosphere as a single, undifferentiated block of greenhouse gases, that is, Callendar urged that we think of it as a number of layers. CO_2 mixes in the atmosphere very well — better than water vapour, for example — and as infrared is emitted from the Earth's surface and moves up through the atmosphere, it encounters CO_2 under a range of conditions at each level. Carbon dioxide just keeps on merrily absorbing at the altitudes you reach long after you've left water vapour behind.

All this burning of coal that people like his clients were going in for, Callendar estimated, had elevated CO_2 by 10% since 1900. He calculated that this had contributed a 0.25°C rise in temperature over the same period. From his assumptions, it followed that a doubling of CO_2 would increase temperature by 2°C.

Wouldn't that be marvellous? he asked the sceptical gents at the Met Office. Imagine how much nicer the world, and London in particular, would be if it were a couple of degrees warmer of a winter. Away with the threat of another ice age, for starters!

Callendar's work put to bed the Angstrom objection, and the similar contention — still trotted out today in Sceptic circles — that there was a point at which the infrared absorption bands for CO_2 would be saturated (sometimes likened to painting a window black: the first coat makes the window nearly opaque, and slapping on more paint has a comparatively less significant effect). But not everyone shared Callendar's pleasure at the prospect of CO_2-induced warming, which for a time was known as the Callendar Effect in his honour.

Now that CO_2 was back on the list of things to worry about, other scientists began asking themselves Arrhenius's and Callendar's question all over again. How, and by how much, did CO_2 affect temp-erature? It wasn't quite universally accepted that Milankovic's cycles of orbital eccentricity were the cause of the ice ages, but it was pretty much universally accepted that the role of CO_2 and water vapour was to act as 'feedbacks' — of reinforcement and amplification — rather than the cause of major climate shifts. From the 1950s, a whole series of primitive models were constructed to try to explain how climate worked and to assign values to the effects of the greenhouse gases. But little headway was made until American Gilbert Plass, tinkering with the problem after work at his job developing guidance systems for heat-seeking missiles, developed one of the very first computer-based, as opposed to graphically based (sometimes called 'hand-waving'), models of the climate.

Subsequent work built on his pioneering efforts. In 1957, Drs Revelle and Suess (not Seuss, the *Lorax* man) published a paper on the exchange of CO_2 between the atmosphere and the ocean, and provided the first estimates of the amount of carbon stored in the atmosphere, oceans, biosphere and lithosphere respectively. A more sophisticated understanding of oceanic circulation came next, growing throughout the 1960s.

Just how badly climate science needed a computer model that took into account all of these new-found complexities was thrown into sharp relief in 1963, when American scientist Fritz Möller used a similar model to Gilbert Plass's and similar assumptions to Arrhenius's about the way a CO_2-induced warming might trigger increased evaporation and a water vapour feedback, and found that — whoops! — doubling the CO_2 concentration would fill the atmosphere with steam and raise the temperature by 10°C. This result was so preposterous that it precipitated the building of full-scale computer models all over the world to try to take account of all of the processes at work in the climate system.

Trouble was, with all the best will in the information technology world at that time, modellers had neither the computing power nor the several dozen airport hangars needed for the hardware, let alone the quality input data at their disposal to make it fly, even if they could recruit an army of secretaries to enter it all via several hundred metric tonnes of punch cards. Even the Earth's energy budget — solar radiation in as against heat energy out — was known only very approximately, and solely from theoretical calculations.

But as computing power increased, the once-impossible dream of representing the circulation of the atmosphere in three dimensions came closer to being a reality. In 1965, Russian climatologist Mikhail Budyko (and soon afterward, William Sellers at the University of Arizona) built a model that differentiated between climate at different latitudes across the planet. The increased resolution yielded impressive results: at last, a computer program could replicate the present climate — the minimum standard, if their forecasts for the future were to be credible. But the models were still unstable: it didn't seem as though the climate could withstand anything much in the way of a shock before runaway warming or snap cooling ensued. The real climate seemed rather more robust, and the consensus seemed to be that it was clouds — high clouds, low clouds, big fluffy clouds, thin wispy clouds, rainy clouds, clouds ephemeral and impossible to model — that functioned as some kind of stabilising influence in the whole set-up and were the missing parameter in the most sophisticated computer representations of climate.

By the end of the 1970s, detailed, three-dimensional, grid-style models of the Earth's atmosphere, with their plethora of altitude-by-latitude-by-longitude representations of the atmosphere that included a working understanding of the dynamics of vertical convection and of horizontal circulation, were being assembled and run on super-computers. These have come a long way since then, too. As we've seen, at their grandest, these are now coupled with representations of ocean systems as well, just to narrow the gap still further between the way the climate works in reality and how representations work on a computer.

Among the results of modelling announced by the fledgling IPCC in its first report in 1990 was its prediction of a rise in temperature by the year 2100 of 2–3°C above 1990 levels, based on climate sensitivity to CO_2 (that is, the impact on temperature of doubling pre-industrial levels of CO_2) calculated at 2.5°C. The second IPCC report of 1995 stuck with the same sensitivity to CO_2 (namely 2.5°C), and now predicted a temperature rise of between 1 and 3.5°C above 1990 levels by 2100. The third report, in 2001, introduced a range in the sensitivity estimate, expecting an increase of 1.5 to 4.5°C, with a (higher) average of 3°C, for a doubling of pre-industrial CO_2 levels, and forecast a temperature rise of between 1.4 and 5.8°C over 1990 levels by 2100, depending what happened with the world's rate of emissions. The latest (fourth) IPCC report expects the temperature by 2100 to have climbed from 1990 levels by between 1.1 and 6.4°C, depending on whether humankind can cut emissions, or whether the rate at which CO_2 is emitted just keeps on going up. The Fourth Assessment Report estimates a doubling of CO_2 would result in a temperature increase of 2 to 4.5°C, with an average of 3°C.

The range in the estimated value for temperature sensitivity to CO_2 indicates that the IPCC can't be entirely sure what will happen to temperature when atmospheric CO_2 levels reach 560 ppm (double their pre-industrial levels). Let's have a look at the source of this uncertainty.

When positive feedback can be a bad thing

When Svante Arrhenius did his pioneering (and tedious) calculations on the climate effects of increasing carbon dioxide, he started from the belief that there was a simple relationship between the gas (cause) and temperature (effect). He was wrong — luckily, because if he'd been right, we'd have been well on the way to frying by now: as we've seen, the good Swede calculated that doubling his contemporary atmospheric levels (giving a total concentration of 600 ppm) would produce a 5 to 6°C rise in temperature. What he didn't count on — and what John Tyndall didn't count on when he decided that variations in water vapour was the cause of the ice ages — was the interplay between different climate influences. Let's have a look at some of the terms in the equation, the 'feedbacks' that are expected to come into play when atmospheric CO_2 concentrations are increased, that complicate calculations of climate sensitivity to CO_2.

Positive feedbacks

▷ Water — a rise in atmospheric temperature leads to greater evaporation of water, and since water vapour is a

Anecdotal Evidence of Climate Shift

Icing Up In February 2007, at the height of the Antarctic summer, we travelled to the Ross Sea and found the re-freeze in full swing. An expanse of beautiful 'pancake ice' (where a sheet of new ice has been fractured by a swell, that causes each plate to butt up against its neighbours, giving it those rounded edges) has formed between the vessel and the glorious ice cliffs of the Ross Ice Shelf several kilometres distant. Sea ice prevented us from reaching McMurdo Base through the shipping channel, which is usually ice-free at this time of year. So how does an anomalous sea ice year such as this square with the notion of 'global warming'? Well, although such phenomena as an apparently colder Ross Sea are seized upon by Sceptics, they can actually support the theory of anthropogenic global warming. It's a complex nexus of winds and currents that determines when and how completely the Ross Sea pack breaks up and empties. Changes in those winds and currents may well be an indicator of change in regional sea and weather patterns attributable to change in the global climate. That said, while some areas of the Antarctic continent have experienced pronounced warming, there has been little effect obvious in sea ice extent since satellite measurement began in 1978, as the graph overleaf indicates.

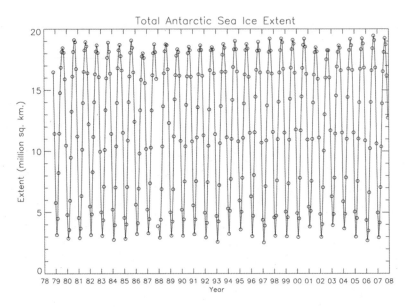

Total Antarctic Sea Ice Extent

Source: Total Antarctic sea ice extent, 1978–2006. Image courtesy of the National Snow and Ice Data Center, University of Colorado, Boulder, CO.

Beetle Bomb   We thought the swathes of browned-off foliage we kept seeing in Douglas fir plantations as we motorcycled north on the highway in British Columbia were due to forest fires or disease. Then we learned a little six-legged, quarter-inch-long bug is to blame. The pine beetle has been feeding on small patches of trees in this part of the world for thousands of years. But traditionally, the several weeks of intense cold at the pit of winter kept the bugs in check. Occasionally, a string of warm winters will allow the beetles to get the upper hand and expand their range. But the devastation now taking place is unprecedented, at least in human memory — the voracious feeding cycle that used to play itself out after three or four years has now gone on for 18. The area affected by the pine beetle has increased by 30% over the last 30 years — both northward and to higher elevations, and the infestation in British Columbia is supposed to have destroyed $6 billion worth of forest.

Reality Bites The pine beetle is not the only pesky critter making its way northward in North America. Several plant species, notably willows, are invading the tundra and encroaching on waterways formerly too cold for them.

When everything freezes up, moose are adapted to stripping the bark and small branches off trees, so where the willows go, the moose follows. Over the last 15 years, biologists surveying the northern Richardson Mountains and their adjacent coastal plain have found moose numbers have increased by 67%. It seems the point at which trees meet the zone formerly covered by the grass and moss of the tundra is moving northward. Meanwhile, Alaska's mosquitoes, so big they're often referred to as the state bird, have spread north to irritate the few residents who used to escape their attentions — as we found out when we motorcycled up to the Beaufort Sea along the Alaskan pipeline (to the right in the shot), itself under threat as the permafrost upon which its supports are built melts and causes the pipe to buckle.

Buckle Up — This is Going to be Some Ride Over the last 30 years, the temperature in Alaska has risen about 4°C. This has given rise to some interesting changes in lifestyle. Residents living from Fairbanks north now commonly yawn, stretch and wander outside to give a few pumps on the handle of the hydraulic jacks that keep their houses from slouching and buckling as the ground beneath their foundations softens up. Permafrost, they say, is no longer permanent. Forests in the far north appear to be sinking or drowning as melting permafrost forces water up. Alaskans have taken to calling the phenomenon 'drunken trees'. The 1200-kilometre Trans-Alaska Pipeline (above) is also feeling the impact. Concern that melting permafrost will destabilise the 640 km of pipeline that is

suspended above the ground (ironically so that the warm oil flowing through it wouldn't melt the permafrost) has meant the construction of new supports, some fastened deeper than 20 m underground.

Anyone for Desert?   On a recent motorcycling trip through Africa, we were able to observe the process of desertification at first hand. The picture above is the southern Sahara in Darfur, South Sudan, once rolling grassland and now . . . not. Desertification is commonly caused by poor agricultural methods in fragile near-desert areas (such as the savannah or grassland at the margins of the Sahara). Irrigation accelerates salination (as trace minerals in irrigation water build up as water is spread and evaporates). Overgrazing, deforestation, and over-cultivation don't help, either, and they're nowhere more obvious than in Africa. Fossil records confirm that the Sahara has alternated between savannah and desert through the ages. Studies also show that, prehistorically, the advance and retreat of deserts — including in Darfur — has tracked annual rainfall, whereas desertification has arisen alongside, and presumably due to, human activities as listed above. Since the 1930s, the deserts of Sudan have expanded almost

200 km southward. The impact on the growing population of nomadic herdsmen is obvious — the search for adequate grazing for their herds has become a lot harder. There are 135 million animals in Darfur now compared to the long-term average of 27 million. In no small part, the story of the recent conflict in Darfur between rival ethnic groups and tribes is sourced from the tension arising from competition for water and grazing. As desertification advances, rainfall decreases and a vicious spiral is established. Not that Africa is the only continent with this problem. As we rode across China we passed whole cities that are being excavated from the desert, and we saw plenty of examples where efforts are being made to hold the desert at bay on modern cities and brand-new highways (right), all under threat from the expanding Taklamakan and Gobi deserts.

Slow Drip to No Drip Speleotherms (stalagmites and stalactites) we photographed in the Carlsbad Caves in New Mexico (below), which have ceased to grow because the water that used to leach through from the ground above has dried up. The caves are in a state of suspended animation, until such a time as the desertification of the land above reverses and the rains come again. Quite close by are several of the sites associated with the Pueblo Indian civilisation. They flourished during the period commonly known as the Mediaeval Warm Period (between roughly AD 900 and 1100), building comparatively permanent settlements in cities hewn from mesas, before a sustained drought seems to have forced them to abandon these areas. Other North American cultures collapsed around the same time.

High and Dry If anyone doubts that human beings can influence local and regional climate and quickly, they need look no further than the Aral Sea, where we found fishing boats parked near the wharf on the former shores of the Aral Sea, 200 km from the nearest significant body of water. From the 1930s, the former Soviet Union built large-scale canals to divert water to vast cotton fields in a grand plan to make cotton a great export earner. The water was sourced from the Syr Darya and the Amu Darya rivers that used to feed the (then) world's fourth largest lake (the Aral was 10% larger than Lake Michigan). The project was successful — the canal-fed cotton fields boosted Soviet cotton production by an impressive 70% between 1960 and 1980. But all the canals were built on the cheap, most were never lined and consequently between 35 and 70% of the water from the river system is lost to evaporation and seepage. By 1990, as a result of the continuing water loss, the shrinking Aral divided in two and its salinity increased threefold. The once-thriving fishing industry was destroyed along with the fish and most of the flora and fauna that depended on the Aral. Of the region's 73 species of birds, 70 of mammals and 24 of fish, most have either perished or moved on. The Aral is thought to have mitigated cold winds blowing from Siberia and to have reduced the heat in summer. Now winters have become harsher and longer, summers hotter and shorter. The drying off of the Aral Sea is also believed to have contributed to the increasing degradation of the glaciers of the Himalayas, Pamir, Tien-Shan, and Altay, which feed the Syr Darya and Amu Darya. More dust on glacier surfaces and the mineralisation of precipitation has led to intensive melting of glaciers. At present, 1081 glaciers have disappeared in the Pamir-Altay area, 71 glaciers in the Zaili Alatau area, and the volume of glaciers in Akshirak has been sharply reduced. Oops! It's that law of unintended consequences again!

Anyone's Guess In Dawson City, Yukon, they've run an annual competition since 1896 to guess the date of the melt of the river. It's measured by fastening a tripod on the frozen river. A wire is connected to the tripod and is run to a clock secure in a box and firmly mounted

Time of the Annual Melt, Yukon River

(Number of days after start of April)

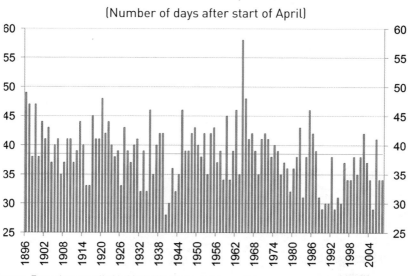

Source: From data supplied by Judy Westberg and Joyce Caley.

on a wall on the shore. The clock stops when the ice moves the tripod and trips the wire. Over the 113 years that the competition has run, the melt date has been 38.5 days from the start of April, so either on May 8th or 9th. But as the graph above illustrates, over the 22 years since 1987 it has only been later than that time twice. This squares with anecdotal evidence from elsewhere in Alaska that the onset and duration of the seasons is changing, with shorter, milder winters and longer, warmer summers. This prompted a little town by the name of Kivalina, well north of the Yukon, to file a lawsuit against several energy companies, including Exxon Mobil, under the same legal principles that have enabled smokers to sue tobacco companies. The case is ongoing.

Tipping Your Cap A shady customer revs her motorbike away from the tongue of a glacier in Iceland. Vatnajökull is the largest ice cap in Iceland and around one kilometre thick in parts. Vatnajökull was growing up until the 1930s, but of late has been shrinking by around five cubic kilometres per year. This is a turbocharged

version of ice loss due to warming. As the ice disappears, it relieves the pressure exerted on the crust deep under the ice sheet, increasing the rate at which the lurking volcanoes there convert rock to magma. An average of 140,000 cubic metres of magma has been produced every decade since 1890, a 10% increase on the usual rate. And the more magma, the faster the ice loss, and the more magma. It's a little-known and fascinating effect of ice loss. It makes you wonder what unforeseen effects there might be as the Earth loses ice.

Long Range

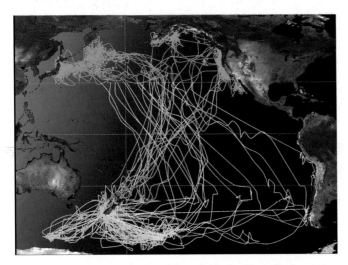

Reproduced by permission of Scott A. Shaffer. From Shaffer et al (2006). 'Migratory shearwaters integrate oceanic resources across the Pacific Ocean in an endless summer.' *Proceedings of the National Academy of Science*, 103, 12799–12802. © 2006, National Academy of Science.

Sooty shearwaters were our constant companion en route from Bluff to the Ross Sea. Amazingly, these birds range between the sub-Antarctic islands south of New Zealand where they breed and the Aleutian Islands in the Bering Sea where they spend the southern hemisphere winter. The tracks of 19 individual birds originating from colonies in New Zealand fitted with transmitters are shown on their annual migration. Their flights during the breeding season are coloured blue. Their migration paths are yellow, arcing right across the Pacific, presumably following food. Their northern holiday flight paths are shown in orange, and their return tracks in green. In all, they travel more than 70,000 km each year in pursuit of an endless summer — the longest known migration of any species. Shearwater numbers are falling, with most colonies experiencing a 40% drop. This is attributed to the reduced supply of food as warming of the oceans results in reduced mixing with the colder, nutrient-rich waters from the depths. This, in turn, limits the growth of plankton and everything that feeds upon it. Such are the subtle, yet profound, effects of warming.

greenhouse gas, the increase in atmospheric water vapour enhances the heat-absorbing properties of the lower atmosphere.

▷ Stored greenhouse gases — as the oceans warm, they absorb less CO_2 (which has a similar net effect to the oceans *emitting* the gas). Atmospheric warming alters wind patterns and the associated ocean current systems. In the Southern Ocean, the southward migration of strong westerly winds enhances upwelling of CO_2-rich deep water (and changes in oceanic currents likely play a part in accelerating the collapse of ice shelves). While not strictly a climate effect, the acidification of the oceans that accompanies an increase in dissolved CO_2 impairs the ability of shell-building creatures to do their thing, further reducing the potential of the oceans to absorb CO_2. At a certain point, the oceans may even begin to release the CO_2 they store into the atmosphere. Similarly, as the permafrost thaws, it releases the vast stores of methane from the decay of deep-frozen plant material. As the deep oceans warm, the 'clathrates' — strange, jelly-like structures in the seabed — release still more methane.

▷ Albedo — reduces as ice loss accelerates due to warming, exposing surface area that previously reflected incoming radiation, so that it absorbs it instead.

▷ Tropical rainforests switching from being a net CO_2 sink to a net source — as tree growth is retarded by higher temperatures they absorb less CO_2 and, meanwhile, the decay of plant material on the forest floor accelerates, emitting more methane.

▷ Warming of the land increases the risk of forest fires and desertification, which has a complex effect. The loss of vegetation reduces the potential of the land area affected to act as a carbon sink, although desert surfaces have a higher albedo than forests, slightly offsetting the positive effect.

Positive or negative feedbacks

▷ Increasing cloud cover is both positive and negative depending on where the clouds are and what type they are. Dick Lindzen's iris hypothesis (described in Chapter 5) supposed that high, cirrus clouds are heat-retaining, whereas low clouds are sunlight-reflecting, but the post-9/11 experience, where the skies were cleared of both aircraft and their cirrus-like contrails, tended to suggest that the albedo effect of cirrus dominates, too.

Negative feedbacks

▷ Water again — as we saw in the previous chapter, it's proposed that there are several ways in which water can act as a negative driver of climate. As water vapour rises to altitudes of lower pressure, it condenses, releasing latent heat at a higher point in the atmosphere, where it has a greater chance of escaping to space. Some water vapour is removed from the atmosphere as rain; some forms ice crystals around aerosols and constitutes radiation-reflecting clouds (i.e., increasing albedo). Or, if increased precipitation reduces high-level cloud cover, this allows greater amounts of heat to escape to space.

▷ Aerosols — naturally injected into the atmosphere by volcanoes, or unnaturally by 'the human volcano'; in either case reflecting incoming solar radiation and causing global 'dimming'.

▷ Oceans — absorb and redistribute heat, sequestering it in the deeps and hence at least delaying any impact of greater CO_2 concentrations on atmospheric temperature.

▷ Biological sinks — terrestrial plants and marine algae absorb CO_2, so as its concentration rises in the atmosphere, the growth rate of photosynthesising plants and algae increases, more effectively removing CO_2 from the atmosphere and sequestering or locking it up in living and dead tissue. Similarly, marine organisms building shells from carbonate remove dissolved carbon from the oceans and sequester it.

Of course, none of these effects can be measured through observation, as none of them will have come to pass until the conditions are there — that is, when the Earth has *already* warmed by a couple of degrees, whereupon any debate over further effects will likely have become academic, too. So the argument over what the net effect of feedbacks is necessarily takes place on a theoretical level. Calculating climate sensitivity to CO_2 is at the cutting edge of contemporary climate science, and the single most useful tool in performing those calculations is the much-maligned climate model.

Let's have a look at what the climate models are, what they're saying about feedbacks, and why.

Model, model on the wall . . .

Climate models are just big computer programs. They're big primarily because they tend to divide the atmosphere up into myriad latitude-by-longitude-by-altitude grid boxes and replicate the gaseous composition of each box, allowing for a number of different layers to represent the heterogeneous zones of the atmosphere. The properties of each box — with respect to the physical processes of radiative transfer, conservation of momentum, mass, energy, water mass (including state changes from ice to water to gas), gas laws, and surface exchange processes — can be deduced using the same basic equations that Jozef Stefan used over a century ago.

By adding effects for the dynamic of convection (yielding an atmospheric circulation model), and in some cases coupling this atmospheric circulation model to an analogous, three-dimensional model of ocean circulation (producing an AOGCM), a coarse replication of the present-day climate can be made.

To see feedback mechanisms at work, models are subjected to shocks, or the model is told to treat a given feedback as constant, the better to see the effect of the others. Such are the internal mechanisms of models that they can work out without being told what water vapour's going to do, what effect more methane will have, what a loss of sea ice means for albedo and temperature, and so on, all based on physical and chemical first principles. That is, calculations of feedbacks are part of what comes out the other end of a modelling experiment, rather than anything the person running the experiment plugs in. In other words, if you assume that a model is a computer representation of our aggregate knowledge of the scientific principles involved in the climate system, the feedbacks they develop for themselves as they process the data that are fed in are realistic estimations of the real-world feedback mechanisms that will occur, based on the state of our knowledge.

The first step in getting a realistic answer is correctly initialising the program — starting the model off on the right foot, as it were, by getting it to represent the present state of the climate with a reasonable degree of accuracy. This work can be — and commonly is — handled by less sophisticated versions of the same models, and Figure iii in the first colour section shows how their representations of the present climate stack up against observations.

Interestingly, the models that produced these results do not allow for the contribution of ice sheets or the biosphere to climate. Still, at a casual glance, using a visual 'goodness-of-fit' criterion, the modelled results appear pretty plausible compared to the observed data. (Be warned, however, that goodness-of-fit tests are notorious for their circularity — the very data on which the model is being tested are the data that were used to set up the model in the first place. This is what we were discussing at the end of Chapter 2.)

Figure iv (also from the IPCC WG1 report, 2007) in the first colour section compares the annual mean precipitation as observed (a) with the average from a range of simulations produced by different climate models (b). Again on a casual, first-glance, visual goodness-of-fit basis (and with the same proviso), the results align plausibly.

Not, of course, that all models give the same results, or even that the same model will give the same results every time if parameters are changed. These figures show the averaged results of a number of model simulations by a number of different models. And differences don't just arise between models of full-scale complexity on the one hand and simple versions on the other: even full-scale, deluxe models, with everything that opens and shuts on the ocean-atmospheric coupling front, disagree among themselves.

The main reason for this is the different ways in which they model the various feedbacks, and the different weights they assign to them. That's why the IPCC takes averages or 'the consensus' from a range of models and model iterations. It's merely a reflection of where major uncertainties remain in the state of our knowledge about climate, namely in the scale of the role of feedbacks.

It's interesting to look at how the different models handle them. The averages of the four feedback values the various models derive from scientific first principles are:

▷ water vapour at 1.8 (± 0.18) W/m²/°C (that is, a rise in energy of 1.8 watts per square metre for every °C rise in temperature)

▷ convection at −0.84 (± 0.26) W/m²/°C

▷ surface albedo at 0.26 (± 0.08) W/m²/°C

▷ clouds at 0.69 (± 0.38) W/m²/°C. Note that this fourth value cannot be estimated in the same way as the other three feedbacks — namely by subjecting models to shocks to see what the effect of a given feedback is — because we don't know enough about the physics of clouds. Instead, the cloud feedback must be parameterised, and the figure assigned to cloud effects is an average of the range of values assigned to its clouds, that is, may be responsible for between 0.31 and 1.07 W/m²/°C.

Now let's put these numbers in perspective. In Chapter 4, we noted that the total incoming solar radiation ranges between 1366.5 and 1368.5 W/m² per year — a variation of only 1.8 W/m². But the energy impacts of water vapour above is reckoned to be the equivalent of the entire difference between a cold and a hot year.

Water vapour is the strongest positive feedback included in models, and there's least disagreement in its significance across models. This suggests that the state of knowledge on this factor is quite uniform (although it could be uniformly wrong, of course!). Another large feedback is albedo, and it too is reckoned to be positive — the amount of incoming solar radiation reflected back to space by ice and snow reduces as greenhouse gas concentrations rise, causing warming, causing melting, causing further reduction in albedo (etc.).

The effect of convection is the greatest negative feedback the models envisage from a rise in greenhouse gases. As greenhouse gas concentrations rise, the difference in temperature between the top and the bottom of the troposphere (technically known as the 'lapse rate') reduces, as water vapour carries more heat from lower regions and releases it in the upper, from where it can more readily escape into space.

The second-largest feedback in the models also happens to be the biggest bone of contention, as we saw in the previous chapter: the net climate effect of clouds and cloudiness. We'll have more to say about this shortly.

Another point of difference between different models and between different model runs is the way in which feedbacks interact with one another. Feedbacks are not independent of one another, and can't be considered in isolation from one another. Some can (and do) influence others — so when these models get run to estimate the overall climate sensitivity to a CO_2 doubling, each feedback is arranged in a hierarchy of significance depending on how the interrelations of feedbacks are believed to operate. Consider the two crudest possible approaches to feedbacks. First, if you ignore them altogether, the equation becomes simple, and the models (and even the Sceptics) readily agree that doubling CO$_2$ will produce a rise of 1.1°C. Second, if you simply add the effects of the various feedbacks together, the computers are again in good agreement: doubling CO$_2$ will produce a warming of 2.6°C.

But there's an unhealthy co-dependence at work among feedbacks, and while the IPCC can give us a figure taking a nuanced view of this relationship — doubling CO$_2$ will produce a warming of 3.2°C — the models tend to bicker a bit about it, based mostly on the precise nature of the relationship they presume to operate among the feedbacks.

Figure 34 shows the overall probability when you take the range of answers you get when you ask models the question 'what's likely to happen to temperature when you double CO$_2$?' and graph it.

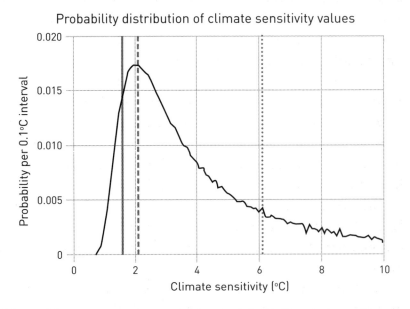

Figure 34. Crisis of confidence: this is what it looks like when you chart what temperature increase the models think we're likely to get from doubling atmospheric CO$_2$. Most of them think we'll get something to the order of 2.5 degrees Celsius. Very few of them think we'll get anything less, and a worrying proportion of them think it could go way, way higher.

Source: Gregory et al (2002),
http://www.gfdl.gov/reference/bibliography/2002/jmgregory0201.pdf

The 'consensus' of the models is clear to see. So, too, is the slim hope they hold out that we'll get away with less than 2°C warming from a doubling of CO_2 — and the worrying lack of confidence with which you'd be able to predict a much higher temperature rise.

So can these models be trusted? Well, compelling work on the radiative balance of the Earth — the amount of radiation incident from the sun, compared with the amount of outgoing radiation — tends to support the results yielded by the models, and can be verified by cross-checking with measurements of ocean and surface temperatures. These analyses are consistent with the modelled finding that temperature sensitivity to CO_2 will lie between 1.5°C and 6°C. Calculating water vapour feedbacks alone — which can be done by studying the effect on temperatures in the wake of volcanic eruptions, which inject aerosols into the upper atmosphere, 'seeding' precipitation and having a temporary drying effect on the atmosphere — has indicated that the chances of getting away with a rise of less than 1.5°C from a doubling of CO_2 are vanishingly small.[2]

The clouds in our eyes

It's about time we heard from the Sceptics. Many — that might even be most — Sceptics are allergic to any talk of models being useful to climate science. But there are some exceptions, notably American-born Israeli astrophysicist Nir Shaviv, whose correlations of cloud cover and cosmic ray flux we came across in the last chapter. Shaviv has much to say in praise of global circulation models (GCMs):

> Global circulation models are very powerful tools. Because in principle all the different aspects of the simulations can be controlled and studied, they can serve as detailed 'climate laboratories', and thus have notable advantages. Specifically,
>
> • GCMs can be used to analyze the effect of different components in the climate system. For example, one can

separate the behavior of different feedbacks (e.g., water vapour, ice, etc.).

- GCMs can be used to estimate the effects of different types of forcing. This is because different geographic distribution of forcings can in principle cause different regional variations and in principle even different global temperature variations (even if the net change to the radiative budget is the same!).[3]

But Shaviv also identifies what he calls the 'Achilles' heel' of GCMs in producing meaningful estimates of future temperature trends, and it's no surprise, given what we were discussing in the previous chapter, that this has to do with clouds. Clouds, he argues, are too tricky to build into the models, as they change minute-by-minute and across spaces of a matter of a few kilometres — beneath the resolution threshold, then, for climate models. That may soon change, as the ever-industrious Japanese have embarked on a programme to build a model with a surface grid size of one kilometre by one kilometre, precisely to deal with this problem. Trouble is, even if they had the computing grunt at their disposal to run it, they'd need a coal-fired electricity plant dedicated to powering it!

Even 30 years' worth of satellite observations haven't helped much, since not only do satellites have trouble sorting out what kinds of cloud they're looking at, they can't see through high cloud to work out what kind of cloud is hanging about beneath it. Since the behaviour of clouds isn't known well enough to be built into models in the way that other feedbacks are, they have to be 'parameterised' (that is, an estimate made of the significance of their effect, and this value 'fed in'). The output of the model (or that particular iteration of the model) is therefore at the mercy of whichever cloud 'recipe' the modeller chooses. This is why, Shaviv argues, model results can vary by as much as a factor of three and are next to worthless. It must be the clouds in our eyes.

The IPCC acknowledges that there is considerable uncertainty around its figure of 0.69 W/m²/°C for cloud effects — which is the average of the values used in the models considered in the 2007 IPCC report — but insists that it is not so great as Shaviv claims.

What does this mean? It casts doubt on the IPCC's gloomy estimates of climate sensitivity. And if further evidence were to emerge (perhaps following the work of Svensmark, as outlined in the previous chapter) that shed further light on the climate effect of clouds and found them to be a significant negative feedback, then it could be that the models would produce different and more reassuring results. But the critical issue here is: what is the significance of this uncertainty, in light of the present state of our knowledge?

Reaching our view on climate sensitivity

Sceptics like Shaviv tend to regard the higher end of the range of predictions that the IPCC produces as next to worthless, as they're the product of calculations performed by models that are fatally ill-informed about the effect of clouds. Better, they argue, to stick to what the observations suggest is the sensitivity of temperature to CO_2. Data such as those produced by Gregory et al. (2002)point to a temperature rise of around 1 to 1.5°C if pre-industrial CO_2 levels are doubled.[4] This is very low, and to be correct, it would need the IPCC to have erred on the high side with the feedbacks other than clouds, or to have mistaken clouds for a net positive feedback when their net effect is really negative. There's pretty good observational support for the calculations of the other feedbacks (and the models construct their own estimates from first principles), so it seems the matter rests with clouds.

There are a number of reasons why the Sceptics' low, low estimate of sensitivity seems Pollyanna-ish, to put it mildly, and why it appears they're pushing the uncertainty over cloud effects too far.

First, atmospheric CO_2 is already a mere 38% higher than pre-industrial levels and yet global average temperatures have risen by around 0.8°C, with a further 0.6°C in the pipeline as the oceans release their latent heat, if the energy budget stuff is to be believed. That's a total of 1.4°C, so the Sceptics are asking us to believe that depositing the remaining 62% of the increase of CO_2 over pre-industrial levels will result in a temperature rise of just 0.1°C.

Clouds might achieve a partial cancellation of other combined feedbacks, but based on our present understanding of cloud behaviour, it seems it's unlikely it will significantly offset them. If the effect of clouds were assumed at zero, then the sensitivity of temperature to a doubling of CO_2 would reduce from 3.2 to 1.9°C.

Third, like it or not, models are the best tool to evaluate climate effects. Observations of cloud behaviour are still too 'noisy' for us to be certain about the signal they're sending, so models are the only useful means of evaluating cloud effects that we currently have, and a degree of confidence in their performance can be gleaned from the limited observational support they enjoy. There's no known model that uses a strong negative feedback value for clouds and a low climate sensitivity to CO_2 that's capable of simulating twentieth-century climate movements and the present state of the climate. On the other hand, models that use a negligible value for cloud feedbacks and a high CO_2 sensitivity can track the climate past and present with a fair degree of accuracy. This doesn't mean cloud feedbacks are *necessarily* positive, but on the strength of modelling results, the estimate used in IPCC modelling commands more respect than mere speculation that cloud effects 'may be negative'.

Fourth, there seems to be no way of squaring the notion of a strong negative cloud feedback (so strong it cancels out other feedbacks or even offsets some degree of radiative forcing) with the observationally verified imbalance in the Earth's radiation budget. If clouds do indeed cancel all other feedbacks, or even cancel some of the greenhouse gas radiative warming, then we have a problem with the way we have used observations to affirm our calculations of basic energy balance. Even allowing for uncertainties in the various measurements in calculations, the chances that clouds can have an effect of this magnitude are less than 10%.

In short, then, we can be reasonably satisfied with the IPCC's estimates of climate sensitivity. It could be that doubling pre-industrial

CO_2 levels may only produce a 2°C rise (the 'coolest' model in the IPCC's 2007 Assessment Report suite of models has about 2.1°C as climate sensitivity). On the other hand, a few of the 'warmer' models lead us to expect a sensitivity of 4.4°C. There's no way at present of determining whether the 'coolest' model is 'better' than the 'warmer' ones. That's simply the uncertainty range, and for the time being we have to live with it.

To claim that climate sensitivity is *much less* than 2°C, then you would need to do one of three things:

(a)   Construct a model that is as competent as the average of the IPCC's models in simulating observed current and past climatic features even though it ran a large negative cloud feedback and low climate sensitivity;

(b)   Find an alternative way of balancing the Earth's energy books (or taking measurements), because they would no longer stack up if climate sensitivity were below 1.5°C; or

(c)   Take the intellectual Fifth Amendment, cop out on the maths, and plead that science knows too little to say anything of value on the matter.

Option (c) appeals to the majority of deniers as the line of least resistance!

How long have we got, Doc?

Let's assume for the moment that the massed chorus of models has got it right, and a doubling of CO_2 will bring about the kind of warming the IPCC forecasts (namely 3°C, or the mean in the range of model results). The range is calculated to indicate how much the Earth would have to warm up before the Earth-atmosphere system re-radiated enough energy to return to equilibrium, following a doubling of CO_2 from pre-industrial levels. It tells us nothing about how long this might take.

Doubling CO_2 concentrations to 560 ppm from their pre-industrial levels of 280 ppm would mean the full equilibrium temperature effect would be a 3°C lift above pre-industrial temperatures. But it's thought that due to inertia in the climate system, only about 70% of the total radiative forcing will be realised by 2100, so that amends the figure to a rise of 2.1°C by that time. Now 0.8°C of that has already occurred, so that leaves a further 1.3°C of warming to eventuate by 2100. That doesn't seem so bad, now, does it?

But a word of caution. Doubling CO_2 concentrations to 560 ppm by 2100 is the IPCC's low-emissions scenario, the result we'll get if we drastically cut the rate at which emissions are growing year by year. A more mid-range scenario has us hitting concentrations of around 800 ppm by 2100, which would yield an equilibrium temperature rise of 4.1°C from pre-industrial times, or 3.3°C above the present. And there's no sign yet that we're getting our emissions under control, or that we're likely to any time soon.

That Proves It — Or Does It?

In the panel 'Data Hockey', in the first colour section, we give the Alarmists a hard time about their handling and presentation of data. But it would be wrong to think the Sceptics are immune to this affliction.

Noted Sceptic and respected geologist Bob Carter of Queensland University has subjected the theory (that human activity is leading to dangerous global warming) to five 'tests' against the historical data, and he has found (surprise, surprise) that it fails all five. He claims, paraphrasing Albert Einstein, that failing one test would prove it was wrong. So if it fails all five, human-induced climate change must be a myth, right?

Not only does the Carter quiz get a lot of airtime in the popular press, but it turns out that his method and conclusions are pretty typical of the method and conclusions you'll find scattered throughout sceptical literature, so we thought it would be worth taking a closer look.

Test 1: Is there warming?
If not, then it can hardly be dangerous

Bob Carter points out that temperature hasn't risen since 1998, which is true but largely irrelevant in the study of climate, which tends to have regard for longer-term trends (and intervals of 30 years are conventional). So Carter argues that even over the last 28 years, the trend is only slight and has been centred in the northern hemisphere, so can hardly be considered 'global'. The observations are true. Such warming as there has been has been more pronounced in the northern hemisphere than in the south, but the theory allows for this, given that it is predicted the Arctic will warm faster than other regions. And the trend over the last 28 years has been slight. But the significance of this finding is doubtful, because the issue is what has caused that warming. Just because observed warming over a single 28-year period hasn't been rapid isn't necessarily any grounds to breathe a sigh of relief, if the causes of that warming aren't known (or can be explained by anthropogenic global warming). All you can claim is that warming is not dangerous — yet. It's not the same as saying there has been no warming. And it's not the same as saying warming won't be dangerous in the future. The professor's test is a straw man.

Test 2: Is temperature outside the range of natural variation?

Here Carter is on firmer ground when he answers in the negative. We have seen that it cannot really be claimed that we have exceeded the bounds even of recent (the last 2000 years) natural variation. But again, this finding is irrelevant. If there has been warming, we need to know what has caused it. Merely to point out that nature is capable of delivering climatic changes of a given magnitude is not the same as saying that nature *has* delivered this one.

Test 3: Does CO$_2$ output correlate with temperature change?

You can't argue that there's a strong correlation between global average temperature curves and CO$_2$, as we've seen. But there are good reasons for this. CO$_2$ is a bit player in a grand opera of feedbacks and amplifying (and mitigating) mechanisms, so to look for a simple, direct, linear correlation is to misrepresent the science of how climate works. There's also the matter of the time lag between climate forcing and observed warming, brought about by the capacity of the oceans to absorb excess energy and to release it slowly over time. It's for these reasons that climate scientists look at the multi-decadal trend rather than at year-by-year variation.

Test 4: Does CO$_2$ lead or lag temperature?

Historically, temperature rises have always preceded rises in atmospheric concentrations of CO$_2$: granted. But surely Carter doesn't expect us to accept that, because of this, it necessarily follows that rising CO$_2$ cannot cause and therefore precede temperature rise? All of our paleoclimate records relate to the way nature works. By its very definition, anthropogenic global warming describes an unnatural act. So more than a simple error in logic would be needed to show that CO$_2$ cannot cause a rise in temperature.

Test 5: The 'fingerprint' expected from anthropogenic global warming does not exist

This is perhaps the strongest of the five proofs, and that isn't saying a great deal. Climate modelling has long predicted that warming will occur faster in the northern hemisphere than in the south, fastest of all in the Arctic and over the Antarctic Peninsula, and that the troposphere over the tropics will warm faster than other regions in the atmosphere. The last is contestable (see page 148) as the only evidence of prodigal tropical tropospheric warming relies upon data acquired measuring a second-order effect of temperature. This hasn't been corroborated by satellite or other measurement techniques — yet. But such evidence as has been emerging from other sources tends to support rather than contradict this prediction (and the thermal wind analysis). Rather than concede this point, it's more a question of watching this space.

Standing the test

In summary, the barrage of the five Carter 'tests' is really a very poorly constructed 'weight of evidence' audit of the historical evidence for anthropogenic global warming. Carter claims that if the theory fails just one of these tests, then it is false. But the whole exercise has been undertaken on the quite false presumption that if it hasn't shown up by now, then it doesn't exist. And each of the tests has been carefully tailored to ensure that on the present state of the data, the theory will fail. Another classic example of 'straw man testing'.

The major concern that arises from Carter's five tests is that they have gone unchallenged by his colleagues on the sceptical side. If anything resembling a peer review process existed among climate sceptics, you'd expect the lightweight Carter tests to have been disowned and their author admonished for bringing serious scepticism into disrepute.

Chapter 7

The Overheated Debate

Doubt it

Scientists are comfortable with uncertainty.

The very basis of the scientific method is radical doubt — doubt your assumptions, your methods, your findings, everything, until you've repeated the experiment so often and it has produced such consistent results that you can chalk your theory up as valid (or at least, not invalidated) and move on to something else. And even then, you must always entertain the possibility that new techniques will yield new data that will show your theory to be inadequate. If enough of that kind of anomalous data comes along, it's time you got a new theory.

What's more, and more disconcertingly, the observed universe and the universe as it exists independent of our observations are an imperfect match. After all, matter — the stuff the universe is made of — is in a constant state of flux, and the very act of measuring it introduces uncertainty. The more accurately we can know the position of a sub-atomic particle, for example, the less we can know how fast or in what direction it's moving.

Scientists are cool with all that.

Just because in the world of science nothing can ever be said to have been proven, to be known 'for certain', doesn't mean you can't claim to have a pretty good working knowledge of things.

That's good enough for the rest of us most of the time, too. The science behind the transmission of television signals is not fully understood — there's still the chance that some property of electromagnetic radiation will be discovered that will radically change the way we understand it — but that doesn't stop us expecting to see a picture when we sit down and press a button on the remote.

Indeed, sometimes discoveries are made that make it seem downright miraculous that we got anything done on the basis of our previous understanding. There's a cute story about the great Austrian philosopher Ludwig Wittgenstein, who was out walking with a student one day. The student was holding forth on how absurd it was that humankind had ever imagined that the sun orbited the Earth.

'Quite,' Herr Professor is said to have replied. 'But I wonder what it would have looked like if the sun *did* orbit the Earth?'

Prior to the 1400s, the prevailing, settled view of the universe was that the Earth lay at its centre and the rest of the heavenly bodies, including the sun, circled around it. That was the theory, and it squared with casual observation, too. It wasn't until Galileo used his brand-new telescope to make more detailed observations of the movements of sun, moon and stars that an alternative possibility emerged. The new theory, which eventually gained universal acceptance, held that the Earth and the rest of the planets orbited the sun, and that far from being part of the terrestrial system, the stars were remote and aloof from us. Curiously, casual observation couldn't tell the difference. The sun still rose and set. The stars still wheeled across the night sky.

Of course, that was a triumph of the new-born scientific method over superstition, wasn't it? That kind of sea change in our world view can't happen these days, can it, when most of our knowledge is the product of three or four centuries' worth of scientific scrutiny, and scientists know just about everything there is to know about the universe?

This hubris has been common to every generation of scientists, including those whose entire theoretical framework was turned on its head by new discoveries.

In short, then, certainty is impossible. The most we can hope for is that our level of uncertainty is quantifiable, and that it is not so great that it renders our information useless for the purposes of decision-making. And according to the 'precautionary principle' — assuming you think it's a good idea: not everyone does — 'where there are threats of harm or irreversible damage, lack of full scientific certainty shall not be used as a reason for postponing cost-effective measures to prevent environmental degradation'.

So where are we with anthropogenic global warming? Given how high the stakes in this debate are, how far short of 'full scientific certainty' do we fall?

The stakes

While it's not part of the scope of this book to canvass possible policy responses to climate change, it's timely to remind ourselves how high the stakes in fact are.

Virtually the entire standard of living we in the West enjoy is based on the so-called 'carbon economy' — the production of energy from fossil fuels. If we consider it to be imperative to wean ourselves off fossil carbon, then it is likely we must resign ourselves to a drop in our standard of living, at least while new technologies, infrastructure and public consciousness are installed. Of course, this is a cost that must be gauged against the likely costs of *not* weaning ourselves off fossil carbon: there has already been an attempt to do this, namely the so-called 'Stern Review on the Economics of Climate Change', commissioned by the British government and published in October 2006, but both costs and benefits change daily as new information becomes available.

Since one of the more popular (among policy-makers, at least) methods of creating an incentive to reduce fossil fuel dependency is some form of tax on greenhouse gas emissions, many — if not most — economic activities will incur an extra cost. This will ultimately be borne by the consumer. Similarly, technologies to reduce greenhouse emissions will be expensive to introduce, and the cost of implementing these will likewise finish up hitting the consumer.

And that's supposing those technologies exist and can be deployed immediately. We presently have no universally acceptable alternative to fossil fuels as an energy source. 'Distributed' energy systems (where each household or business is responsible for generating some of its own energy needs, with photovoltaic or micro wind generators, for example) look promising, and have made some inroads in countries such as Germany where a long-term subsidy regime encourages their adoption. Large-scale 'peak load' generation remains a problem in the immediate future. Wind and hydro cannot yet altogether replace coal- and gas-fired electricity generation. Both wind and hydro generators are expensive to construct, and their cost must be reckoned not only in dollar terms, but also in terms of their impact upon the environment. Conventional, large-scale hydro dams inundate vast tracts of land; and even their reputation as our saviours from carbon-fuelled ruin can't persuade folk that it would be a good thing to live next door to a wind farm. These days, we have the curious spectacle of environmentalists campaigning against the very installations that on another level they are demanding: build hydro and wind farms to curb our carbon emissions by all means — just not in my backyard.

This paradox is especially true, of course, where the most promising technology to re-emerge as an alternative to coal and gas is concerned. Try getting the most committed climate change activist to accept nuclear power as our friend in need and see how far you get.

Despite the emergence of several speculative technologies to replace fossil fuels in powering transport, none has yet emerged as a viable alternative. So-called hybrid cars still use fossil fuels, although, driven properly, they are more fuel-efficient. Rechargeable, fully electric 'battery electric vehicles', or BEVs, are poised to enter mass production which will bring their very high cost to the car buyer down, but not immediately. BEVs have fewer moving parts and will be more reliable and lower-maintenance than cars powered by traditional internal combustion engines. Battery technologies are likely to improve enormously now that significant demand exists. But the ultimate limitation of BEVs is that they are powered by the electricity grid (or the distributed network of micro-generators) and that means we're back where we were a couple of paragraphs ago. It doesn't matter how clean and green your wheels are if they're drawing power from a grid supplied by coal- or gas-fired generators.

The partial substitution of fossil fuels with biofuels looks good in theory, but in practice the sudden boom in the crops that serve as feedstocks for biofuel production has been responsible for deforestation and even declines in land area devoted to staple food production, causing sharply rising prices. Other, more sustainable biofuel options are promising but are barely out of the laboratory; the holy grail of transport fuels, hydrogen, remains out of reach, because while the engine technology to burn hydrogen as fuel and produce water as waste has been around for years, viable methods of producing, storing and delivering enough hydrogen to anything resembling our existing transport fleets don't exist.

Nor, at the moment or in the foreseeable future, are any of the various techniques for carbon sequestration (capturing carbon from the atmosphere, or trapping it at the smokestack) close to presenting a solution. The injection of CO_2 into the same subterranean reservoirs from which fossil fuels have been drawn has been demonstrated to work (one such facility, at Statoil's North Sea Sleipner West well, has been operating since 1996). The artificial acceleration of the capture of atmospheric CO_2 through the weathering of minerals also looks promising, but it's still in the development stages. And even successful methods of sequestering CO_2 will come at a cost, and that cost will ultimately be borne by you and me.

So a society committed to doing something about reducing carbon emissions must accept major changes, most of which will entail a reduction in the amount of energy it consumes and a concomitant drop in the standard of living of its citizens.

But it's not just a few bucks a week and freedom from the need to (gulp) use public transport for the denizens of the developed world that are at stake. Our standard of living, even in carbon-straitened times, still looks fantastic to inhabitants of the developing world — where China and India are at the head of the queue, and other populous nations crowd in behind — even if we have to catch the odd bus. In the absence of some revolutionary, viable alternative, the path to a similar standard of living for the vast populations of these countries is paved with carbon, and a new round of industrialisation taking off in the developing world will make any lengths we go to in the West — turning the plasma TV off at the wall, fitting compact fluorescent lightbulbs — seem puny.

But on what grounds are we to deny to these emerging nations the same lifestyle that we currently enjoy? There's no moral basis to do so, and there's no practical means to do so, as things stand. Energy-efficient technologies or alternatives to fossil fuels could be made available to them to minimise their carbon footprint, but this would require a total transformation in the way in which intellectual property usually changes hands. Any other course of action is likely to involve confrontation, perhaps even conflict.

So to pose the earlier question again: how sure can we be that these kinds of actions are necessary, and that anthropogenic global warming is not (as you'll occasionally hear) merely a pretext for the implementation of other agendas?

Peer group pressure

There's a whole branch of philosophy devoted to asking (and attempt-ing to answer) the question: 'How do we know the truth when it's staring us in the face?' This line of enquiry goes by the name of 'epistemology'. Humankind has had many answers to the Great Epistemological Question down the years. Once upon a time, the answer was: 'The truth is what your tribal elders tell you.' Then it was: 'The truth is what the Bible says, as interpreted by the Pope.' Later still, it was: 'The truth is the conviction you reach when, with a pure and open heart, you apply the divine gift of reason to the two books in which God has revealed His truth, namely Scripture and Nature.' More recently, it was: 'The truth is unknowable, but approximations of the truth can be arrived at by demonstrating through repeated trials that a theory can make predictions that are borne out by observations.'

In the 1980s, it was briefly fashionable (just one of the fashion disasters of that decade, along with New Wave music, shiny dress suits, beige carpets and smoked glass) to say: 'The truth is whatever you believe it to be, as your interpretation of reality is as valid as anyone else's.'

The answer in the IPCC world is hardly less wacky: 'The truth is whatever is published in a select bunch of peer-reviewed journals.'

Apart from criticising Sceptics' personal credentials — the quality of the institution from which they hold degrees, or (in the case of easy targets such as outspoken British Sceptic the Viscount of Brenchley, Christopher Monckton) the fact that they don't hold relevant degrees at all — Alarmists tend to disparage sceptical arguments on the grounds that they don't appear in 'reputable' journals. Willie Soon's 2007 paper on the environmental effect of carbon dioxide, for example, appeared in a publication called the *Journal of the American Physicians and Surgeons* which, while it is a reputable scientific journal, doesn't make it onto the Alarmists' list of sources of information worth anything more than the paper they're written on.

Why, you may ask (and we did), do Alarmists insist that contributions to the climate change debate appear in 'respectable', which is to say peer-reviewed, journals?

As we've noted, the Earth's climate is among the more complex objects of scientific enquiry you could care to name. As indicated in Chapter 3, determining the present state of the world's climate is not just a matter of averaging out thermometer readings taken from sites distributed evenly around the globe. As we've seen, the climate involves the radiative influences of the sun and the cosmos at large, and the dynamic responses of the atmosphere, the oceans, the biosphere, and the geosphere. Each element is only partially understood; some are considerably better understood than others, and some considerably worse.

Climate science is naturally complex, too. It draws together many different disciplines — physics, chemistry, biology, geology, higher mathematics — and involves a vast array of the sub-disciplines within each. As we noted at the outset, it's a feature of modern science that it is highly specialised, and consequently, you'll never see anyone claiming to be an authority on climate science as a whole (and if you do, you should never trust them with your credit card details or contemplate buying a used car from them). Faced with science emerging from an unfamiliar branch of climate science, even the most well-respected scientists in the IPCC network have little advantage over the interested layperson, except they're likely to have paid more attention in college science classes, and have some experience of the cut-and-thrust, hurly-burly of scientific debate.

If it's not feasible to judge the correctness of a given scientific paper personally, then there must be some gold standard by which to judge a paper's validity. The criterion that is used is whether a paper has stood up to the critical scrutiny of the authors' peers. If an atmospheric chemist sees that an oceanographer's paper has been put through the intellectual wringer by other oceanographers before appearing in the pages of some august journal, s/he will take it more seriously than if it were to appear in a journal that did not insist on this. It's a kind of procedural check on the quality of an argument for those who are not personally equipped to judge the argument's content.

A Jury of One's Peers

During the 1850s, traders on the California goldfields used to submerge nuggets they were offered in a vial of nitric acid, which tends to corrode base metals and leave gold unscathed.

One of the more interesting aspects of the climate change debate is the spotlight it has thrown onto the whole process by which scientific research is validated. Modern science subjects new work to an acid test of its own, immersing it in the highly corrosive critical scrutiny of the authors' peers.

Dubious claims, faulty assumptions or methodology fall
apart; anything that survives the process is presumed to be
the knowledge equivalent of gold, and is allowed to pass into
currency.

So how does peer review work? It occurs principally when
a piece of scientific work is submitted to a journal for
publication. There are squillions of journals out there, with
every minute specialisation within every scientific discipline
having its own publication or publications, avidly read by
practitioners who dream that their work, too, will one day be
read and admired in the *American Journal of Proctology*, for
example, or the *Journal of the Lepidopterists' Society*.
    Some journals are global, and publish short articles (four
to eight pages) interesting, and accessible to, a readership
that isn't necessarily specialist in that field, but which
is nevertheless scientifically literate. Others are global
and publish short articles of interest to practitioners in a
particular, broad field. Some are global and publish long
(between eight and 30 pages) papers in a particular broad
field. Others are global and publish long articles of interest
to specialists in a narrow field. Still other, regional journals
run long, highly specialised papers, and it's in this tier
that much of the fruit of the painstaking research of the
world's scientists sees the light of day. More and more, and
especially in a fast-moving field such as climate science,
scientists get their information by scanning the proceedings
of conferences for papers relevant to their own interests, and
by retrieving data posted on websites by other researchers.
But journals remain the major means by which hypotheses
and experimental results are promulgated by researchers,
not least because of the prestige factor that accrues to
publication therein.
    Most scientists are capable of working out for themselves
which journals are authoritative within their own field. But
they stand as little chance as the next person of making

the same pronouncement on journals in other fields, and after all, not all journals are equal. Some are more highly regarded, prestigious and authoritative than others. Some have become highly regarded, prestigious and authoritative by virtue of having been around for a long time and having been responsible for the publication of important research, and enjoying a large circulation.

The journal *Science* was founded in 1880, its inaugural publication largely funded by Thomas Edison (the American inventor who brought us the lightbulb, the gramophone, and the electric chair). It is published weekly by the American Association for the Advancement of Science, which was founded in 1848. *Nature* was first published in 1869, largely at the instigation of a group of English scientists who were admirers of Charles Darwin. John Tyndall, whose work we have referred to in this book, was one; the great naturalists Thomas Huxley and Joseph Hooker were others.

But long before the science-minded gents of England were settling into their leather armchairs with a snifter and the first number of *Nature*, England already had what has become the oldest surviving scientific journal of them all, *The Philosophical Transactions of the Royal Society*, first published in 1665.

Age is a great winnower. But to enable scientists to sort the wheat from the chaff among the rest, the majority of which are much younger than the leathery old guard, there's a rating system.

The 'Web of Science' was the brainchild of American scientist Eugene Garfield, who began to compile a 'citation index' in 1945. The purpose of this was to enable scientists to see which articles had been cited (referred to) in other works. It was based more or less on the kind of citation index used in law, where 'authority' — decisions made on the same or similar issues in previous cases — is a guiding principle in decision-making.

In 1955, Garfield founded the Institute for Scientific

Information (ISI), which sought to provide rating information on scientific journals as well (and which still exists, albeit as part of the Thomson Reuters media empire).

Key to the indexing enterprise was Garfield's very own invention, the 'impact factor', which assigns a value to the 'impact' a journal has based on the number of times articles published in that journal are cited over a two-year period. One of the curious findings of the ISI when it performed its first analyses was that a very few journals comprise the beating heart of world science. *Nature* and *Science* are high on the list, and top dogs in the earth sciences. This has partly to do with their general appeal — they publish short pieces of wide interest rather than longer, more specialised papers. But if you looked at their prestige today, a large component of it would doubtless be owed to the circular logic of ratings systems: a journal is regarded (and read) as prestigious because it is rated as prestigious, and it is rated as prestigious because it is regarded as prestigious.

Needless to say, computers vastly lightened the workload for the ISI. Journals are rated in the ISI Web of Science not only in terms of 'impact', but also of 'influence, timeliness, peer review [yes or no] and geographic representation'. It's possible for a scientist considering research by a scientist in a different field to get a handle on the quality of that research simply by looking up the journal's rating — or so scientists believe.

Computers have also made it possible not only to see how often work in a given journal has been cited, but also to see how often work by a particular author has been cited (and in what journals they published). Thus, the ISI's Web of Science also provides a method of working out to whom it's worth giving time of day — or so scientists believe.

In the course of writing this book, we became very accustomed to the almost automatic response of our panel of Alarmists to much of the work that we showed them from the Sceptics' side: 'We couldn't find them on Web of Science, and the journal they've published in isn't on our list of reputable, peer-reviewed publications.'

Web of Science appears to be a kind of kingmaker in the field of scientific enquiry. The risk is that the 'scientific community' will pay attention to work emanating from sources that Web of Science endorses (and to authors whom it rates), and will disregard without so much as a hearing work by authors unknown to Web of Science or published in lowly ranked (or unranked) journals. Since the top journals are exclusive indeed — *Science* publishes only 8% of around 12,000 papers it receives annually; *Nature* only 8% of 10,500 — that's an awful lot of work that's slipping down the rankings, if it's finding its way into the respectable end of the ratings market at all. Even some of the regional, highly specialised journals have a rejection rate as high as 70%.

So how does peer review work? We were given a look at the entire process involved in a paper gaining the status of 'valid research', from original submission to ultimate publication in a peer-reviewed journal.

The paper in question was submitted to a prestigious journal (that is, one with a high impact factor) in April 2007. Who knows how long the research took that culminated in the writing of the paper, by 11 authors from three English and one Northern European institutions, in order to reach the stage where they collectively judged it fit for submission. In accordance with the journal's policy, the paper was discussed by staff editors and an editorial board convened electronically, and possible reviewers discussed. The board screened it for originality of research, scientific importance and the level of interest of its findings for 'an interdisciplinary readership'. It was one of the chosen few (only 25% for this journal) that make it through this first pass.

Once the nominated referees had agreed to review it, the paper was sent to three 'peer' reviewers, who were selected for their expertise in the field to which the paper purported to contribute. According to policy, since the paper was taking issue with the findings of another piece of work recently published in the journal, the lead author of that study was also given a right of reply.

Within a couple of months, the journal editors had all relevant comments — one reviewer in favour of publication, one against, one persuadable either way and, predictably, a defensive response from the author of the earlier paper — and were in a position to write to the authors rejecting the work in June 2007.

The letter of rejection offered the lead author the chance to address the reviewers' criticisms and resubmit the paper. The revised paper, now sporting 14 authors, was duly resubmitted, and sent back to the same three reviewers for reconsideration. Their opinions hardly changed, although the fence-sitter first time around hardened his/her attitude in favour of rejection (although this person also remarked that the authors' hypothesis was likely to be correct). The paper was duly declined in January 2008, nearly a year after its first submission.

Somehow the authors found the energy to keep trying, this time submitting to another prestigious (that is, also with a high impact factor) journal. This time, and doubtless with another set of ups and downs in the review process, they were successful, and the paper was accepted, fully 18 months after its initial submission. This was a comparatively simple path to publication. Many authors whose papers are submitted to (and rejected by) top-drawer journals will try their luck with many others before seeing the light of day. Some, inevitably, will not see the light of day at all.

Once published, of course, the work and its conclusions are in the public domain and it is at this point that their review by the authors' peers really begins. The significance and validity of the research and findings will be challenged, questioned, pondered and perhaps even accepted by other researchers. And it's only with this kind of scrutiny and the fullness of time that a contribution to the body of scientific knowledge can be considered to have been made.

That's the peer review process in action. It doubtless serves to weed out much material that doesn't deserve to survive the acid test. But it's the threshold examples that are most troubling in any case, and in the special case of climate science — which seems to have the power to turn kindly, mild-mannered scientists into closed-minded, ranting evangelists — you have to worry how objective the review process can really be. In other words, it would be useful to see an analysis of what kinds of publication bias — if any — exist, and how much research is not admitted into the pool from which conclusions about the climate are ultimately drawn.

Certainly the Sceptics argue that they're forced to publish in pseudo-scientific comics and tabloid rags because they're shut out of the reputable journals — that ever since the climate debate, like hostilities in Iraq, was declared over, any paper presenting a thesis that goes against the IPCC orthodoxy won't get a look-in. It's hard to gauge the truth of such claims, although in the 20-odd years in which climate science has been topping the scientific bill, few examples of quality sceptical research that have evaded any such Alarmist blockade have emerged. In fact, it's hard to point to any. Conversely, despite intense scrutiny by sceptical consumers of the peer-reviewed literature, remarkably few pieces of research have appeared in support of the anthropogenic global warming hypothesis that have subsequently been discredited and shown to have been given an 'easy ride' to respectability by biases in the peer review process. The 'hockey stick' controversy (see 'Data Hockey' panel, in the first colour section) is probably the closest we can point to.

That said, it's still easy to be bothered by the way in

which research is sorted into 'good' science and 'bad' science. Science is supposed to be indomitable, disdainful of authority. Yet the whole ISI project seems to be contrary to this spirit. The Web of Science, the Journal Citation Reports and the 'impact factor' have become a kind of new magisterium. It certainly does nothing to reassure anyone who feels the scientific community is in danger of becoming inbred.

You'll readily see that the peer review system places an enormous amount of power in the hands of the editors of the 'respectable' scientific journals. Rejecting a paper out of hand (that is, without putting it out for review) would be to declare the information it contains to be false dogma, and nothing the author(s) could do will change that status — publishing in a lesser (non-peer-reviewed) journal wouldn't do it, and nor would promulgating its contents in the popular press or on the internet.

Even the selection of peer reviewers is an act of power: sending a paper out to reviewers known to be hostile to the proposition it contains — or indeed, to the author(s) proposing it — could be as effective a means of anathematising it as straightforward rejection. Of course, in a world where scientists strive to be objective, and to assess arguments and evidence purely on their own merits, this kind of thing just couldn't happen. But we're not talking about that world here. We're talking about the small, phenomenally catty world of climate science. In this world, journal editors are the new arbiters of truth; and given the scope and breadth of the policy initiatives poised to be implemented across the world based on the doctrine promulgated in their publications, it's no exaggeration whatsoever to say that they are among the most influential one hundred-odd people alive today.

Climate change Sceptics often suggest that this power is abused. Editors who are converts to the anthropogenic global warming cause, they allege, will give an easier ride to papers that support that cause and, further, it's the capture of the majority of Earth science journals by such editors that accounts for the absence of sceptical opinion in those journals. They simply aren't let in the door.

How seriously you take these claims is probably indexed to whether you regard *The Da Vinci Code* as a work of fiction or non-fiction, how fervently you believe the Apollo lunar landings were staged in a New Mexico warehouse, and how earnestly you're keeping your diary open for Elvis Presley's comeback gig. After all, it's asking you to believe that there's an active conspiracy on the part of a cabal of environmentalist scientific journal editors to suppress science — even good science — that calls the theory of anthropogenic global warming into question.

What's more, the claim is occasionally made that the majority of the world's scientists who are aligned behind the IPCC are there because the theory of global warming is the single best source of funding for scientific research that money-grubbing scientific minds could contrive. And so venal are the majority of the world's scientists that they have joined up simply because they know which side of their bread the butter is.

It's all possible. The truth, as they say, is out there.

Of more concern is just how susceptible to the phenomenon known as 'publication bias' climate science may be. It's been shown in other scientific disciplines with their own caste system of journal classification that much of the information generated in research never sees the light of day because it's excluded from the respectable, peer-reviewed journals. This becomes a problem for what's called 'meta-analysis', the pulling-together of the disparate information in the discipline in order to draw conclusions from the totality of research — precisely the kind of task that climate science sets itself. Comparisons of the kind of findings that can be reached by including data and information from outside the peer-reviewed literature and those that are reached solely by considering published results show that there are significant differences. Of course, the less objective Alarmist would say that there's a difference, all right:

the stuff in the peer-reviewed literature is right and the rest is wrong. But other disciplines find that certain publications prefer data to be presented in a certain way, and the mere failure to meet that expectation can be used as a reason for rejection. This is tantamount to saying that meta-analysis will be deprived of potentially useful data, purely because the authors used the wrong spreadsheeting package.

The rejection rate for papers submitted to the most 'prestigious' of the Earth science journals is high — over 90% for *Science* and *Nature* — and while it declines as you go down the ranks of the journals into less general and more regional publications, there is still the potential for work to slip through the cracks. How can we, or anyone else, be sure that the data upon which the entire edifice of anthropogenic global warming is based is not seriously skewed by a slavish insistence on publication in peer-reviewed journals?

Sceptics also claim that academia is complicit in the attempt to silence dissent from the IPCC orthodoxy. We're aware of a couple of examples where (it's claimed) sceptical academics have received rough treatment from their institutions — being shifted to an inferior office in a far-flung part of the campus, for example — apparently because they were swimming against the global warming tide.

The Alarmist camp is not above indulging in conspiracy theories, either. One nice example is the explanation for the embarrassing announcement in the 1970s in populist publications such as *Newsweek* and *Time* that a body of scientific opinion saw the Earth staring down the barrel of a period of pronounced cooling, perhaps even portending the onset of the next ice age. Alarmists are fond of pointing out (and have assembled an impressive body of evidence to show) that there was more scientific discussion of the prospects of anthropogenic global warming at the same time, but they can't resist discrediting the school of cool. The brief run in the sun of 'global cooling' scaremongering is said to have been the fruit of intensive research sponsored by a struggling coal industry.

More relevant to the present-day debate, it's often noted in Alarmist literature that the opponents of the IPCC use the same tactics — and even some of the same people — that have served the tobacco lobby so faithfully down the years. In many cases, the search has paid off: important-sounding outfits such as The Heartland Foundation, the George C. Marshall Institute, the Competitive Enterprise Institute, the Center for the Study of Carbon Dioxide and Global Change, the Science and Environmental Project and the Lavoisier Institute have all proved to be funded by organisations with vested interests in the carbon economy. This had been suspected long before the massive US oil conglomerate Exxon Mobil, under pressure from the American National Academy of Sciences and the British Royal Society, declared that it was no longer funding such organisations, and disclosed some of the past recipients of its funding. It turned out that the 1998 Oregon Petition, signed by 31,000 graduates all claiming that in their considered opinion there was 'no convincing evidence' for anthropogenic global warming, and urging the US government not to sign the Kyoto Protocol, was organised by John Speitz, a past president of the National Academy of Sciences (in the 1960s) who had served as a consultant to the tobacco lobby in the 1970s. His funding came from the George C. Marshall Institute, which was in turn funded by Exxon Mobil, among others. The investigation that turned this up (conducted by Greenpeace, and so hardly objective) also claimed that few, if any, of the 31,000 signatories to the Oregon Petition had any standing whatsoever in the field of climate science.

It sometimes seems as though more effort goes into tracing the funding of any given piece of sceptical research than has gone into addressing its findings, and while this kind of attempt to discredit climate change scepticism is all very well, it eschews debate on the strict scientific merits of sceptical research in favour of a distinctly unscientific moralism.

For anyone who has yet to be convinced that the burning of fossil fuels is a mortal sin, the fact that the coal industry is funding its own research into carbon dioxide's influence on the Earth's climate will seem not only perfectly understandable, but also quite benign. After all, it's the research itself that counts, isn't it? Or if it's possible, as the converse line of argument seems to suggest, that scientific research can be used to 'find' the answer that best suits the sponsor, the general lay public would do well to treat both sides in the climate change debate with a good deal of caution.

The numbers game

When told that a book had been published entitled *100 Authors Against Einstein*, Einstein apparently quipped, 'If I were wrong, one would have done!'

We noted in the Introduction to this book that it's pretty common o hear proponents of anthropogenic global warming insisting that there's a scientific consensus on the subject, as though that carries any weight whatsoever. In fact, as the Sceptics rightly argue, it's distinctly unsettling to see what ought to be the last bastion of freedom of thought and speech given over to the potential tyranny of majorities. Science can't operate on a truth-by-majority-decision basis. It doesn't matter how many scientists believe, any more than it matters how many don't — for yes, the Sceptics can't resist playing this game, either: lists of the names of 'eminent scientists', PhDs, former IPCC expert reviewers and so on, who have now seen the light and nailed their colours to the mast of scepticism, emerge with monotonous regularity (the Oregon Petition, the Morano List, etc.).

The same game is played with institutions and governmental organisations, with lists of the bureaucratic organs that have pro-nounced on the matter adduced as some kind of validation, even though this mass acquiescence can only ever show how convincing the case has appeared to them.

It is played with scientific papers, where anything that makes even the slightest concession to your own case is grabbed and cited as corroboration, often to the discomfort of its author(s). And it's done all over the place with data, where any kink in a curve that suits your claims is carefully snipped out of context and packaged up with other such cherry-picked values. These tactics are distractions at best, or distortions at worst, and can't advance the quest for certainty one iota.

Left and right

Part of the reason that the entire debate over climate change has become so fraught is that it has fitted snugly over existing contours of the sociopolitical landscape. The moralism referred to above, which looks to expose climate change deniers as the stooges of multinational corporations seeking to protect the fossil carbon basis of their own wealth-creation machinery, appeals to anti-consumerist sentiment at least as strongly as it does to environmentalism. After all, much of the developed world has a conflicted attitude to its own affluence, and it's generally not too hard to get the liberal middle classes to concede that not only does having money and shed-loads of material goods not buy happiness, but having too much may actually be immoral, or dangerous in some vaguely karmic sense.

In other words, there is a widely held belief that the average citizen of the First World doesn't exactly tread lightly on the Earth.

What's more, many of the ways in which it is suggested we might reduce our carbon footprint have their own distinct appeal. We like clean, and we like green. Energy efficiency seems like a good thing. So does anything that reduces our dependence on the oil- and trouble-rich Middle East.

Conversely — or perhaps that should be perversely — we're quite attached to our cars, our plasma-screen televisions, our energy-hungry gadgets of every description — and there's no sense in denying that there's a whole economic superstructure founded upon the credo of consume, consume, consume. This creates inertia at best, in the form of an unwillingness to heed the doomsayers and change our daily lives, or outright hostility to the climate change message on the part of those whose commercial interests are deeply vested in the 'carbon economy', never mind those who are simply too attached to their Hummers. This is how it's possible to have a government that has a Climate Change Minister calling a press conference to pass on the latest dire warnings from the IPCC while down the corridor an Energy Minister is calling another to celebrate the latest successful exploration for coal seam gas.

Of course, we had environmentalism and anti-consumerism long before the theory of anthropogenic global warming gained much traction, and alongside them we had corporations with entrenched interests in fostering capitalism and consumerism. The two camps were aligned with liberal and conservative political strands, and that is how, broadly speaking, the two sides in the debate on climate change have fallen, too. How disposed you are to accept the IPCC message is probably closely related to whether your politics are liberal or conservative.

The conservative end of the spectrum tends to regard the whole theory of anthropogenic global warming as a stalking horse for anti-consumerist Greenies and interventionist liberals, and to regard any attempt to introduce policies to curb greenhouse emissions as an unconscionable interference with the workings of the 'free market'. (Of course, the activities of some of those who occupy this end of the spectrum in deliberately spreading misinformation and creating confusion around the topic of climate change are based on a gross misunderstanding of how 'free' markets work. It's not just freedom from interference that defines a free market: it's the freedom of information flow, without barriers or asymmetries where one party has more information, and a concomitant transactional advantage, over the other. Tampering with the easy and complete flow of information is about as antithetical to free-market ideals as it's possible to get.)

Greenies and liberals, on the other hand, based on the nefarious tactics of some deniers, tend to regard all climate change scepticism as nothing more than a rearguard action by hard-pressed corporations whose interests are mortgaged to the fossil fuel economy. But pious refusal to tolerate any opposition to the IPCC orthodoxy in any of its particulars, or worse, the mantra-like repetition of the slogan that the science is settled and the debate's over, are just as injurious to the search for clarity. Tarring all gainsayers or questioners of the science of anthropogenic global warming with the brush of denial and obfuscation is to throw the baby out with the bathwater.

In the end, throwing politics into the mix has only created more heat around an already hot topic without necessarily producing much light. Under these circumstances, only the science, clearly explained and made available to anyone who is interested, has the power to change hearts and (far more importantly) minds. Yet not enough has been done to address the knowledge gap that exists between the scientific elite and the rest of us, and this gulf ultimately threatens the entire IPCC mission.

IPCC, speak to me

There was a picturesque moment during question time in the public forum held at Victoria University in Wellington, New Zealand in early 2008 on the topic of 'Toward a Carbon-Free World', where a white-haired woman produced a book from her bag and, holding it evangelically aloft, paced across the front of the overflow auditorium. Upon reaching the exit, after giving the book a final triumphant flourish, she walked out.

A few minutes later, she could be heard over the public address feed from the main auditorium asking whether any of the panel — which comprised august members of the IPCC, politicians (the Prime Minister of soon-to-be-inundated Kiribati and New Zealand's then Climate Change Minister, David Parker) and scientists — whether any of them had read the book in question, *Unstoppable Global Warming* by Fred Singer and Dennis Avery, one of the seminal works in the literature of climate change scepticism. If so, she went on, how did they answer the irrefutable proof it contained that the present warming of the world climate was due to the natural variability of solar irradiance and was therefore unstoppable?

After a short, sotto voce consultation with his co-panellists, Rajendra Pachauri, the IPCC's suave and debonair chair, volunteered to grasp the poisoned chalice and give an answer. No, he hadn't heard of the book in question, he said, let alone read it. And however exalted the credentials of its authors might be in their respective fields — be that astrology or spiritualism — he doubted they had anything to contribute to the discussion on global warming, which was being conducted by scientists.

The riposte was greeted with a titter in both auditoria. So much for Singer and Avery and climate Sceptics everywhere. The discussion moved on. But that moment — the heretical question and the dismissive, magisterial response — was illustrative of the way in which the IPCC risks failing to achieve the very kind of meaningful and timely change that the Panel itself argues is needed to avert deleterious climate effects.

Curious that we should have been using religious vocabulary in this context, but it's hardly coincidental, because this language so neatly fits the global warming debate. After all, here we have an orthodoxy and a whole index of heresies, a magisterium and a crowd of schismatics, an exalted elite prescribing an ascetic, sanctified lifestyle abstaining from grubby carbon while the corrupt, worldly crowd urges you to carry on guzzling. And hovering over our heads if we fail to mend our ways, suppose our scientific counsellors are correct, there's even a version of good old-fashioned fiery damnation.

There's another parallel, too. One of the aspects of the sixteenth-century Catholic Church to which the instigators of the European Reformation — Luther first, and later Zwingli and Calvin — objected was the way priests celebrated the entire Mass facing the altar and with their backs to the congregation. Worse, the ceremony, just like the church-approved Vulgate Bible itself, was in Latin, which nobody but a tiny, educated elite understood. The message was clear: never mind working it all out for yourself. Just believe what the church says you should believe.

This aspect of the analogy of religion with the IPCC is remarkably apt. What's more, each of the four Assessment Reports that it has so far produced might as well have been written in Latin for all the use they are to the layperson. And as far as communicating the detail of the scientific discussion that the reports contain to the general public goes, the IPCC has been conducting the ceremony with its back as resolutely turned to the congregation as any pre-Reformation priest. For as its very name suggests, the Inter-Governmental Panel on Climate Change only really deigns (and was only ever intended) to talk to those responsible for making policy. Indeed, it's the most efficient clutch ever devised between the scientific community and policy-makers, the point at which the rubber meets the road. On the one hand, this has seen the dire warnings of climate scientists echoed in the corridors of power throughout much of the Western world far faster than could ever have been dreamed possible before the round of meetings that led to the 1987 Montreal Protocol on ozone-depleting substances. On the other, negative side, however, the arrangement that has policy-makers in direct communion with science while those whom policy directly affects — the general public — are left in the dark poses the single greatest threat to the IPCC's mission. There's a gap where some organ of the media willing and able to interpret complex science to the general public should be. Strange that at the pinnacle of the Age of Information we should be confronted by as much (if not more) falsehood and disinformation as by the good oil. For as our means of acquiring and storing information have attained miraculous proportions, the sources we've traditionally relied upon for the information we need to make important decisions in our lives, notably the popular media, have been dumbed down to the point where they simply aren't capable of speaking in other than monosyllables of shock, drama and tragedy.

The fourth and latest IPCC report declares with greater than 90% certainty that human-induced global warming is a fact, and has supported the conclusion that we must make profound changes to avoid its potentially catastrophic consequences. Curiously, this aggregate level of certainty is hardly borne out by the circumspection of the scientists contributing to the report, and nor can there be much certainty over how much warming, with what impacts, is likely to follow. It's as though there has been a general agreement to bring back a verdict before all the evidence has been heard. Even if you don't believe that the IPCC is a grand conspiracy on the part of environmentalists and left-wing politicians to derail capitalism, you can still believe that there is a conspiracy of sorts at work — a conspiracy to overstate the case.

The obvious rejoinder, of course, is that if the science is correct, there simply isn't time to wait until the theory is uncontroversial in all its detail before we start to act. This is one scientific question that can't wait for 'full scientific certainty' to emerge from the stately progress of scientific research.

And this is where the arrogance of the IPCC may well prove to be its — and everyone's — undoing. Avoiding the worst consequences of global warming is going to require changes at every level and in every aspect of the world order. People have already died in its name — those who have starved as food crops have been ripped out and different species planted to supply the more lucrative market for biofuel feedstocks — and many more stand to die yet. The stakes are high indeed.

But it is a feature of our style of democracy that a population that won't go willingly can't be led by the nose. Worse, it will actually hold policy back as it tugs on the bridle. You need only look at the extreme reluctance of the US administration of George W. Bush and the Australian regime of John Howard to ratify the Kyoto Protocol to see at work the diluting effect that realpolitik has on political resolve.

Where the electorate stands to lose so much — the convenience of the unfettered use of private transport, a proportion of its standard of living (as carbon taxes dampen economic growth), its flat-screen televisions, its beloved SUVs — it will need to be convinced that it's all in a good cause. It sure as hell won't vote for a government that promises to hike fuel prices and pay a surcharge on consumer goods to reflect their carbon content if it's not.

Complicating matters is the fact that the conversion of our leaders themselves to the climate change cause seems to have been somewhat less than wholehearted. Governments thunder about the need for emissions trading schemes, even as they encourage exploration for new fossil fuel resources.

The solution, if political action is to be taken, is to create a motivated electorate, and this can only be achieved by educating the general public. This will require embarking upon a whole lot of tedious exegesis of the science and the maths of the thing, and it will certainly mean the dark superstitions abroad among laypeople — fostered by the deniers — need to be actively disproven rather than simply dismissed.

It's high time, in short, that the priests turned to face the congregation. The people are waiting.

Reaching a verdict

Religious disputation is one thing. The other language that recommends itself as an analogy for the climate change debate is that of the legal process. In trying to make up our minds on the question of anthropogenic global warming, we placed ourselves in a position similar to that of jurors trying to decide a complex case involving expert testimony from both sides. After all, the conviction — if that's quite the right word — was identical: the jury are not experts in the high-flown science being used to try to prove guilt or innocence, but it's essential if they're to reach a verdict that they reach some basic understanding of it, and so it must be broken down into terms and concepts that they can grasp.

That's what we tried to get our experts from both poles to focus on: presenting their evidence in a clear and orderly manner, and explaining its significance without venturing their own opinions on the merits of the case.

Meanwhile, we were barracked by barristers on both sides. One side traded heavily on sheer institutional gravitas, as the police and prosecution occasionally do, and sought to undermine the credibility of the other side's witnesses. The other side tried every trick of the trade to raise reasonable doubt: confronting the prosecution's case head-on, impugning the prosecution's witnesses, hinting darkly at corruption and witness-coaching, constructing plausible-sounding counter-scenarios and alibis, probing loopholes . . . the whole gamut.

Our task was to ignore all the distractions and to concentrate on the evidence, reminding ourselves each step of the way what it was we were here to decide. Is there a coherent scientific theory of dangerous anthropogenic global warming, and does the evidence garnered from observations of the natural world corroborate it?

The Courage of Their Convictions

The purpose of this book has been to examine the current state of the scientific evidence for the anthropogenic global warming hypothesis and from that to arrive at a reasonable person's view on whether sufficient corroboration exists to warrant taking the next step (namely, evaluating policies to address the likely consequences of warming). As we've sifted through the arguments and data, it's become clear that it's all coming down to a weight-of-evidence decision.

But along the way, as we've noted, we couldn't help but fear for the objectivity of some of the participants in the debate. It would be funny if the stakes weren't so high.

There's no shortage of scientists who are convinced either one way or the other about global warming, and they're all prepared to argue with equal (and opposite) conviction. This gets confusing for the public: on the one hand, we're being asked to implement a raft of policies to combat warming, while on the other we're being assured by people with impressive credentials and plausible-sounding arguments that these policies are unnecessary and unnecessarily costly.

This lack of unanimity amongst experts leaves the public feeling it's damned if it does, damned if it doesn't — at least if it's open-minded enough to listen to anyone from the scientific fraternity who claims they're a climate expert.

So when it was suggested to us that we try our experts out on a little thought experiment, we could see the merits right away. At the very least, we thought, it would give a sense of the consistency of the thinking on both sides of the divide.

The suggestion was that we asked our 'experts':

'What single piece of evidence would it take to change your mind about the theory of anthropogenic global warming?'

The suggestion was made by former chair of the OECD Roundtable on Sustainable Development, Simon Upton.

Clearly he, too, had got frustrated with the seemingly endless litany of pieces of evidence dragged up by both sides to stuff their claim that their side had a monopoly on the scientific merits.

We hoped that each respondent would identify for us the cornerstone (for them) of their beliefs in the matter. If, from the various answers, three or four of these 'cornerstones' emerged, it would be more than a little reassuring. If, on the other hand, answers were all over the shop with little consistency, then we'd have a reason to doubt the collective understanding of one side or the other (or both).

So that's the question we put to the experts, on both sides of the debate, who'd been assisting us. With the same zeal as that with which they had so patiently and enthusiastically helped out with the rest of the book, they canvassed their colleagues, and we saw with delight some very prominent names in world climate science attached to the responses we began to receive.

Baulkers

We received quite a few responses from Alarmists along the lines of 'If anyone can show me any evidence that such-and-such a Sceptic has a good degree from a respectable university.'

We've come to expect that kind of thing in this game.

We were more perturbed by the number from both sides — around 5% of those asked — who refused to give us an answer at all. Disappointingly, it was our scientist friends who are staunchly of the belief that the theory of anthropogenic global warming is false that were mostly afflicted by this condition. A common refrain was that since global warming is naturally driven, there's no need for Sceptics to adduce any evidence whatsoever. You can take this line of argument at face value, or you can interpret it as caginess, and insecurity over their own position, as you like.

But it wasn't just the staunch Sceptics. A number of
Alarmists refused to answer, too, and the main reason
they cited was that 'the evidence is so overwhelming it
can't be boiled down to a single item or items'. This was no
more reassuring than the Sceptics' position, and certainly
indicated minds that were every bit as closed.

Answers

In terms of the valid (rather than flippant and off-topic)
responses we received, we were gratified by the consistency
on both sides.

On the Alarmist side, 90% of our respondents named
the calculations carried out over a century ago by Svante
Arrhenius (that suggested a doubling of CO_2 concentration
would raise temperatures by 5–6^{0}C as it absorbed infrared)
as the principal plank in the edifice of the theory of
anthropogenic global warming. That's why the Alarmists are
able to stare down a decade of cooling (according to global
average temperatures), for example, without blinking: the
purity of the science assures them that human-sourced CO_2
emissions must raise temperatures. But if a fault were ever
found with Arrhenius's logic, which has stood the test of
time, you get the impression scientists would be fighting to
man the boats as the Alarmist cause foundered.

The Sceptics came up with a wider range of factors
that might undermine the courage of their convictions if
shown to be true. The majority (60%) cited the lack of a
correlation between rising CO_2 and measurements of world
temperature as lying at the core of their doubt. Again,
you got the impression that if you could demonstrate that
correlation, the noise from the sceptical side would calm
right down — little wonder the 'hockey stick' controversy
(see 'Data Hockey' panel, in the first colour section), which
purported to show identical curves for CO_2 and temperature
measurements, was so divisive! Other factors that the

Sceptics acknowledged to have the power to change their minds were any hard evidence that warming was occurring (apart from a measurable temperature rise) and 'any evidence that climate models could predict climate'.

We'd embarked on this exercise imagining that both camps would be all over the place in terms of the things they saw as fundamental to their conviction about anthropogenic global warming. However, if the results of our little straw poll are anything to go by, the issue can be boiled down quite simply.

So here's a heads-up to protagonists on both sides as to where the chink lies in the armour of their opponents' convictions. Shake the Alarmists' faith in the demonstrated ability of atmospheric CO_2 to absorb infrared (and produce warming) that convinces them that rising CO_2 must produce warming, and it's victory to the Sceptics. On the other hand, find more convincing evidence that rising CO_2 concentrations are causing warming and you'll likely separate the true Sceptics from the true deniers.

Chapter 8

The Verdict

Phew! At last we can wrap it up.

Law textbooks used to appeal to a mythical individual known as 'the rational man on the Clapham omnibus' to refer to the way common sense would construe a set of facts. Our mission from the outset was to try to gather enough information from both sides of the argument to make up our minds, as rational laypeople, about the climate change debate. The rational man on the Clapham omnibus is not an expert — that's the point of him, and that's presumably why he's on the Clapham omnibus in the first place, rather than driving something fancy somewhere fancier than Clapham — and nor are we. For all our reading, and for all the superb tuition we've received along the way from our admirable panels of long-suffering experts, we've learned only just enough to know how little we know. But society thinks nothing of taking 12 rational men or women from the Clapham omnibus and trusting them to get it right when they grapple with technical legal and scientific issues in the courtroom, and the electoral rolls, too (or at least, the roll for Clapham), are full of such people, whom we trust to make informed, responsible decisions on policy in difficult and complex areas every time a general election rolls around. There's a point at which the reasonable person is going to have to make decisions on climate change, and making no pretentions to be anything other than reasonable laypeople, we believe we've heard enough to be able to make some pronouncements on the matter.

The very first of these is that contrary to the protestations of your average environmentalist, the science on this whole thing is *not* settled. The hypothesis of anthropogenic global warming is impressive, as it's based on well-established principles of physics and chemistry. The greenhouse gases *do* absorb infrared. They *do* punch above their weight in terms of atmospheric concentration — they're mere whiffs compared to the major atmospheric constituents, but they're the reason our Earth isn't just another frigid rock drifting through space. And it has been shown to general satisfaction that human beings *have* been responsible for a dramatic increase in the concentrations of the greenhouse gases since the industrial revolution.

But the climate is complex, and greenhouse gases are but one of the influences tugging and pushing at it. Just how it all works is not fully understood. In fact, parts of it are hardly understood at all.

This is only to be expected, as the über-discipline known as climate science is comparatively young, and the tools with which it makes sense of the chaos that is climate-in-the-making are younger still. Our knowledge of the precise effect on global climate of the shock that human activity has been delivering to it for the last 150 years is in a state of flux. Any statement to the contrary is nothing more than a kind of apostle's creed. The *theory* is settled, that is; the *evidence* has been something less than unequivocal.

Still, given the stakes involved, and with due deference to the 'precautionary principle' of responsible policy-making, we can't wait for full scientific certainty before we act (or refrain from acting). Probabilities will have to do, and we feel we can say which way they point. We also hope to have shown which way they point in the preceding chapters.

So before we make our pronouncement on the matter, let's take a brief trip down memory lane, and look at some of the things we've seen en route.

We began our discussion at the beginning, with the science of anthropogenic warming — the comparatively basic chemistry and physics by which the Earth maintains such an equable climate, and how those same principles suggest that the 150-year orgy of fossil fuel consumption that's given us such a heady lifestyle is likely to bring on a nasty hangover if we don't lay off the stuff quick.

In Chapter 2, we had a look at the extraordinary range of ways in which we can tell how much energy there is in the Earth system, and got a fascinating glimpse of how the modern climate scientist spends his or her time. Working out whether the Earth is warming is not, as it turns out, just a matter of looking at what all the thermometers in the history of the world have said about it and are saying now, partly because thermometers haven't been around for very long, and they haven't been waved about at all the necessary points on the Earth's surface, let alone on, under and over the sea, and in the thin air of the atmosphere. Climate scientists these days have got techniques for measuring climate parameters past, present and, if you're inclined to believe in the usefulness of computer modelling, future. Each technique has its limitations, and consequently, any statement that's made about what the Earth's climate has done in the past and what it's doing now (let alone what it will do in the future) has to be qualified.

Nonetheless, as was seen in Chapter 3, there are a number of points of agreement between all parties to the debate on anthropogenic global warming:

▷ The climate is naturally changeable, and it has changed dramatically in the past without any help from human beings.

▷ Global average sea and surface temperatures have been rising. Carbon dioxide levels have been rising, too.

▷ Historically, it looks as though there's a link between these two things (which stands to reason, given the ability of CO_2 and other greenhouse gases to absorb infrared radiation).

▷ Significant global warming would likely have deleterious consequences for the human and natural worlds.

That's about all the two sides agree on, and it has to be repeated that this is general agreement only. You'll find a diehard Sceptic to argue practically every item on this list, except the first. And there's not even general agreement over the combined significance of all these 'facts'.

Chapter 4 presented the evidential basis for believing that the theory of anthropogenic global warming is more than academic speculation. It's not just direct instrumental records of surface, sea and atmospheric temperatures that attest to an energy imbalance in the Earth system (and it's not just that measurements of radiation coming into the Earth system show it to be greater than the radiation leaving it). Various effects of warming can be seen in its various components:

▷ The cryosphere, where the Earth is losing ice at an unprecedented rate, with the rapid and general retreat of glaciers, the shrinkage of annual Arctic sea ice, and the collapse of ancient ice shelves.

▷ The aquasphere, where the world's oceans are warming, growing more saline, sea levels are rising and seawater is absorbing less CO_2.

▷ The atmosphere, where weather patterns (which, ultimately, are driven by temperatures, particularly of the oceans) are changing, with the tropics expanding, the belts of westerly winds in the high latitudes migrating polewards.

▷ The biosphere, where the range of a number of species is changing, with the retreat to higher altitudes and latitudes of creatures adapted to cooler climes.

What's more, certain aspects of the warming that's going on seem unnatural, or at least atypical, of the way in which natural warmings are thought to have occurred in the past:

▷ The rate and scale of warming, which looks fishy. The proxy records considered reliable — such as the measurement of isotopic ratios in ice cores — indicate that the rate and scale of the change in global average temperatures is unprecedented in the last 2000 years, and perhaps as much as 5000, and this squares with some of the other evidence, too. We seem to be losing ice at present that the Earth hasn't seen the back of for 5000 years.

▷ The pattern of warming, which looks fishy too. The strongest warming trend is detectable at the poles and (maybe) in the troposphere over the tropics, and it's the northern hemisphere leading the southern this time around, contrary to other instances of warming as recorded in the ice cores, where the south has invariably led the north. The troposphere has been getting warmer, while the stratosphere has been getting cooler, and while the picture is complicated by the stratospheric cooling effects of ozone depletion, this pattern is consistent with the effect of excess greenhouse gases in the atmosphere.

▷ Measurements of solar irradiance seem to suggest the climate should be getting cooler rather than warmer, as since records began in the 1970s, the Earth has been receiving progressively less radiation while temperatures have (mostly) risen.

And lastly, it can be shown by isotopic analysis of atmospheric carbon that the source of the measured (and uncontroversial) increase in carbon dioxide is due to the combustion of fossil fuels.

Chapter 5 presented the case against the theory of anthropogenic warming, or at least, the theory as formulated by the IPCC. This qualification is necessary, because the harder you look, the more you detect two kinds of sceptical argument. There is the ubiquitous nit-picking at every aspect of the theory and its evidential basis, which tends to play to the uncertainties over climate — we don't know precisely how nature has contrived to plunge the Earth into ice ages, let alone thaw it out again — so we can't possibly know what's going on at the moment, although (as some add) it's likely to have something to do with the sun. To put it politely, this approach lacks scientific rigour, and indeed, there's every reason to believe much of it is advanced as an attempt to delay action on climate change rather than as any kind of objective challenge to the science. This school of sceptical thought seizes every scrap of corroborating evidence, even if it has to be lifted out of context or subtly manipulated in order to appear to add corroboration. But it has to be said that the failure of global average temperatures to show an orderly rise in recent years has played into the hands of climate change deniers — with no cherry-picking, data-mining or massaging required.

Scientifically meritorious sceptical argument against the theory of anthropogenic global warming tends to be thin on the ground. There is some interesting work that challenges the relationship between CO_2 concentrations and warming, based on proxy evidence suggesting that atmospheric carbon dioxide is more variable than the ice cores give it credit for. The fact that the steep rise of carbon dioxide is not tightly correlated with temperature, which is highly variable, helps this argument to fly. So, too, does the evidence of the ice cores, which show that in every single instance in history, temperature rises have led CO_2, even if the further step — to say that rises in CO_2 *cannot* lead temperature rises — is a step too far, logically speaking.

The remaining sceptical arguments tend not to be arguments against the science of anthropogenic global warming so much as attacks on the IPCC's certainty over the numbers. There's further interesting work on the way in which clouds might help stabilise the Earth's climate in the face of shocks such as a rise in greenhouse gas concentrations. One theory speculates that warming might lead to a decrease in radiation-trapping clouds, allowing more radiation to escape to space and cooling the surface and lower atmosphere. Another, noting the attractive correlation of variations in cosmic ray flux and temperature, speculates that the creation of charged particles in the upper atmosphere by the collision of cosmic rays with atmospheric gases forms condensation nuclei and thus radiation-reflecting low cloud, dimming (and cooling) the surface. By contrast with most sceptical arguments, this one can boast laboratory evidence that tends to corroborate its proposed mechanism.

It's possible for proponents of both of these sceptical arguments to accept the theory of anthropogenic global warming lock, stock and barrel but to part company with the IPCC where it predicts dangerous temperature rises. For the respectable end of the sceptical spectrum tends to dispute the numbers, as we saw in Chapter 6, where we tried to get a feel for what expected rises in CO_2 and attendant feedbacks would mean in temperature terms. Here, we were interested to discover that there are considerable uncertainties in the IPCC attempts to quantify anthropogenic warming, and that these uncertainties have to do with the behaviour and interrelationship of the various feedback mechanisms involved in determining the climate's response to forcing.

And of the various uncertainties that exist, by far the biggest and foggiest is the effect of clouds. The trouble with clouds is that we just don't know how they behave, or how they've behaved in the past. No proxy records of cloudiness exist. Anecdotal records are hopelessly patchy. Measuring them with any precision is impossible, not least because satellites — the most reliable and globally consistent measurers of other climate parameters since the late 1970s — can't see clouds through other clouds. And even if they could, clouds change so rapidly and are so infinitely variable that they defy explanation in terms of mathematical algorithms. That makes them imponderable for climate models, the most potent tool we presently possess to test our knowledge of climate and the closest thing we have to a laboratory in which to experiment upon it.

So what does this mean? Well, if the Sceptics are right about clouds, any effect of human activity on climate is largely cancelled out by changes in cloudiness and the level of anthropogenic global warming is too slight to cause any real concern. If the IPCC is right about clouds, their net effect is either to aggravate warming, or alternatively, if mitigating, too slight to offset warming due to anthropogenic greenhouse gases and other feedbacks. Who knows who's right?

After we'd reached this point, by way of diversion and because we couldn't resist, we had a look in Chapter 7 at a few implications of the climate change debate for politics. We noted that what we'd witnessed since we began studying the issue was an extraordinarily heated debate, more what you'd expect in a disputation over religious doctrine than in a supposedly cool, rational discussion of scientific theory and empirically gathered evidence. This seemed to be a product of uncertainty, with both sides — *both* sides — choosing their position and closing their minds to alternatives. One guy, who responded to our request for assistance and provided much valuable material, claimed to be open-minded and to be interested in the pure science of the matter. But of the 200-odd emails he sent in a three-year period, each with references and suggestions for further reading attached, he didn't manage to supply us with a single reference or suggestion that supported the side opposite to his own. How scary is *that*, given how much science is going on around the world every single day on every aspect of climate science, by turns supportive of or antagonistic to the theory of global warming?

The polarising effect of the climate change question is partly due to its tendency to appeal to forces massed along the borders of existing political territories, such as between laissez-faire (that is, dog-eat-dog) 'free marketeers' on one hand and interventionist, anti-consumerist Greenies on the other. Each side accused the other of using climate change as a Trojan horse for their own, ulterior agenda.

Stuck in the middle, of course, is the layperson — the poor old put-upon rational man on the Clapham omnibus — who just seeks clarity but, in the absence of clear, intelligible information on the subject, provides easy meat for sector interests if either side proves to be right about the dark motives of the other. Informing the public is the only way to protect them against the blandishments of slick, highly organised partisan lobby groups — and we could just as easily be talking about the IPCC here as about the marketing arm of any fossil-fuel-mongering evil empire.

The envelope please . . .

The verdict we're about to reveal, in case it hasn't already emerged like a signal from noise, is based on the weight of evidence as at the end of 2008. Climate change is probably the fastest-growing body of research in the world today, with a huge array of scientific disciplines and sub-disciplines contributing new material on a daily basis. We have, therefore, to state our own uncertainty principle: we can state our position as at the end of 2008, but that pronouncement will obscure the speed with which it will change in light of new information.

After what we strove to make a fair hearing, and fighting our way through the distractions, diversions, smokescreens and other courtroom histrionics that both sides went in for, we have to say that we were more impressed with the case for anthropogenic global warming than with the case against.

The science is practically irrefutable. The evidence isn't overwhelming, but it's certainly mounting. It's hard to argue against some of the anecdotal signs of warming, many of which we've seen with our own eyes from the saddle of a motorbike or the deck of an icebreaker. Much of the more technical evidence is compelling, too. If the Earth is warming, since we have a highly plausible scientific explanation for it, the common-sense response is to deduce that greenhouse gases, the concentrations of which are increasing due to human activity, are behind it.

But we can't declare total victory to the pro-anthropogenic warming camp. The most convincing of the sceptical arguments have clustered around the uncertainties in the IPCC's calculations of the effects of the anthropogenically enhanced greenhouse effect, most notably in the behaviour of clouds. So the debate isn't over: it's moved on, and is now concerned with how the climate will respond to the increase in greenhouse gases due to human activity. Although we don't regard climate models as truth machines, unlike many followers of the IPCC, nor do we regard them as of about as much practical use in predicting future climate as Frogger, as do some Sceptics. We regard the IPCC range of values for sensitivity to carbon dioxide — between 1.8°C and

4.4°C — as plausible, or more plausible, at any rate, than the Sceptics' unreasonably low 1.5°C. That means we're bound to accept the range of temperature increases we face by 2100 — between 1.1°C and 6.4°C, depending on which emissions scenario plays out — that the IPCC derives. That's a huge margin of error for those trying to formulate policy to respond to global warming. There's plenty of work to do yet before science can claim to understand how the climate really works, to the point where there can be very high confidence in its numbers. Clouds are definitely worth a closer look.

Whaddawedo? Whaddawedo?

In terms of the three possible positions we thought we'd be in by this stage of proceedings way back there in the Introduction, we are in position (1):

On the balance of evidence, observations of the natural world would support a coherent theory of why increased concentrations of greenhouse gases due to human activity will produce significant global warming, in which case policy initiatives to address global warming and its consequences were worth evaluating.

The Alarmists were right, and we shouldn't call them alarmists any more — or at least, not all of them! And further, it has to be said that only a few of the Sceptics are actually sceptics: too many are mere gadflies and deniers.

Policy initiatives to address (that is, to mitigate and to adapt to) global warming are worth evaluating, as we see it. Because of the uncertainty that surrounds the extent of the climate change, let alone the extent of the impact of that change, advocates of public policy to address this issue face the additional hurdle of dealing with the constraints of designing policy under conditions of substantial uncertainty. This means that policy must be more risk-averse than normal: they must not use a sledgehammer, that is, to crack a nut. Policies to address climate change and its effects come at a substantial economic cost — and may even cost lives in some of the less well-off parts of our world.

That's a huge responsibility for public policy. The last thing it can afford — in terms of net national social and economic benefit — is to be held to ransom by myopic, single-issue activists. Not only is a comprehensive cost/benefit analysis of the policy options called for, but a substantial resourcing of scientific research into global warming aimed at reducing the uncomfortably wide bands of uncertainty surrounding the quantitative effects of various CO_2 emissions scenarios is indicated.

But then that's another book.

And at all times, policy-makers and the lay public alike must keep a weather eye open for evidence or arguments that have the potential to prove us wrong. After all, we embarked on this enterprise with the words of famous economist Lord Keynes at the forefront of our minds:

> *When the facts change, I change my mind.*
> *What do you do, sir?*

And that's one thing we won't change our minds about.

Abbreviations

ACC   Antarctic Circumpolar Current

AOGCM   Atmosphere–Ocean General Circulation Model

CFC   chlorofluorocarbon

CO_2 carbon dioxide

DTR   diurnal temperature range

EPICA   European Project for Ice Coring in Antarctica

GCM   global circulation model

IMO   International Meteorological Organization

IPCC   Intergovernmental Panel on Climate Change

IR   infrared radiation

NOAA   American National Oceanic and Atmospheric Administration

OLR   outgoing longwave radiation

pH   potential of Hydrogen; measure of the acidity or alkalinity of a solution. The higher the pH the more alkaline (less acidic) it is.

ppb   parts per billion

ppm   parts per million

ppmv   parts per million by volume

SLE   sea level equivalent

TSI   total solar irradiance; measure of radiance emitted from the sun

UV   ultraviolet

VOC   volatile organic compound

WMO   World Meteorological Organization

Glossary

aerosol   A suspension of fine solid particles or liquid droplets in a gas (smoke or smog, for example). However, in everyday use, 'aerosol' usually refers to the output of an aerosol spray can. In order for the content of the can to be 'sprayed out', it must be pushed out by a 'propellant'. Historically, chlorofluorocarbons (CFCs) were used, but these have since been replaced (mostly by hydrocarbons) due to the harmful effect these long-lived CFCs were found to be having on the ozone layer. Confusion over aerosols — which are mentioned in the context of two discrete atmospheric crises — is rife.

alarmist   The dictionary definition of an 'alarmist' is 'a person who tends to raise alarms, esp. without sufficient reason, as by exaggerating dangers or prophesying calamities'. However, we use the term in this book to mean a proponent, or someone who accepts the truth, of the theory of human-induced global warming.

albedo   A unitless measure of the extent to which an object reflects and scatters light from the sun; that is, the incident rays are reflected at a number of random angles. Often thought of as the proportion of the rays that are hitting the object or surface that are reflected.

algorithm   A series of calculations or operations that, when given an initial state (or value), will proceed through a series of successive states and eventually terminate at an end state. Very common in mathematics and computing.

altitude   The height measured from sea level up to a given point.

anemometer   A device used for measuring wind speed.

anthropogenic   Caused by human activity.

aquasphere   The Earth's bodies of water, including streams, rivers, lakes, seas, oceans etc., and their interrelationships with one another.

atmosphere   A layer of gases surrounding a planet, held in place by the planet's gravitational field. Earth's atmosphere is divided up into five layers, including the troposphere and the stratosphere.

atom   A basic unit of matter consisting of a positively charged nucleus (containing protons and neutrons) surrounded by a cloud of electrically charged electrons. The number of protons in the atom determines the chemical element of the atom: for example, an oxygen atom has eight protons whereas a carbon atom has only six.

atomic mass   The total mass of protons, neutrons and electrons of an atom (and since electrons are of negligible atomic mass, usually the atomic mass is the same as the number of protons and neutrons). This differs between isotopes of the same element, as the number of neutrons in the nucleus varies from isotope to isotope.

atomic nucleus   The very dense region of neutrons and protons at the centre of an atom.

barometer   An instrument used to measure atmospheric pressure (i.e. the force per unit area exerted by the air in an atmosphere on a surface).

bathythermograph   An instrument used to detect changes in hydrostatic pressure (pressure in a liquid), from which temperature can be deduced. When lowered into water, it records pressure (and temperature) changes as it descends through the water.

belemnites   An extinct group of marine molluscs, very similar to squid. They were abundant throughout the Mesozoic era (250–65 million years ago) and thus their fossils are commonly found in Mesozoic marine rocks. During the Mesozoic era the continents shifted from a connected state into their current configuration. This period was also host to a particularly warm climate, allowing evolution and diversification of new animal species. Belemnites are used by geologists to determine the age of rocks in which they are found.

bimetal   Composed of two different metals, not like an alloy in which the metals are mixed, but instead consisting of layers of separate metals.

biosphere   The broadest level of ecological study; the global ecological system integrating all living beings and their relationships, including their interaction with the elements of the lithosphere, hydrosphere and atmosphere.

blackbody   An object that absorbs all electromagnetic radiation (EMR) that falls on it. As no radiation passes through it and none is reflected by it, the object appears black when cold. If hot a black body is an ideal source of thermal radiation: that is, it emits EMR.

calcite   A mineral (naturally occurring solid) containing the carbonate ion (CO_3^{2-}).

calcium carbonate   A chemical compound ($CaCO_3$) consisting of calcium, carbon and oxygen atoms. Commonly found as rock, and the main component in the shells of many organisms.

carbohydrates   The most abundant of the major classes of biomolecules (organic molecules produced by living organisms). They are responsible for the storage and transport of energy in living organisms.

carbon 12 (^{12}C)   The most abundant of the two stable isotopes of carbon; it accounts for 98.89% of carbon.

carbon 13 (^{13}C)   The second stable isotope of carbon; it accounts for approximately 1.1% of carbon.

carbon 14 (^{14}C)   A radioactive isotope of carbon, which means it undergoes radioactive decay. It is used in radiocarbon dating, which is a method that can be used to determine the age of materials up to about 60,000 years old.

chlorofluorocarbon (CFC)   A group of chemical compounds that are known to deplete ozone. They are widely used as propellants in fire extinguishers and spray cans, and as refrigerants in fridges, freezers and air conditioners.

cirrus clouds   Thin wispy clouds that are usually indistinguishable from each other and appear like a gauzy sheet in the sky. They trap and reflect infrared radiation (heat) beneath them, but also reflect sunlight arriving from above.

clathrates   More properly (for our purposes) termed clathrate hydrates, these comprise a 'lattice' of water molecules entrapping gas molecules, notably methane. The name is derived from the Latin word 'clatratus', meaning 'barred'. Methane clathrate hydrates have been found in permafrost and in the seabed.

climate   Refers to the temperatures, rainfall, humidity and behaviour of other meteorological factors over a period of time, usually 30 years. Climate is different from 'weather', which refers to transient, short-term meterological phenomena such as storms, wind, rain and so on.

climatology   The study of climate.

CO_2 equivalent   A measure for describing how much global warming a given greenhouse gas may cause, using the equivalent amount of CO_2 as the reference.

compound   A chemical compound consists of atoms of two or more elements bonded together.

condensation   The transition of a gas into liquid, commonly occurring when the gas is cooled but can also occur when it's compressed.

condensation nuclei   Also known as 'cloud condensation nuclei' (CCN), these are small solid or liquid particles about which water can change from a gas to a liquid (that is, condense).

conduction   Heat conduction is the transfer of heat energy between materials by direct contact. Conduction is one of the three major forms of heat transfer between substances, the others being convection and radiation.

convection   The movement of molecules within fluids or gases as the result of heating. Convection is one of the three major forms of heat transfer between substances, the others being conduction and radiation.

cosmic rays   Energetic particles originating from space; 90% of all the incoming cosmic ray particles are protons, about 9% are helium nuclei (alpha particles) and about 1% are electrons. The term 'ray' is a misnomer, as they are particulates. Solar cosmic rays come from the sun, galactic cosmic rays from throughout the galaxy.

cosmic ray flux   The flow-rate of cosmic particulates.

cryosphere   The portions of the Earth's surface that are covered by ice or snow. This can take the form of sea ice, river ice, snow, glaciers, ice caps and sheets, and more.

decomposition   The process by which dead organisms break down into their constituent, simple compounds.

diatoms   One of the most common types of phytoplankton.

diurnal   Literally, 'of the daytime'. A diurnal animal is one that is active during the day and rests at night, human beings being a prime example. Diurnal temperatures are daytime temperatures.

Earth system   The interconnecting systems of all components of the solid Earth, its living residents, its oceans and its atmosphere.

El Niño Southern Oscillation (ENSO)   The seesaw shift in surface air pressure between the east and west of the Pacific. The extreme phases of the Southern Oscillation are El Niño and La Niña. El Niño is Spanish for 'little boy', and more specifically, Christ child, as it was a term coined by the fishermen of Ecuador to refer to times around Christmas when the waters of the eastern Pacific are abnormally warm, low on nutrients, and sea level air pressure drops there, bringing dismal fishing, heavy rain and often catastrophic flooding. Meanwhile, on the other side of the Pacific, Australia will typically be suffering from drought and its sea temperatures will be lower than usual. It's vice-versa for La Niña (Spanish for 'little girl') which is simply the label for the other extreme of the Southern Oscillation. When the oscillation isn't occurring, then typically sea surface temperatures in the tropics off Australia are 6–8°C warmer than on the tropical west coast of South America, which enjoys the upwelling of the nutrient-rich cold Antarctic waters that support large fish populations. Easterly trade winds blowing the warm waters to the western side of the Pacific cause the sea level in Indonesia to be some 50 cm higher than that in Ecuador. When the Southern Oscillation enters a strong El Niño phase, the air pressure differential drops and the trade winds abate, allowing warm water to move slowly back eastward.

electromagnetic radiation (EMR)   Sometimes called 'radiation' or 'light', EMR takes the form of waves of electrical and magnetic energy moving together through space. These are classified according to wave frequency, and the entire range of EMR types includes radio waves, microwaves, infrared light, visible light, ultraviolet (UV) light, X-rays, and gamma rays.

emissions   Literally, things that are sent out or 'given off'. In the context of climate science, this is often used to refer to the introduction of air pollutants into our atmosphere from the burning of fossil fuels.

empiricism A theory that suggests that knowledge arises from experience. It is a branch of epistemology.

epistemology A branch of philosophy concerned with the nature and extent of knowledge. It focuses on what knowledge is, how it is acquired, what we know and how we know it.

equator An imaginary line that intersects the Earth's surface and the plane perpendicular to the Earth's axis of rotation. It is seen on a map as a horizontal line around the middle of the Earth.

equilibrium When two opposing processes proceed at the same rate, thus there is no change in the concentrations, or amounts, of the products of either process (for example, water flowing into a bathtub at the same rate as water is flowing down the drain). Basically it looks as if nothing is happening because the things that are occurring are essentially 'cancelling each other out'.

eustatic Refers to global changes in sea level due to the addition (or removal) of water to (from) the oceans.

evaporation The transition of a liquid into gas that occurs at temperatures below boiling point. This usually occurs at the surface of the liquid when it is exposed to a significant volume of gas.

evapotranspiration The evaporation of water from the Earth's surface and anything on it (e.g. plants, oceans, etc.) to the atmosphere.

exosphere The uppermost layer of the atmosphere, which consists mainly of hydrogen; sometimes used synonymously with the term 'outer space'.

feedback When an output from an event in the past will influence the continuing event in the future.

firn Ice that is at a stage between snow and glacial ice. It is left over from past seasons, so becomes denser and thus closer to the firm ice of glaciers.

foraminifera Literally, 'hole bearers'— possessing a shell with a pore (or pores). Single-celled organisms characterised by the absence of specialised tissues and organs. While they are some of the simplest organisms in the animal kingdom, they create some of the most beautiful and complicated shells. They typically take the form of a linear, spiral, or concentrically circled shell perforated by small holes or pores through which the organism can extend. The evolution of foraminifera (often referred to by scientists as 'forams') is well enough known for the fossil presence of species or combinations of species to be used to date rock samples. Since they construct their shells of calcite, incorporating carbon lately drawn from the atmopshere, they are also useful as a proxy measurement of atmospheric carbon isotopes of past atmospheres.

forcing   A technical term used by climatologists to refer to anything that 'perturbs' or upsets the equilibrium of climate. An increase or decrease in solar radiation is a forcing (positive and negative respectively); so too is an increase or decrease in greenhouse gas concentrations, or cloudiness, or albedo, and so on.

fossil carbon   Carbon that has been 'fixed' from the atmosphere by plants or shell-building organisms and 'sequestered', or stored underground in the form of hydrocarbons (such as coal, oil and gas) or limestones. Fossil carbon was once part of the living carbon cycle, but the present climate equilibrium would not naturally include it.

fossil fuels   Compounds found in the Earth's crust that have been used as energy sources. Coal and petroleum, for example, are mined and burned to power cars and electricity grids. In the United States, 90% of greenhouse gas emissions come from the burning of fossil fuels.

frequency (waves)   The number of waves passing a given point per unit of time. This is inversely proportional to the wavelength of the wave — in other words, the longer (greater) the wavelength, the lower the frequency.

geosphere   The solid parts of the Earth, e.g. crust, mantle and core.

glacial   Frozen, or related to glaciers.

glacial period   An interval of geological time within an ice age, where the Earth's temperatures are colder and thus our glaciers grow.

glaciation   The establishment and growth of glaciers.

glacier   A large, slow-moving mass of ice. The Earth's glaciers are the largest reservoir of fresh water, second only to oceans as the planet's largest reservoir of total water.

global warming   The increase of the average temperature of the oceans and the air closely surrounding the Earth. Sometimes used as a term for the specific period of human-induced global warming since industrialisation.

greenhouse effect   Change in the steady state temperature of a planet (in this case Earth) by the presence of an atmosphere containing gases that absorb and emit infrared radiation. The natural greenhouse effect is due to the insulating property of several trace gases in the atmosphere, which contrive to ensure the planet's average surface temperature is +15°C rather than −17°C. The 'greenhouse effect' is sometimes (inaccurately) used as a term for human-induced global warming (which can acceptably be called the 'enhanced greenhouse effect').

greenhouse gases   Trace atmospheric gases that absorb and emit infrared radiation within the thermal infrared range (just one of the bands of wavelengths in the spectrum of infrared radiation). These notably include water vapour, carbon dioxide and methane.

halocarbon   A compound containing carbon atoms and one or more halogen atoms.

heat   Best defined as 'energy in transit', or the transfer of energy from one object to another of a different temperature. When we touch a hot cup of coffee, the sensation we're feeling is the nervous response to a movement of energy from the hotter cup to the cooler tissue of our hand. Similarly, a hot cup of coffee left on a table will cool, as it loses heat to the surrounding air by conduction and radiation. Both conduction and radiation will cease when the coffee reaches 'room temperature' — that is, reaches equilibrium with the surrounding air.

Holocene   Literally, 'entirely recent': the period of geological time which began approximately 11,000 years ago and continues until the present.

humidity   The amount of water vapour in the air.

hydrological cycle   Also known as the 'water cycle', this is the continuous movement of water (in its various states, e.g. liquid, vapour and ice) on, above, or below the surface of the Earth.

hydrosphere   The combined mass of liquid, solid and gaseous water found on, under and over the surface of a planet.

hygrometer   An instrument used for measuring relative humidity.

hypothesis   Literally, a 'sub-theory': a proposed, or suggested, explanation for an observed phenomenon that requires validation by experimental observations before it can be accorded the status of a theory.

ice age   A period when a long-term cooling of the Earth's surface occurs and results in the drastic expansion of ice sheets and glaciers. The most recent ice age occurred around 20,000 years ago when ice sheets covered much of the North American and Eurasian continents.

ice sheet   A mass of glacier ice greater than 50,000 km². Currently, ice sheets are only found in Antarctica and Greenland, whereas during the last ice age they covered much of Canada, Europe and the Americas.

infrared   Infrared radiation (IR) is a subset of electromagnetic radiation (EMR) which is more commonly called 'heat'. It consists of waves with a wavelength longer than that of visible light (400–700 nm — hence its name, 'beneath red') but shorter than that of terahertz radiation (3–300 µm, made famous by cooking technology as 'microwaves'). A significant proportion (47%) of direct sunlight consists of infrared radiation.

insolation   A word coined to describe 'incident solar radiation', a measure of solar radiation energy (i.e. energy from the sun) received on a given surface area over a given unit of time. It is measured in watts per square metre (W/m²).

interglacial   A period in geological time that separates glacial periods, or ice ages. The Earth's average temperature is warmer during an interglacial than during a glacial period so our glaciers grow little or not at all, or even retreat and vanish. We're currently enjoying an interglacial, technically referred to as the Holocene interglacial.

ionosphere   The uppermost part of the atmosphere. Aptly named, as it is 'ionised' (given an electrical charge) by the radiation from the sun.

iris effect   A hypothesis, proposed by Professor Richard Lindzen in 2001, whereby an increase in sea surface temperature in the tropics would reduce the quantity of cirrus clouds and thus more infrared radiation would be leaked from the Earth's atmosphere. This, in turn, was proposed to have a net cooling effect on the Earth's surface.

irradiance   A measure of the power of electromagnetic radiation (at all frequencies) on a surface per unit of area. It is usually expressed in watts per square metre (W/m^2).

irradiation   The exposure of an object to radiation.

isotope   Atoms of the same chemical element with different atomic mass. Different isotopes have the same number of protons (this is why they are the same element) but differ in the number of neutrons. Protons and neutrons are each assigned the atomic mass of 1. In general, different isotopes have nearly identical chemical and physical properties; the main exception to this rule is that isotopes with higher atomic mass seem to react more slowly than 'lighter' isotopes.

isotope ratio mass spectrometer (IRMS)   An instrument used to measure the relative abundance of different isotopes of an element in a given sample. Crudely, it works by accelerating atoms of the sample down an evacuated tube and past a magnet. This has the effect of deflecting the stream of atoms. Lighter nuclei deflect more than heavier nuclei. By collecting and 'counting' the number of nuclei so deflected, the ratio of 'light' and 'heavy' nuclei (and therefore relative abundance of isotopes) can be determined.

lapse rate   The negative change in temperature with height in the troposphere.

latitude   An expression of the location of a point on the Earth's surface relative to the equator. It's essentially a north–south measurement (the east–west measurement is given by longitude). Latitude appears as horizontal lines on a map of the Earth's surface.

lithosphere   The outermost shell, or crust, of a planet, the surface directly adjacent to the atmosphere.

living carbon cycle   The cycle by which carbon is exchanged between all things on Earth (including the rocks comprising Earth itself) and the Earth's atmosphere. Carbon is considered to be the 'backbone' of all life on Earth, thus this cycle is essential to life as we know it. Carbon is combined and recombined in molecules of varying degrees of complexity in a continuous set of processes that can range from photosynthesis to the incineration of limestone in a volcanic eruption.

longitude   The expression of the location of a point on the Earth's surface relative to the 'prime meridian' (an arbitrarily chosen line drawn from pole to pole on the Earth's orb). It's essentially an east–west measurement. Lines of longitude appear as vertical lines on a map of the Earth.

mesosphere   A layer of the Earth's atmosphere that lies above the stratosphere, approximately between 50 and 90 km above the Earth's surface.

metabolism   The set of chemical reactions occurring in living organisms that release energy for life processes. These reactions, in turn, depend on some external source. Green plants are able to store energy in molecules created from water, carbon dioxide and sunlight in a process called photosynthesis. Animals acquire energy from the ingestion and digestion of tissues from plants or other animals.

meteorograph   An instrument that measures and automatically records (without transmitting) weather features, such as temperature, atmospheric pressure, humidity, etc. With luck, the record can later be retrieved.

meteorology   The scientific study of the dynamic processes of the lower atmosphere, and in particular, weather processes. The best-known branch of meteorology is weather forecasting (the observing of the present state of the various short-term processes that comprise local and regional weather and their extrapolation into predictions of future weather states, usually a matter of days or weeks hence). Although they are related — in the same way that weather and climate are related — meteorology and climatology are not to be confused.

Milankovic cycles   A set of cycles (named after their postulator, Milutin Milankovic) with differing periods that reflect the effect of changes in the Earth's motion (on its axis and in its orbit) on climate. As the position and orientation of the Earth (relative to the sun) changes, so does the distribution of the sun's rays reaching the Earth. This is what causes the daily variations of night and day, and the annual variations we know as the seasons. Eccentricities in orbit and spin thus cause slight variations in the regular cycles and are responsible for corresponding climatic changes.

molecule   A stable (electrically neutral) group of atoms held together by molecular bonds. An oxygen atom is expressed as O. An oxygen molecule — two oxygen atoms strongly bonded together — is expressed as O_2. Similarly, CO_2 is a carbon atom bonded with two oxygen atoms.

molecular energy   A technical definition of heat, describing the energy present in the movement of the molecules of a substance.

monsoon   A seasonal prevailing wind that lasts for several months. Often used to refer to monsoon rainfall, this is when a susceptible region receives the majority of its annual rainfall.

neutron   A neutral (that is, with no electrical charge) nuclear particle that is found in the nucleus of an atom.

névé   Type of snow that has been partially melted, refrozen and compacted. This type of snow is associated with glacier formation. Also used to refer to the basin of snow that 'feeds' a glacier.

North Atlantic Oscillation   Sometimes referred to as the Northern Oscillation, this is the seesaw in the difference between the high air pressure of the tropics and the low air pressure of the Arctic. When the oscillation is in its positive phase, it implies stronger northerly winds and wet and warm winters in Europe, with cold and dry winters in Canada and Greenland. In its negative phase, the oscillation implies the opposite — calmer, dryer and cooler winters in Europe and warmer, windier and wetter winters in Canada and Greenland.

organic compound   A compound containing carbon.

ozone   A molecule consisting of three oxygen atoms (O_3). It is much less stable than the commonly occurring molecular oxygen (O_2), which we breathe.

paleoclimate   The climate of the Earth over its entire history (approximately 4.5 billion years). The knowledge we have about this is from the study of climate 'proxies' such as ice cores, tree rings, sediment and rocks.

permafrost   Ground that has been frozen for two or more years. Mostly located around the poles, but also exists closer to the equator at high altitudes.

pH   A measure of the acidity or alkalinity of a solution. A neutral substance (e.g. pure water) is described as having a pH of 7. Acidic solutions have a pH lower than 7, whereas solutions with a pH greater than 7 are described as alkaline.

photolysis   A chemical reaction in which a compound is broken down by photons (that is, light).

photon   A particle which carries electromagnetic force. It is the basic unit of light and all other forms of electromagnetic radiation. A photon has no mass, thus can interact with things at long distances: e.g. sunlight affecting things on Earth.

photosynthesis   A series of chemical reactions that converts carbon dioxide (CO_2) and water into organic compounds such as sugars, using the energy from sunlight in the presence of a compound named chlorophyll. A prime example of this is plants 'breathing' CO_2 to 'fix' and store the energy they need for their life processes. Conveniently (for animal life) oxygen is a waste product of these reactions.

phytoplankton   The 'autotrophic' component of the plankton community — that is, plankton that are able to use energy from sunlight to produce compounds that can be used in metabolic processes. Phytoplankton perform in the oceans the same basic role as green plants do in terrestrial systems.

plankton   Drifting organisms that live in the surface layers of oceans, seas and fresh water. They are a vital food source for aquatic life.

Pleistocene   The Pleistocene is the epoch that began 1.8 million years ago and ended about 11,500 years ago. It was characterised by lengthy ice ages, when glaciers covered large regions of the continents, interrupted by short interglacial periods, when the climate was temperate.

poles   The areas of the Earth around the North and South Poles. These are the two points at which the (invisible) axis around which the Earth rotates intersects with the Earth's surface. On a map of the Earth they appear as the top and bottom of the Earth.

pollution   The introduction of contaminants into an environment which can cause instability or harm to living organisms and physical systems. It's important to realise that pollution is not just human-generated: it can refer to naturally occurring substances (or energy) if they occur in excess.

precipitation   A product of the water vapour in the atmosphere condensing and then falling to the Earth's surface. Examples of this are rain, hail, snow, sleet, etc. It occurs when a region of the atmosphere becomes saturated (full) of water vapour and thus condenses.

proton   A positively charged particle that is found within the nucleus of an atom.

radiation   The process by which energy emitted by one discrete body travels to ultimately be absorbed by another discrete body.

radiometer   A device for measuring the power of electromagnetic radiation.

radiosonde   A device that is used in weather balloons to measure a range of parameters that describe the atmosphere — for example, pressure and temperature — then transmit these data to a fixed receiver back on Earth.

re-radiation   The radiation of energy by a body subsequent to its absorption; for example, when concrete warmed by sunlight is still warm to the touch (and thus emitting infrared radiation) after the sun has set.

remote sensing   The acquisition of information about an object or phenomenon by the use of sensors that aren't in direct contact with the object. For example the data acquired by weather satellites (usually by measuring infrared radiation emitted by the Earth's surface) and ultrasound scans for pregnancy.

salinity   The saltiness of a body of water.

sceptic   The dictionary definition of a 'sceptic' is 'a person who habitually doubts generally accepted beliefs', although we use it in a sense nearer its secondary sense of 'a person who doubts the truth of a religion'. We use it to mean anyone who doubts the theory of human-induced global warming or its generally agreed implications. That is, our sceptics range from those who doubt that human activity is causing climate change to those who accept that human activity is causing climate change, but believe that the magnitude or the nature of that change is other than it is generally held to be.

sensitivity   A technical term used in statistical analysis to describe the change in one quality consequent to a change in another, related quality. 'Climate sensitivity' is used in the debate over human-induced global warming as a shorthand for the relationship of global average surface temperature to a doubling of pre-industrial atmospheric concentrations of carbon dioxide, but it could just as easily refer to the 'sensitivity' of climate to a given change in other parameters, such as insolation, cloudiness, etc.

sequestration   Long-term storage (of carbon dioxide).

smog   A kind of visible air pollution which appears as a smoky haze (smog + fog). Usually seen over cities, as it occurs when emissions from vehicle exhausts and industry react with sunlight.

solar cycles   Eleven-year cycles of sunspot activity. Total solar output varies over a solar cycle by around approximately 0.1% or about 1.3 W/m^2 peak-to-trough.

solar flares   Abrupt, violent explosions from the sun's surface that can occur in complex sunspot groups. They are thought to be caused by sudden magnetic field changes.

Southern Oscillation   See El Niño Southern Oscillation.

southern annular mode (SAM)   Also known as the Antarctic Oscillation (AAO), this is a large-scale seesaw in atmospheric pressure between the western and eastern hemispheres.

spectrophotometer   An instrument used to measure the intensity of electromagnetic radiation at different wavelengths. Specifically, it is used to study visible light, and more specifically, light absorption.

spectrum   A range or continuous set. Commonly used to refer to the electromagnetic spectrum, which is the range of all electromagnetic radiation frequencies. This includes X-rays, visible light, UV light and more.

speleotherm   Commonly known as a cave formation, a mineral deposit formed in a cave. These are usually made from calcite and aragonite.

steric   Refers to the amount of space each atom within a molecule takes up. More specifically in the context of this book, a steric sea level rise is that associated with the thermal expansion of seawater due to warming.

Heat, as we know, causes the molecules in a substance to move in their random manner with more energy. This causes an expansion of the space over which this random movement occurs, and ultimately, the expansion of the volume occupied by the substance itself.

stochastic   Random.

stratigraphy   The study of the layers in rock, ice or other media. This is helpful in ageing or dating samples for the study of the Earth's history.

stratosphere   The second major layer of the Earth's atmosphere, directly above the troposphere. It is stratified, with the cooler layers closer to the Earth, by contrast with the troposphere, which has its coolest layers higher up.

sunspots   These always appear in pairs, as dark spots on the sun's surface. They are intense magnetic fields that break through the solar surface. Magnetic field lines leave through one sunspot and re-enter through its twin. Sunspot activity appears as part of an 11-year cycle.

telemetry   A technology that allows the remote measurement and reporting of information. This typically refers to wireless communications, e.g. radio, telephone and computer networks.

temperature anomaly   It is common practice in climate science to refer to temperature anomalies — indeed, many of the graphs in this book are depictions of such anomalies. A temperature anomaly is defined as the difference in temperature, over the time period in question, from the average temperature of some arbitrarily chosen base period, commonly a decade or longer average temperature measure.

test   The shell of sea urchins and certain microorganisms.

theodolite   An instrument for measuring both horizontal and vertical angles, useful for calculating distance and height relative to the observer.

thermal energy   The form of energy that is evident as an increase in temperature.

thermal inertia   The ability of a substance to undergo a change in temperature without changing states (e.g. changing from liquid to gas). Basically how much heat the substance can absorb without changing its form.

thermistor   A type of resistor, with resistance inversely proportional to its temperature. So as a thermistor's temperature increases its resistance to electrical current decreases, a change that can be measured with a voltmeter or ammeter in the circuit.

thermodynamic   Relating to the conversion of heat into other forms of energy via conduction, convection or radiation.

thermohaline circulation (THC)   The part of the complex ocean circulation that is thought to be created by surface heating and changes in the freshwater concentration.

thermometer   A device that measures temperature.

thermoscope   An early form of thermometer. Commonly known as a Galileo thermometer after the Italian physicist Galileo Galilei. It consists of a glass tube filled with a clear liquid and various objects that sink in a known sequence as the temperature of the liquid increases. The fact that liquids decrease in density when heated is essential to the thermoscope. The temperature at any given time can thus be approximately known by observing which objects have sunk and which are still buoyant.

total solar irradiance (TSI)   The amount of solar energy striking the top of the Earth's atmosphere.

trace element   An element in a sample that has a concentration of less than 100 parts per million atoms (100 micrograms per gram).

tropics   The area of the Earth closest to the equator, approximately 23.4 degrees latitude on either side. Also more technically defined by certain patterns of circulation and precipitation distinctive to the torrid zone.

tropopause   The boundary between the troposphere and the stratosphere. Ascending from the Earth, it is the point at which air stops getting cooler the higher you go and begins increasing in temperature again. It's also the point at which the atmosphere becomes almost completely dry.

troposphere   The part of the Earth's atmosphere that is adjacent to its surface. It averages an 11-km thickness, although it is thinner at the poles and thicker over the tropics. It contains around 75% of the atmosphere's mass and almost all of its water vapour and aerosols. For the latter reason, it's also the region of the atmosphere in which practically all of the Earth's weather occurs.

tundra   An area where tree growth is hindered by low temperatures and short growing seasons. There are two types: Arctic tundra (which occurs in the Arctic and, to a far more limited extent, in the Antarctic) and alpine tundra.

ultraviolet (UV)   Electromagnetic radiation with a wavelength shorter than that of visible light (hence the name 'beyond violet'), but longer than X-rays. UV light is found in sunlight and the most notorious effect in human experience is sunburn, which is radiation damage to the outer layers of human skin by UV.

urban heat island   A metropolitan area (city) which is significantly warmer than its surrounding rural areas.

volatility   A measure of how easily a substance changes from a liquid to a gas (via evaporation), or the high degree of random variability in some quantity (for example, a stockmarket index, a commodity price, or year-to-year local average temperatures).

wavelength   The distance between repeating units of a wave. Wavelength is inversely proportional to frequency, i.e. waves with longer wavelength have a shorter frequency.

weather   The current phenomena occurring in the atmosphere at a given place at a given time. Be careful not to confuse this with climate, which is the behaviour of the atmosphere over a longer period of time. 'Weather' can also be used in a slightly more technical sense to refer to the combination of convection, circulation, condensation and precipitation of water vapour.

References

Introduction

1. Bryden, .H.L. 'Slowing of the Atlantic Meridional Overturning Circulation at 25°N', *Nature*, 438, 2005, 655–657.

2. Cunningham, S.A. 'Temporal Variability of the Atlantic Meriodonal Overturning Circulation at 25°N', *Science*, 317, 2007, 938–941.

Chapter 2: Taking the Earth's Temperature

1. Oke, T.R. 'The Energetic Basis of the Urban Heat Island', *Quarterly Journal of the Royal Meteorological Society*, 108, 1982, 1–24.

2. Karl, T.R., H.F. Diaz, and G. Kukla. 'Urbanization: Its Detection and Effect in the United States Climate Record', *Journal of Climate*, 1, 1988, 1099–1123.

3. Hansen, J.E., R. Ruedy, Mki. Sato, M. Imhoff, W. Lawrence, D. Easterling, T. Peterson, and T. Karl. 'A Closer Look at United States and Global SurfaceTemperature Change', *Journal of Geophysical Research*, 106, 2001, 23947–23963.

4. http://wattsupwiththat.com/2008/09/23/adjusting-pristine-data/

5. www.climateaudit.org/?p=2964

6. www.pik-potsdam.de/~stefan/Publications/Book_chapters/essay.pdf

7. Thompson, D.W.J. 'A Large Discontinuity in the Mid-twentieth Century in Observed Global-mean Surface Temperature', *Nature*, 453, 2008, 646–649.

8. Gaillard F., E. Autret, V. Thierry, and P. Galaup. 'Quality Control of Large Argo Datasets', *Journal of Atmospheric and Oceanic Technology*, 2008.

9. www.ncdc.noaa.gov/oa/climate/ratpac/index.php

10. www.niwa.cri.nz/__data/assets/pdf_file/0005/55634/ice.pdf

11. Kuilian Tang, Xiahong Feng, and GarY. Funkhouser. 'The $\delta^{13}C$ of Tree Rings in Full-bark and Strip-bark Bristlecone Pine Trees in the White Mountains of California', *Global Change Biology*, 5, 1998, 33–40.

12. According to the findings of Helliker and Richter et al. *Nature*, 454, 2008, 422–423.

13. Dyke, A.S., and J.M. Savelle. 'Holocene History of the Bering Sea Bowhead Whale (*Balaena mysticetus*) in Its Beaufort Sea Summer Grounds off Southwestern Victoria Island, Western Canadian Arctic', *Quaternary Research*, 55, 2001, 371–379.

Chapter 3: Is Anything Agreed?

1. Robinson A.B., N.E. Robinson, and W. Soon. 'Environmental Effects of Increased Atmospheric Carbon Dioxide', *Journal of American Physician and Surgeons*, 12, 2007, 110.

2. Arrhenius, S. 'On the Influence of Carbonic Acid in the Air upon the Temperature of the Ground', *London, Edinburgh, and Dublin Philosophical Magazine and Journal of Science* (fifth series), 41, 1896, 237–275.

3. Arrhenius, S., quoted in R. Kunzig and W. Broeker. *Fixing Climate: the Story of Climate Science — and How to Stop Global Warming*, Profile, London, 2008, 88.

Chapter 4: The Case For Anthropogenic Global Warming

1. Stroeve, J.M., M. Holland, W. Meier, T. Scambos, and M. Serreze. 'Arctic Sea Ice Decline: Faster than Forecast', *Geophysical Research Letters*, 34, 2007; also Maslanik, J.A., C. Fowler, J. Stroeve, S. Drobot, J. Zwally, D. Yi, and W. Emery. 'A Younger, Thinner Arctic Ice Cover: Increased Potential for Rapid, Extensive Sea-ice Loss', *Geophysical Research Letters*, 34, 2007; also Serreze, M.C., M.M. Holland, and J. Stroeve. 'Perspectives on the Arctic's Shrinking Sea-ice Cover', *Science*, 315, 2007, 1533–1536.

2. Overpeck, J.T., K. Hughen, D. Hardy, R. Bradley, R. Case, M. Douglas, B. Finney, K. Gajewski, G. Jacoby, A. Jennings, S. Lamoureux, A Lasca, G. MacDonald, J. Moore, M. Retelle, S. Smith, A. Wolfe, and G. Zielinski. 'Arctic Environmental Change of the Last Four Centuries', *Science*, 278, 1997, 1251–1256.

3. Scambos, T., C. Hulbe, and M. Fahnestock. 'Climate-induced Ice Shelf Disintegration in the Antarctic Peninsula. In 'Antarctic Peninsula Climate Variability: Historical and Paleoenvironmental Perspectives', *Antarctic Research Series*, 79, 2003, 79–92.

4. Steffen, K., and Huff, R. 'A Record Maximum Melt Extent on the Greenland Ice Sheet in 2002', Cooperative Institute for Research in Environmental Sciences (CIRES), University of Colorado at Boulder, http://cires.colorado.edu/steffen/melt/index.html

5. Oerlemans, J. 'Extracting a Climate Signal from 169 Glacier Records', *Science*, 308, 2005, 675–677.

6. Meier, M.F., M.B. Dyurgerov, U.K. Rick, S. O'Neel, W.T. Pfeffer, R.S. Anderson, S.P. Anderson, and A.F. Glazovsky. 'Glaciers Dominate Eustatic Sea-level Rise in the 21st Century', *Science*, 317, 2007, 1064–1067.

7. Curry, R., B. Dickson, I. Yashayaev. 'A Change in the Freshwater Balance of the Atlantic Ocean over the Past Four Decades', *Nature*, 426, 2003, 826–829; also Boyer, T.P., S. Levitus, J.I. Antonov, R.A. Locarnini, and H.E. Garcia. 'Linear Trends in Salinity for the World Ocean, 1955–1998', *Geophysical Research Letters*, 32, 2005.

8. Jacobs, S.S., C.F. Giulivi, and P.A. Mele. 'Freshening of the Ross Sea During the Late 20th Century', *Science*, 297, 2002, 386–389.

9. Le Quéré, C., C. Rödenbeck, E.T. Buitenhuis, T. J. Conway, R. Langenfelds, A. Gomez, C. Labuschagne, M. Ramonet, T. Nakazawa, N. Metzl, N. Gillett, and M, Heimann. 'Saturation of the Southern Ocean CO_2 Sink Due to Recent Climate Change', *Science*, 316, 2007, 1735–1738.

10. Toggweiler J.R., and J. Russell. 'Ocean Circulation in a Warming Climate', *Nature*, 451, 2008, 286–288.

11. Ibid.

12. IPCC WG1-AR4 2007.

13. Webster, P.J., G.J. Holland, J.A. Curry, and H.R. Chang. 'Changes in Tropical Cyclone Number, Duration, and Intensity in a Warming Environment', *Science*, 309, 2005, 1844–1846.

14. Mitchell, T.D., and P.D. Jones. 'An Improved Method of Constructing a Database of Monthly Climate Observations and Associated High-resolution Grids', *International Journal of Climatology*, 25, 2005, 693–712.

15. Brown, S.J., J. Caesar, and C.A.T. Ferro. 'Global Changes in Extreme Daily Temperature since 1950', *Journal of Geophysical Research*, 113, 2008.

16. Alexander, L.V., X. Zhang, T.C. Peterson, J. Caesar, B. Gleason, A.M.G. Klein Tank, M. Haylock, D. Collins, B. Trewin, F. Rahimzadeh, A. Tagipour, P. Ambenje, K. Rupa Kumar, J. Revadekar, and G. Griffiths. 'Global Observed Changes in Daily Climate Extremes of Temperature and Precipitation', *Journal of Geophysical Research*, 111, 2006.

17. IPCC WG1-AR4 2007.

18. Shulmeister, J., I. Goodwin, J. Renwick, K. Harle, L. Armand, M.S. McGlone, E. Cook, J. Dodson, P.P. Hesse, P. Mayewski, and M. Curran. 'The Southern Hemisphere Westerlies in the Australasian Sector during the Last Glaciation Cycle: A Synthesis', *Quaternary International*, 118/119, 2004, 23–53.

19. Ibid.

20. Mayewski, P.A., E. Rohling, C. Stager, K. Karlén, K.A. Maasch, L.D. Meeker,

E. Meyerson, F. Gasse, S. van Kreveld, K. Holmgren, J. Lee-Thorp, G. Rosqvist, F. Rack, M. Staubwasser, and R. Schneider. 'Holocene Climate Variability', *Quaternary Research*, 62, 2004, 243–255.

21. Thompson, D.W.J., and S. Solomon. 'Interpretation of Recent Southern Hemisphere Climate Change', *Science*, 296, 2002, 895.

22. Marshall, G.J, C.M. Johanson, and Q. Fu. 'Trends in Antarctic Geopotential Height and Temperature: A Comparison between Radiosonde and NCEP–NCAR Reanalysis Data', *Journal of Climate*, 15, 2002; also Johansen, C.M., and Q. Fu. 'Antarctic Atmospheric Temperature Trend Patterns from Satellite Observations', *Geophysical Research Letters*, 34, 2007.

23. Toggweiler, J.R., and J. Russell. 'Ocean Circulation in a Warming Climate', *Nature*, 451, 2008, 286–288.

24. Seidel, D.J., Q. Fu, W.J. Randel, and T.J. Reichler. 'Widening of the Tropical Belt in a Changing Climate', *Nature*, 1, 2008, 21–24.

25. See for example G.J. Vermeij and P.D. Roopnarine. 'The Coming Arctic Invasion', *Science*, 321, 2008, 780–781.

26. Dyke, A.S., and J.M. Savelle. 'Holocene History of the Bering Sea Bowhead Whale (*Balaena mysticetus*) in Its Beaufort Sea Summer Grounds off Southwestern Victoria Island, Western Canadian Arctic', *Quaternary Research*, 55, 2001, 371–379.

27. www.spiegel.de/international/world/0,1518,574815,00.html

28. Turner, J.T., A. Lachlan-Cope, S. Colwell, G.J. Marshall, and W.M. Connolley. 'Significant Warming of the Antarctic Winter Troposphere', *Science*, 311, 2006, 1914–1917.

29. Thompson, L., G.E. Mosley-Thompson, M.E. Davis, J.F. Bolzan, J. Dai, L. Klein, T. Yao, X. Wu, Z. Xie, and N. Gundestrup. 'Holocene–Late Pleistocene Climatic Ice Core Records from Qinghai-Tibetan Plateau', *Science*, 246, 1989, 474–477.

30. Ibid.

31. Mayewski, P.A., and K.A. Maasch. 'Recent Warming Inconsistent with Natural Association between Temperature and Atmospheric Circulation over the Last 2000 Years', *Climate Past Discussion*, 2, 2006, 1–29.

32. Brook, Ed. 'Palaeoclimate: Windows on the Greenhouse', *Nature*, 453, 2008, 291–292.

33. Barrows, T., T. Scott, J. Lehman, L.K. Fifield, and P. De Deckker. 'Absence of Cooling in New Zealand and the Adjacent Ocean During the Younger Dryas Chronozone', *Science*, 318, 2007, 86–89.

34. Weaver, A.J., O.A. Saenko, P.U. Clark, and J.X. Mitrovica. 'Meltwater Pulse 1A

from Antarctica as a Trigger of the Bølling-Allerød Warm Interval', *Science*, 299, 2003, 1709–1713.

35. Barnett, T.P., D.W. Pierce, K.M. AchutaRao, P.J. Gleckler, B.D. Santer, J.M. Gregory, and W.M. Washington. 'Penetration of Human-Induced Warming into the World's Oceans', *Science*, 309, 2005, 284–287; also Mayewski, P.A., Maasch, K.A. 'Recent Warming Inconsistent with Natural Association between Temperature and Atmospheric Circulation over the Last 2000 Years', *Climate Past Discussion*, 2, 2006, 1–29.

36. Allen, R.J., and S.C. Sherwood. 'Utility of Radiosonde Wind Data in Representing Climatological Variations of Tropospheric Temperature and Baroclinicity in the Western Tropical Pacific', *Journal of Climate*, 20, 2007, 5229–5243.

37. Hansen, J., L. Nazarenko, R. Ruedy, Mki. Sato, J. Willis, A. Del Genio, D. Koch, A. Lacis, K. Lo, S. Menon, T. Novakov, J. Perlwitz, G. Russell, G.A. Schmidt, and N. Tausnev. 'Earth's Energy Imbalance: Confirmation and Implications', *Science*, 308, 2005, 1431–1435.

38. Pelejero, C.E.C., M.T. McCulloch, J.F. Marshall, M.K. Gagan, J.M. Lough, and B.N. Opdyke. 'Preindustrial to Modern Interdecadal Variability in Coral Reef pH', *Science*, 309, 2005, 2204–2207.

Chapter 5: The Case Against Anthropogenic Global Warming

1. Kouwenberg, L.L.R., J.C. McElwain, W.M. Kurschner, F. Wagner, D.J. Beerling, F.E. Mayle, and H. Visscher. 'Stomatal Frequency Adjustment of Four Conifer Species to Historical Changes in Atmospheric CO_2', *American Journal of Botany*, 90, 2003, 610–619.

2. van Hoof, T.B., F. Wagner-Cremer, W.M. Kürschner, and H. Visscher. 'A Role for Atmospheric CO_2 in Preindustrial Climate Forcing', *Proceedings of the National Academy of Science*, www.pnas.org/content/105/41/15815.full

3. Ibid.

4. Svensmark, H. 'Influence of Cosmic Rays on Earth's Climate', *Physical Review Letters*, 81, 1998, 5027–5030.

5. Ibid.

6. Gettleman, A., J.R. Holton, and A.R. Douglass. 'Simulations of Water Vapor in the Lower Stratosphere and Upper Troposphere', *Journal of Geophysical Research*, 105(D7), 2000, 9003–9023.

7. Lindzen, R.S., M.D. Choub, and A.Y. Houb. 'Does the Earth Have an Adaptive Infrared Iris?', *Bulletin of the American Meteorological Society*, 82, 2001, 417–432.

8.   Hartman, D.L., and M.L. Michelsen. 'No Evidence for Iris', *Bull. Amer. Met. Soc.*, 83, 2002, 249–254.

9.   Travis, D.J., Carleton, A.M., and R. Lauritsen. 'Jet Contrails and Climate: Anomalous Increases in US Diurnal Temperature Range for September 11–14, 2001', *Nature*, 418, 2002, 601.

Chapter 6: How Much CO$_2$ Leads to How Much Warming?

1.   Arrhenius, S. 'On the Influence of Carbonic Acid in the Air upon the Temperature of the Ground', *London, Edinburgh, and Dublin Philosophical Magazine and Journal of Science* (fifth series), 41, 1896, 237–275.

2.   Soden, B.J., R.T. Wetherald, G.L. Stenchikov, and A. Robock. 'Global Cooling after the Eruption of Mount Pinatubo: A Test of Climate Feedback by Water Vapor', *Science*, 296, 2002, 727–730.

3.   Shaviv, N. 'On Climate Sensitivity', 2005, www.sciencebits.com/OnClimateSensitivity

4.   Gregory, J.M., R.J. Stouffer, S.C.B. Raper, P.A. Stott, and N.A. Rayner. 'An Observationally Based Estimate of the Climate Sensitivity', *Journal of Climate*, 15, 2002, 3117–3121.

Colour sections

1.   Mann, M., R.S. Bradley, and M.K. Hughes. 'Global Scale Temperature Patterns and Climate Forcing over the Past Six Centuries', *Nature*, 392, 1998, 779–787.

2.   McIntyre, S., and R. McKitrick. 'Corrections to the Mann et al. (1998) Proxy Data Base and Northern Hemispheric Average Temperature Series', *Energy and Environment*, 14(6), 2003, 751–771.

3.   National Research Council of the National Academies. 'Surface Temperature Reconstructions for the Last 2000 Years', National Academies Press, Washington, 2006, report accessed at www.uoguelph.ca/~rmckitri/research/NRCreport.pdf

4.   Mann M., Z. Zhang, M.K. Hughes, R.S. Bradley, S. K. Miller, S. Rutherford, and F. Ni. 'Proxy-Based Reconstructions of Hemispheric and Global Surface Temperature Variation over the Past Two Millennia', *Proceedings of the National Academy of Science*, 105, 2008, 13252-13257.

Acknowledgements

No one said it would be easy.

For a layperson to try to get to grips with the enormously complex and rapidly changing world of the science of climate change was always going to be demanding, to put it mildly. The sheer volume of academic literature on the subject, not to mention the highly technical nature of most of it, was always going to be beyond our own, unaided efforts to master it.

So our approach was to enlist the help of two panels of experts. Why two, you may well ask? Why not one panel, which could assess the literature and advise us of the relevance and relative scientific merits?

Well, it turned out that finding one, let alone several, experts who are capable of remaining objective and agnostic in this field was among the more difficult of the very difficult tasks we set ourselves. This issue just seems to divide even mild-mannered, rational people, and the two sides are poles apart. So two panels it was — one of scientists who are sceptical about the theory of human-induced climate change, and another of scientists who are convinced that the theory is valid.

For most of the journey we felt like jurors in a case involving expert scientific testimony, stuck in the middle while the boffins argued the finer points of technical detail across a vast range of disciplines.

Each panel pointed us in the direction of key literature and where necessary — most everywhere — helped us to understand its significance. No matter how au fait the layperson is with scientific method, they'll need exactly the kind of mentoring we received from both panels to get a toehold in this stuff. Still, the sheer depth of the ignorance of this pair of climate dummies probably shocked all parties at times. We hope that the glow of satisfaction that rewards educators when they see the lights come on will go some way toward compensating our patient, obliging experts from both camps.

Both sides have our thanks and admiration. It's hard to imagine how we could have been more ably assisted. We are well aware that in many, if not most cases, we will disappoint those who so wholeheartedly helped, because in the end, the intention was always that we should make up our own minds on this subject. That means we're bound to disagree with at least half of the scientists. And it's not just opinion, either: much of the technical detail and the subtlety of the arguments will have been lost or fudged by the need to keep it simple, for our own sakes if not for the reader's. But we hope that in all cases, our panellists will recognise traces of their pearls of wisdom in the footprints of the swine.

Our panel of Sceptics, who directly or indirectly contributed and answered questions arising in the course of our deliberations, included: Dr Fred Singer, Professor Emeritus of Environmental Science, University of Virginia; Dr Bob Carter, Research Professor of Geology, James Cook University; Dr Richard Lindzen, Alfred P. Sloan, Professor of Meteorology, Massachusetts Institute of Technology; Dr Dennis Avery, Director, Center for Global Food Issues, Hudson Institute; Lord Monckton (Christopher Monckton, 3rd Viscount Monckton of Brenchley), politician and business consultant, policy advisor; Dr Kesten Green, Senior Research Fellow, Business and Economic Forecasting Unit, Monash University.

Our panel of Alarmists included: Dr Dave Lowe, Adjunct Professor Atmospheric Chemistry, Antarctic Research Centre, Victoria University of Wellington; Dr Lionel Carter, Professor of Marine Geology, Antarctic Research Centre, Victoria University of Wellington; Dr Peter Barrett, Professor of Geology, Antarctic Research Centre, Victoria University of Wellington; Dr David Etheridge, CSIRO Marine and Atmospheric Research; Dr Jim Renwick, Principal Scientist, Climate Variability and Change, National Institute of Water and Atmospheric Research (NIWA); Dr Andy Reisinger, Senior Research Fellow, New Zealand Climate Change Research Institute, Victoria University of Wellington; Dr Bill Allan, Atmospheric and Space Scientist, Wellington; Dr Ralph Keeling, Professor of Geochemistry, Scripps Institution of Oceanography, University of California; Dr Jeff Sveringhaus, Professor of Geosciences, Scripps Institution of Oceanography, University of California; Dr David Fahey, NOAA Earth System Research Laboratory; Dr Christopher Shuman, Associate Research Scientist, University of Maryland, Goddard Earth Science and Technology Center.

We must make special mention of the three gentlemen who applied themselves to the project with more devotion than we could have hoped for, let alone asked. We came to refer to them as 'Los Banditos', the tight trio of Dave Lowe, Peter Barrett and Lionel Carter. They acted as a cross between a steering committee for our reading, a consultancy on basic (and not so basic) science, and a sounding board for our misguided ideas and interpretations. This book could not have been written without them; we owe to them — and Dave Lowe in particular — a huge debt of gratitude for their good humour under fire, and an apology for every occasion we got up their noses. And if aspects of the finished product represent one final nasal intrusion, then we apologise for that, too, in advance.

As with any project of this nature and magnitude, many others also assisted along the way and we owe a great dollop of thanks to them even if we do not intend, thereby, to implicate them in our conclusions.

To Ruby Morgan, Penny Deans and Andrew Gawith, our sincerest thanks for persevering with early versions of the text, and to Kim, who assisted with the proofreading, thank you, too. To friends and family and random strangers who took an interest in the project, and with many of whom we each had lively discussions: thanks. To Jenny Hellen and her team at Random House — Susan, Graeme, especially Tracey, and nameless others — an equally sincere accolade. This has not been an easy book to bring to fruition. To Michael Bordignon who built the associated website, www.polesapart.com, we are also grateful.

Since the publication of the first edition of this book, several alert readers (notably Paul Broady) have pointed out errors to us. We received all such advice gratefully and have made the necessary corrections with due humility. Thank you!

Scientists don't work for free, and in order to compensate our experts for their time, we drew upon the resources of the Morgan Family Charitable Foundation (www.morgancharity.org), which has as one of its objectives the funding of research into public policy issues and communication of the findings to the public. We are grateful to the Foundation for the not insubstantial funding of this work.

And once again, the disclaimer bears repeating: we, this jury of two, were ably assisted by scientists on both sides of this question, but ultimately our conclusions are all our own work, and so too are any remaining errors of fact or matters of opinion. Your consciences are clear.

Gareth Morgan & John McCrystal

Author Profiles

Gareth Morgan

Gareth is a well-known media figure in New Zealand, whose opinions and expertise on financial economic matters are highly sought after. He's an economist and investment advisor for his day job. He established his own economics consultancy in 1982, and an investment advisory business in the 1990s. His profile meant he was invited to perform a series of popular broadcasts from far-flung corners of the world when he and his wife Jo embarked on a series of international motorcycling expeditions, collectively known as the World By Bike project. Each year since 2001, Gareth and Jo's adventures by motorcycle have been published in radio, television and the print media, and in a series of bestselling books. They have so far ridden their motorcycles on all seven continents and the journey is not over yet.

In recent years, Gareth has found himself in the position to become involved in philanthropy. As UNICEF Ambassadors, he and Jo have visited and contributed to many UNICEF projects and have financed a wide range of social sector projects aimed at providing assistance to the world's most disadvantaged, including at locations the couple have visited on their travels.

It was during these travels that Gareth's interest in the climate change debate first arose. Visiting the Arctic and Antarctic regions exposed him to several of the real-world instances cited as evidence of global warming. What's more, as Gareth's postgraduate work was into macroeconomic modelling, he couldn't resist digging a little deeper into the subject of computer modelling as a contributor to our understanding of what climate is and how it works. Once bitten by a dodgy model, after all, is twice shy.

And above all, the climate change debate appealed to his lifelong interest in bringing clarity to public policy. He was determined to cast light into the dark corners of his understanding of the climate issue — call it ignorance or what you will — for his own sake, if not for his readers'. This was all the motivation he needed.

John McCrystal

John has been working as a freelance writer ever since graduating from Auckland University with a few degrees in Political Studies in the mid-1990s. He has published a small amount of fiction, and rather more non-fiction on subjects as diverse as motoring, meat works, rugby, travel and, now, climate change.

John has collaborated with Gareth on several writing projects to date. His interest in scientific matters — his meandering career at university began with a misguided attempt to become a scientist — recommended this project to him as soon as Gareth proposed it. And his interest in politics meant that even once the joys of the science of climate change had palled, the fascination of the politics kept him going. After all, it's not often that an issue as divisive, as urgent, as politically and socially fraught as climate change arises. In terms of the ancient Chinese curse 'May you live in interesting times', climate change is easily the most interesting issue of the day.

Index